Contending for the Faith

For Suellen Bakleda,
my Lutheran friend
in the Faith

Ralph Wood

November 2,
2005
Wichita
Kansas

Contending
for the
Faith

The Church's Engagement with Culture

Ralph C. Wood

Provost Series

B

Baylor University Press
Waco, Texas USA

This volume is the fortieth published by the Markham Press Fund of Baylor University Press, established in memory of Dr. L. N. and Princess Finch Markham of Longview, Texas, by their daughters, Mrs. R. Matt Dawson of Waco, Texas, and Mrs. B. Reid Clanton of Longview, Texas.

Library of Congress Cataloging-in-Publication Data

Wood, Ralph C.
  Contending for the faith : the church's engagement with culture / Ralph C. Wood.
      p. cm. -- (Interpreting Christian texts and traditions series ; #1)
Includes bibliographical references and index.
  ISBN 091895486X
  1. Christianity and culture. I. Title. II. Series.

BR115.C8W65 2003
261--dc21

                                        2002153708

Printed in the United States of America on acid-free paper

Contents

Preface

The reputations of the foremost American colleges and universities, from the point of view of both academics and the wider public, grow out of several qualities, from their identification with an elite group of institutions such as the Ivy League, to the SAT or ACT averages of their entering undergraduates, to the size and prestige of their graduate schools, to the scientific and literary accomplishments of their faculty, particularly the number of Nobel laureates among their ranks, to the size of their endowments, even to the excellence of their athletic teams. However, at Baylor University, we believe it is fair to say that the positive reputation of our university, unlike many others, has come almost exclusively as a consequence of the impressive achievements of its graduates, whether in law, politics and public service, medicine, nursing, and other health-related fields, the church, education, business and commerce, or cultural and artistic endeavors. And those who know Baylor will testify that one of the most important reasons behind the extraordinary accomplishments of its graduates for over 150 years is the quality of teaching they experienced during their time at Baylor, a benefit of the great teaching tradition that the university has nurtured and rewarded.

More recently, however, the academic leaders of Baylor have urged the university as a whole to recognize the enormous potential of its faculty members not only to influence society indirectly through the accomplishments of their students but also to influence society directly through their own scholarship and other contributions to the public forum of ideas and intellectual discourse. This imperative became particularly important as the Baylor community, first under the presidency of Herbert H. Reynolds and now Robert B. Sloan, has made the commitment to seek to become a nationally recognized Christian university. It was clear to the academic leadership of Baylor that such aspirations could not be achieved without a critical mass of faculty members who were not only excellent teachers but also highly productive scholars in the kind of research and publications that would make an important contribution to the academy and in the wider culture.

Thus, in the fall of 1997, the Provost and Vice President for Academic

Affairs, with the full support and encouragement of the academic deans, proposed to President Sloan the inauguration of the "University and Distinguished Professors Program." While university and distinguished professors were not unprecedented at Baylor, this new effort had four distinctives: first, the recruitment of top-tier faculty was adopted as an institutional strategy to enhance the scholarly reputation of Baylor's faculty; second, all university and distinguished professors in the program would be recruited from outside Baylor; third, those recruited would be foremost scholars in their fields and would be committed to research and teaching emphases relevant to the Christian character of Baylor; and fourth, a specific number—twenty—of such faculty members would be recruited within seven years, starting effectively in the fall of 1998. The first University Professor recruited as part of this new initiative is the author of this book, Ralph C. Wood. Thus has this theologian and literary scholar led the way for Baylor in generating "Christian kinds of knowledge," thoroughly grounded in the Baptist tradition and in the orthodox Christian faith.

Ralph Wood is a native of east Texas and holds degrees from East Texas State University (B.A. M.A.) and the Divinity School of the University of Chicago (Ph.D.). Currently he is University Professor of Theology and Literature at Baylor (1998–present), having previously served as Distinguished Professor of Religion at Samford University (1997–1998) and John Allen Easley Professor of Religion at Wake Forest University (1991–1997). Before that he held various academic ranks in the Department of Religion at Wake Forest (1971–1991). These various teaching assignments reveal that the classroom has remained his first calling over the course of his career. Highly esteemed as a demanding and engaging teacher, Dr. Wood has endeared himself to countless students over the years, earning teaching awards along the way.

Among his many professional activities, Dr. Wood serves on the editorial board for the *Flannery O'Connor Review* and as the book review editor for *Perspectives in Religious Studies*. Dr. Wood is also a regular contributor to the *Christian Century* for which he also serves as editor-at-large. His teaching and research have focused on the relation of Christian theology to the chief literary texts of the West, an interest seen clearly in his main book, *The Comedy of Redemption: Christian Faith and Comic Vision in Four American Novelists* (University of Notre Dame Press, 1988).

His interests in the intersection of theology and literature are also clearly evinced in this present work. Though some of these essays have been previously published, this book is no mere "collection" of essays. Rather, it is a literary mosaic, with each tessera contributing to a beautiful and powerful image of the *alteras civitas*, the "other city," which is Christ's body called the

Church. Wood's introduction is indispensable for understanding the coherence of the argument. Here he makes clear that "Christian existence itself requires a culture; a realm where the most fundamental practices and doctrines of the church can be inculcated" (p.1). Further, Wood argues that "scripture and tradition provide the church with a distinctive kind of existence—with unique ways of birthing and dying, of becoming youthful and growing old, of marrying and remaining single, of celebrating and sacrificing, of thinking and imagining, of worshipping the true God and protesting against the false gods" (p.2). What follows, then, are nine essays, that are a constructive attempt, a contention, to (re-)create a distinctively Christian culture by reforming its institutional and individual practices—in the intellectual tasks of its colleges and universities, and in the worship, liturgy, ethics, and theology of its churches.

Wood is a sure-footed guide through the (post-)modern landscape. At times, he stands atop a high peak ready to make circumspect and insightful comments about the moral condition of our educational institutions or the bankruptcy of our sexual ethics. At other times, he puts an individual thinker and his work under the microscope, with a thick and detailed description, for example of Peter Berger's or Russell Kirk's thought. Wood's literary analysis is balanced and relentless; his autobiographical anecdotes are poignant but never self-indulgent. There is plenty here to offend both conservatives and liberals alike!

Contending for the Faith is a splendid inaugural volume for the Provost's Series, "Interpreting Christian Texts and Traditions." The purpose of the series is twofold. First, the series aims to present the Christian intellectual's reflections on the Christian texts and traditions that shape his or her faith and the implications of those reflections not only for the contemporary Christian church but for our larger society as well. The Series also provides the opportunity to showcase the Distinguished and University Professors Program at Baylor University, since the main contributors to this Series will be those Professors appointed to this program, because their Christian faith has energized their thinking about and participation in their various disciplines. As such, Professor Ralph Wood's *Contending for the Faith* is a significant portent of how this Series will not only expand knowledge in a variety of fields but ultimately bring honor and glory to God, who is himself the Fountain of all Wisdom and Knowledge.

Donald E. Schmeltekopf
Provost and Vice President for Academic Affairs

Mikeal C. Parsons
Professor of Religion and Series Editor

Acknowledgments

This book is dedicated to the entire Baylor community in gratitude for the challenging and gratifying new life that it has made possible for Suzanne and me ever since we arrived here on an August day in 1998 when the temperature stood at 106. We have learned that heat does not indicate hell. Quite to the contrary, Baylor has shown us that redemption is possible in the academy as well as the church—especially when the university is devoted, as it is here at Baylor, to serving the church as well as the world. Here we have found new friends and companions who have taught us what it means to love God with our minds no less than our hearts and souls. There is no greater gift.

The two administrators who first invited me to join the Baylor faculty must be singled out for special praise. President Robert Sloan and Provost Donald Schmeltekopf have worked diligently and courageously to create an ethos of scholarly learning and Christian faith that makes Baylor a university worthy of one's full devotion. I have been honored to have them as my academic and spiritual leaders. They have read much of what I have written, commented wisely upon it, and not hesitated to disagree with me. It is a delight to call them my friends and fellow travelers on the Christian journey.

Many colleagues—not only at Baylor but in many other places as well—have served as my interlocutors along the way, making helpful suggestions for improvement. To list their names is all too inadequate tribute, but at least they cannot be blamed for my faults: Mike Beaty, Peter Berger, Jim Burtchaell, Max Deal, Timothy George, Barry Harvey, Doug Henry, David Jeffrey, Bob Kruschwitz, Roger Lundin, the late Jim McClendon, Scott Moore, Carey Newman, Mark Noll, Mike Parsons, and Dennis Sansom. It is a special honor to name former students who have assisted my efforts in all sorts of ways: Kristen Bargeron, Steve Blakemore, Cindy Caldwell, Pete Candler, Ken and Pam Carter, Marti Greene Eades, Matthews Grant, David Green, John Hayes, Tim Hood, Galen Johnson, Araminta Johnston, Pamela and Jeff Kinlaw, Jim McCoy, Ann and Brewster Rawls, and John Sykes. I have also been aided by four graduate assistants who have labored tirelessly in my behalf: Bryan Hollon, Jennifer Hughes, Don Shipley, and Jonathan Speegle. Diane Smith has also done splendid work as my editor at the Baylor Press. I cannot end my list of friends to thank without the confession that all of my teaching and writing, all of my thinking and living, have been permanently shaped by the faithful witness of Warren Carr, the Baptist preacher and pastor who first taught me that to be Christian is to make witness in and through Christ's church.

All of the chapters are thoroughly reworked versions of previously published essays or addresses, and it is a pleasure to acknowledge their origins. Parts of Chapters 1 and 6 were delivered to the Southwest Lilly Fellows Program in Humanities and the Arts, meeting at the University of Dallas. Chapter 2 originally appeared in the *Christian Century* as "Russell Kirk, Knight of Cheerful Conservatism." Chapter 3 was published as "To the Unknown God: Peter Berger's Theology of Transcendence," first in *Perspectives in Religious Studies*, and then, slightly revised, in *dialog*. Chapter 4 is an elaboration of a review for *First Things* entitled "Evangelicalism, With and Without Reformation." Chapter 5 develops ideas first broached in a *Christian Century* review-essay called "Rest Not in Peace: James Burtchaell on the Death and Rebirth of Christian Colleges." Chapter 7 was originally a *First Things* essay entitled "In Defense of Disbelief." Chapter 8 appeared in a festschrift for William L. Hendricks, *Baptist Reflections on Christianity and the Arts*. Chapter 9 had its origins in a Valentine's Day meditation for the Wake Forest University chapter of InterVarsity Christian Fellowship. Chapter 10 was delivered at a symposium on evangelical theology and Christian spirituality at the Beeson Divinity School of Samford University in Birmingham, and it was printed in *Christian Ethics Today*.

Introduction

The social critic Christopher Clausen argues that we live in a post-cultural age. He maintains that ours is a time of such rampant individualism, such rapid hybridizing and amalgamation of ethnic and linguistic and religious groups, that nearly all cultural distinctions have collapsed. "Twentieth century America is a graveyard of cultures," he declares.[1] Culture once signified the totality of learned behavior that a particular society inculcated in its inhabitants. Such enculturation occurred through various institutions and practices which, though gradually changing, were basically stable: sexual ethics, property divisions, status differentiations, kinship and inheritance rules, arts and athletics, government and trade policies, funeral rites, religious beliefs, etc. Culture in this sense, Clausen contends, is all but dead, at least in the United States. The single remaining universal value, he insists, is self-fulfillment. It is a powerful corrosive against all conviction that we are constrained by, or even obliged to, anything transcending the omnivorous and autonomous self—whether family, school, city, country, or God. Nihilism and atheism are not the right words to describe this condition, in my opinion, since they both imply an overt rejection of transcendent norms. Though Clausen is loath to use the term, I believe that ours is an anticultural era: an era that is rejecting, with increasing vehemence, even the most basic requirements of life together and life before God.

What is to be done about such a massive rebarbarizing of the world? The argument of this book is that Christian existence itself requires a culture: a realm where the most fundamental practices and doctrines of the church can be inculcated. My aim is not, therefore, to offer one of the standard responses to culture described by H. Richard Niebuhr more than fifty years ago in his *Christ and Culture.* As John Howard Yoder and others have shown, Niebuhr viewed culture as monolithic and autonomous, when in fact it is an immensely varied and dependent thing. Yet, if Clausen is right, even a drastically modified notion of culture will no longer suffice. If there is no real culture to affirm or oppose or transform, then the church may be called to create its own culture. I will argue, in fact, that Scripture and Tradition provide the church with a distinctive kind of existence—with unique ways of birthing and dying, of becoming youthful and growing old, of marrying and remaining single, of celebrating and sacrificing, of thinking and imagining,

1

of worshipping the true God and protesting against false gods—and that
these distinctive beliefs and practices constitute the church's own culture.

To make this claim is not to urge the church toward a self-contained life,
much less to form a ghetto of its own over against its new anticultural envi-
rons. Precisely to the contrary: Jesus Christ lived and died and rose, not for
the sake of the church but the world. Better put: the Jesus whom Christians
call Messiah, like Israel itself, constitutes his people as the church in order
that, through them, all the families of the earth might be blessed (Gen. 12:3;
Acts 3:25). And in a world increasingly void even of a culture that would
supply it with the very fundaments of common existence, the church is
called to bless the world by providing it such a culture. Its task is not to create a counter-culture, so much as a new culture based on one so ancient and
nearly forgotten that it looks freshly minted.

Two Unacceptable Alternatives

Before describing what such a Christian cultural alternative might look
like, we must first examine some of the unacceptable cultural alternatives
that have appeared on both the left and the right. The most obvious option
on the left is multiculturalism. It holds that we must learn to tolerate several distinct cultures within our single American society; in fact, that we must
grant each minority culture its own protection from being reduced to mush
in the great American stew. The old melting pot metaphor, once so venerat-
ed, is now considered racist. Though himself a man of the left, Clausen
argues, as we shall see, that the multiculturalist demand for diversity and
inclusiveness is a huge exertion in self-deception. There are virtually no cultures left to protect, he contends, since they are all crumbling under the
hammer of our rampant individualism.

Culture warriors on the right want to combat such individualist nihilism
by reinstantiating family values, respect for the flag, reverence for religion,
and the like. They want to recover the lost culture of small-town America.
Yet the conservative call to restore community life by centering it on a common set of binding assumptions presumes that such shared beliefs and
virtues are still available. Clausen argues, by contrast, that the very notion of
picking-and-choosing one's values, even if they be noble rather than self-
serving, already signals the real death of culture. Cultures come as whole and
organic things developed slowly over time. They are inherited rather than
invented, and they do their work silently and anonymously rather than by
way of overt and conscious choice. Indeed, it is the multiculturalists who
hold that one can choose one's culture. Not only have the left and the right

thus become kinsmen unawares, they have also changed places. Today's conservatives were yesterday's liberals. It was liberals such as John Stuart Mill and Lord Acton who invented the idea that the individual should be freed to make his own life, so long as it doesn't infringe on the right of others to do the same thing. Though these Victorians both believed that conscience and duty would restrain most people from becoming utterly self-serving, they offered no larger conception of the good which might sponsor such constraint.

The upshot of the matter is that both conservatives and liberals, despite their seeming antipodal differences, are very much the products of the Enlightenment. To state the matter oversimply but still truly, our seventeenth- and eighteenth-century forebears sought to solve the ancient problem of oppression by naïve recourse to tolerance, equality, and human rights—without noting the limits of such goods, nor asking whether they must be grounded in historical institutions and faith-sustained communities that serve both to restrain their excesses and to inspire their realization. There is no doubt that the Enlightenment project as supported by the churches accomplished many valuable things—from the abolition of slavery to the public education for the masses, from the establishment of due process to the unfettering of women and the poor from their oppressed condition. Too often, alas, both the churches and their humanist friends failed to ground their common enterprise in any larger conception of the good than the freedom to pursue happiness in one's own individual way.

Christian Contention concerning the Triune Mystery

After Flannery O'Connor had given a lecture at Emory University in 1961, she was approached by a shy freshman who, as a youth called to Christian ministry, was troubled by the doubts that his college courses had raised about the most fundamental concerns of his faith. His name was Alfred Corn, and he was later to become a distinguished poet. Young Corn feared that he had lost his faith. O'Connor later replied to Corn's questions by letter. She insisted that Christian faith is never a thing to be taken for granted, never a set of confident assumptions that one relies on without challenge. It is rather a matter of what this book will call contention. Exactly because faith is God's supreme gift, it requires our constant wrestling and striving, our effortful endeavor to gain greater clarity and conviction, our persistent probing of its mysterious depths, even our Jacob-like grappling with God amidst doubts that, far from being vices, become strange virtues. Hence O'Connor to Corn:

I think that this experience you are having of losing your faith, or as you think, of having lost it, is an experience that in the long run belongs to faith [. . . .]

I don't know how the kind of faith required of a Christian living in the 20th century can be at all if it is not grounded on this experience that you are having right now of unbelief. This may be the case always and not just in the 20th century. [As the father of the epileptic son in Mark's gospel said,] "Lord, I believe. Help my unbelief." It is the most natural and most human and most agonizing prayer in the gospels, and I think it is the foundation prayer of faith [. . . .][2]

As O'Connor makes clear, Christian faith is both engendered and sustained by an entrustment of the will and heart as well as a clarification of the mind. The central thesis of this book is that contemporary Christian existence thus requires contention: a rigorous engagement with the brutal realities of this bloodiest of all epochs, as the church confronts its environing culture with the radical claims and demands of the Gospel. The twin tasks for life in the church today, I shall argue, are to make arguments and to provide alternatives.

The church faces a perennially difficult challenge because the God of the Bible is perennially hidden rather than obvious. He is the God of Abraham, Isaac, and Jacob; the God of Golgotha, the God who remains mysterious, concealed, even unknown. "Truly," cries Isaiah, "thou art a God who hidest thyself, O God of Israel, the Savior" (45:15).[3] Only through God's own acts of self-identification, pre-eminently in Israel and Jesus, does He reveal himself. Even these acts of divine self-disclosure grant no easy certainties or absolute answers. The Cross, as God's largest and most drastic demonstration of his presence in the world, also remains the event of God's most drastic absence. "Let this cup pass from me." "My God, my God, why hast thou forsaken me?" (Matt. 26:39; 27:46.)

This radical sense of God's presence-in-absence has long been a staple of Christian theology. Hans Urs von Balthasar is perhaps its most eloquent twentieth-century advocate. He insists that we in the west have too lightly abandoned the apophatic theology of the Orthodox east, especially as it came to focus in pseudo-Dionysius. The early fathers of the church insisted that we know God truly only as we first acknowledge his overwhelming otherness—his total difference from us and all other created beings. God is not one Being among beings, and certainly not the Supreme Being. Hence von Balthasar's constant recurrence to the formula of the Fourth Lateran Council (1215) concerning the likeness and unlikeness of earthly things to God: *the ever greater dissimilarity to God no matter how great the similarity to Him.*[4]

The more we know about God, even through his own acts of self-demonstration, the greater our unknowing, the fuller our need for further understanding, the deeper our plunge into the one Mystery which produces the humility of ever-increasing knowledge and ever-growing ignorance.

To proclaim this divine Mystery in word, to live it out in deed, to celebrate it in sacrament, is for the church to offer the world a set of drastic alternatives that it cannot offer itself. This book concerns the various forms that these Christian alternatives take—cultural, educational, liturgical, artistic, apologetic, political. It is not a book addressed, therefore, to a purportedly timeless or placeless audience. It is aimed primarily at American Christians living in the prosperous but troublous years of the early twenty-first century. It seeks to engage secular and non-Christian readers as well. While I am myself a Baptist who teaches at a Christian university situated in a city that forms the western terminus of the Old South, my sympathies and convictions are neither denominational nor regional nor merely Protestant. I have been deeply and thankfully formed by Roman Catholic and Eastern Orthodox traditions as well.

All three of the major Christian traditions teach a common lesson, even if they disagree about the way it works itself out in both the church and the world. They teach that the God who has displayed his own triune life, first through the nation Israel, and finally in the life and death and resurrection of Jesus, invites—indeed, requires—his people to participate in it. This is the God who, as Karl Barth liked to say, refuses to be God alone and unto himself, to be God without his People. There is no God-beyond-God, no far-off Father who relativizes all religions, no pre-Trinitarian issuer of the terrible decrees. There is only—but also finally and fully—the God whose life becomes ours when we are baptized in the reality-creating name of the Father and the Son and the Holy Spirit. The late Walker Percy put the matter somewhat amusingly when he hyphenated the inseparable realities which we must simultaneously declare: God-Israel-Christ-Church.

To utter this hyphenated phrase is to admit that Christian faith is not centered in private and inner experience so much as in outer and public life—in an alternative existence to the world's existence, a life displayed in Scripture and tradition and practiced in the church. Rather than identifying itself with various cultural and political endeavors, no matter how worthy and admirable, the church seeks to embody what Barry Harvey, borrowing from St. Augustine, calls an *alteras civitas*, Another City. This city which is not made with hands reveals, as we shall see, that the chief earthly cities that call themselves conservative and liberal are but unwitting twins. Though they polemicize against each other, I will argue that their assumptions are

nearly identical. I will also seek to show that, rather than baptizing the causes of either the right or the left, the church is called to embody a clear
counter-option to both, even as it seeks common cause with various secular
projects that serve as parables or reflections of the Gospel.[5]

The Good News as Argument

The church can pose a distinctive counter-life to a stultified culture only
because it has distinctive doctrines and indispensable practices of its own.
Though hardly reducible to clear and distinct propositions that submit to
logical proof, there would be no Christian existence without them. They
have their validity not merely in being stated. They must also be explained
and defended. Contention of another kind is thus required of Christians.
The word *contentio* means not only struggle and exertion but also dispute
and argument. Christians are called, therefore, to make their own case—
their *apologia* as it is called in 1 Peter 3:15—for the hope which has laid hold
on them. The central Christian claim that the Truth has become flesh and
dwelt among us allows for no ghetto-faith. Jesus is not only the Christ for
Christians alone, but for the whole world. He is Lord not only for those who
believe in Him but, in ways often staggeringly strange, even for those who
do not. To claim the finality and absoluteness of the Christian revelation has
become exceedingly difficult in our pluralistic and relativistic age. Yet nothing less is required if Jesus is indeed the single name given throughout history by which human existence is to be saved. Hence our summons to a
Christian existence that requires argument. Truth which is true only for me,
as Augustine tartly remarked, is not true even for me. Christ is not the center of a circle inhabited by Christians alone: He is the core of the entire cosmos. The truth revealed in the God of the Gospel is not local and partial but
universal and absolute.

Such assertions require arguments, and one aim of this book is to supply them. Apologetics of the traditional sort, we must confess, is not the tack
taken here. To defend God, said Barth, is to insult God. The Gospel would
no longer require our scandalous obedience if its truth could be demonstrated by proofs. Søren Kierkegaard wittily dismissed apologetics as "the old
military science," a blunderbuss shot fired across the bow of faith's cultured
despisers and deniers. Thus put on the defensive, the enemies of Christianity
volley back their own missiles. The resulting battle bloodies both sides but
leaves no one edified, much less converted. Hence Kierkegaard's cunning
suggestion that the best apologetic approach is to attack from the rear, to
sting pagans and secularists alike into a surprising consideration of the

Gospel, not by the cannonade of a frontal assault but by the gadfly's satirical bite.

Kierkegaard possessed a hornet-like dexterity of imaginative movement, but we of less nimble gifts must resort to more pedestrian engagements of the world with the witness of the Gospel. John Howard Yoder has taught us, in his important critique of H. Richard Niebuhr's *Christ and Culture*, that culture is no monolithic and autonomous thing that requires a single Christian response. Rather does it come in many varieties and require several responses. Yet Yoder is no advocate of a convenient sort of Christian pluralism which assumes that all theological positions, because they are all so severely limited, somehow interlock into an ever-so-vague unity. Appeals to divine sovereignty and ecumenical openness, Yoder observes by contrast, cannot obscure the fact that "there is such a thing as *binding* revelation, valid knowledge, or a firm moral imperative. [. . .] God's transcendence is [. . .] the ground of the assurance that our knowledge of God's call, and to some extent of his nature, is reliable and binding because, even though partial, it comes from God when it encounters us in Christ."[6]

The task of Christians in seeking to make arguments that are bound by the definitive call and revelation given in Jesus Christ is a task of discrimination and discernment, a labor of analogy and connection. Some forms of culture—Nazi and Soviet totalitarianism, for example—are clearly inimical to the Gospel. Freedom-granting cultures, especially when they do not hinder the church's liberty to announce and enact its own scandalous Gospel—demand the church's qualified assent. So do sentimental and moralistic forms of worship remain deeply alien to the Faith, even when the church endorses them. Secular forms of art, by contrast, when they denounce churchly sentimentality and hold hard to the integrity of human doubt and fear, require Christian confirmation. Thus does the range of Christian discernment run from vehement rejection to charitable approval. Yoder demonstrates both the obvious and subtle judgments that Christian discrimination requires:

> Some elements of culture the church categorically rejects (pornography, tyranny, cultic idolatry). Other dimensions of culture it accepts within clear limits (economic production, commerce, the graphic arts, paying taxes for peacetime civil government). To still other dimensions of culture Christian faith gives a new motivation and coherence (agriculture, family life, literacy, conflict resolution, empowerment). Still others it strips of their claims to possess autonomous truth and value, and uses them as vehicles of communication (philosophy, language, Old Testament ritual, music). Still other forms of culture are created by the Christian churches

(hospitals, service of the poor, generalized education, egalitarianism, abolitionism, feminism).[7]

The Piquancy of the Particular

Rather than letting such judgments remain stratospheric in their abstraction, this book aims to make such discriminations while engaged with concrete problems and texts and authors. In every case, I will seek to provide more than merely theoretical answers, even when the questions are in fact theoretical. Rather will I examine particular thinkers and writers, many of whom do not make their way into most discussions of the church-and-culture question. Concerning the controversy about culture as being an entirely human creation or as arising out of an eternal order, for example, I will examine the work of Peter Berger and Russell Kirk, the one a sociologist of religion and the other a cultural critic. When wrestling with the character of the Christian academy, I will enter dialogue with James Burtchaell and Robert Benne, the one a Roman Catholic and the other an Evangelical Lutheran. In assessing the church's worship, I have drawn primarily on the work of G. K. Chesterton and Flannery O'Connor, both of them Roman Catholics. In seeking to provide an alternative to the sentimental unbelief that pervades much of Christian culture, I will draw upon the work of Christopher Morse as well as Peter De Vries, the one a United Methodist theologian and the other a lapsed Dutch Calvinist novelist. In assessing the state of evangelicalism and the vogue for spirituality, I will have recourse to the work of Mark Noll, a contemporary church historian, on the one hand, and to Charles and John Wesley, the eighteenth-century founders of Methodism, among others. And in seeking to describe the burden of a distinctively Christian kind of education, I will make appeal to such notably non-Christian writers as Mark Twain, William Faulkner and Emily Dickinson.

My purpose in examining these particular figures is not to locate some safe middle position, nor to play opposites against each other for the sake of some putative higher synthesis. Neither do I seek to provoke a conversation that knows no terminus. As G. K. Chesterton famously reminded H. G. Wells, "the object of opening the mind, as of opening the mouth, is to shut it again on something solid."[8] My aim, therefore, is to put countervailing viewpoints into a conversation that produces something substantial, even when they clash and contradict no less than complement each other. My hope is to arrive at conclusions that may be of use both to the academy and the church. Whether the effort succeeds or fails, I will abide by my most basic conviction: that Christian faith cannot be identified with any particular cultural program, with any conservative or liberal politics, with any literary or philosophical school. Rather will I attempt to show that the Gospel produces arguments and embodies alternatives, not only to its many secular substitutes, but also to allegedly Christian options that lack the tang and piquancy of Christian particularity.

Karl Barth spent his entire career reiterating the basic truth that all attempts to identify the Gospel with this or that worldly enterprise, no matter how worthy, end in the worst of all idolatries. They make Christ the servant of such endeavors, when he is meant to be their Lord. As one who had witnessed at first hand the terrible work of the *Deutschen Christen*—and who had authored the Barmen Declaration in refutation of them—Barth knew that an acculturated Christian existence can offer no prophetic critique of culture, even against a culture as palpably evil as Nazi Germany. Hence his unwillingness, as a convinced lifelong socialist, to retain membership in the Christian Socialist Party. For Barth there was no such thing as a Christian politics or Christian culture, a Christian music or Christian philosophy. He was extraordinarily chary about using the word "Christian" as an adjective of any kind—convinced, as he was, that nouns govern adjectives and that "Christian" refers to members of the Body of Christ.

In one of his wittiest sayings, hidden amidst the eye-straining small print of the Church Dogmatics, Barth declared that God's greatest enemy is the fatal little word "and." The heart of the Old Testament attack on the worship of other gods, as well as the New Testament attack on belief in other gospels, Barth insists, lies in their dread fear of combining and coordinating the Word of God with "the authority and contents of other supposed revelations and truths of God."[9] The moment we speak of "the Gospel and," we have ceased to speak of the Gospel at all. Barth supplies discomfiting examples of secondary truths that bid for Christian endorsement:

> There are [. . .] Christian nations in which it is customary to find a prominent place in the church for national flags as well as the pulpit and the Lord's table, just as there are evangelical churches which substitute for the Lord's table a meaningfully furnished apparatus for the accomplishment of baptism by immersion. These externals, of course, are trivial in themselves. But as such they may well be symptoms of the attempt [. . .] to incorporate that which is alien in other prophecies into what is proper to that of Jesus Christ. If these [alien] prophecies are prepared for this—and sooner or later they will make their bid for sole dominion—the prophecy of Jesus Christ asks to be excused and avoids such incorporation. If it is subjected to such combinations, the living Lord Jesus and His Word

depart, and all that usually remains is the suspiciously loud but empty utterance of the familiar name of [Jesus Christ]. "No man can serve two masters" (Mt. 6:24). No man can serve both the one Word of God called Jesus Christ and other divine words.[10]

Barth's radical claims do not sequester the Gospel in some remote Olympian eyrie, high above all earthly goods, looking down with immaculate disdain on their impurity. As Barth notes, there are indeed other manifestations of God that Christians must honor, but never in a way that makes them equivalent to the singular revelation given in Israel and Christ. Idolphobia can be as dangerous as idolatry, if it encourages Christians to remain righteously aloof from the human fray. As Stanley Hauerwas and William Willimon have observed, the real threat of idolatry may be found less in worshipping false gods than in attempting to use the true God for our own ends. They offer a sharp rejoinder, therefore, to an Alabama supreme court judge as well as to Ted Koppel, both of whom want to make the Ten Commandments into ethical guidelines for overcoming the moral problems of our culture:

> We cannot understand the commandments, the Decalogue ("Ten Words"), apart from the worship of the true God. Those who do not worship God will catch a glimpse of that God when they, for example, tell the truth. But the obeying of an isolated commandment is not to know the commandment "perfectly." The Ten Commandments are meant for those who are known in the God of Abraham, Isaac, Jacob, the God of Jesus Christ. The commandments are the way we learn to worship the true God truthfully, not the way we make American democratic pluralism work.[11]

This is not to say, of course, that the Gospel is intended only for the church's justification when, in fact, it is meant for the world's salvation. But the church will offer the world real hope only as it becomes clear about the unique character of its own Message as it is worked out in the midst of the world. Hence the aim of this book: to take the measure of culture through the focus of the cross, the narrowest of apertures which opens onto the widest of worlds, affirming what is good in the various expressions of culture, decrying what is evil, engaging both friends and enemies alike with the Good News of Jesus Christ. To this privileged task we now turn.

Chapter 1

The Crisis Afflicting Church and Culture Alike

Our first task is to define the nature of the crisis that besets not only the church but also its environing culture. Though the church exists to make witness to the world, it often serves as a mere mirror to it. Nowhere is this malady more evident than in the massive ignorance about Christian culture and traditions that any college teacher of the humanities repeatedly encounters. In her story entitled "Greenleaf," Flannery O'Connor names two of her child characters Wesley and Scofield, yet almost none of my students ever catch either allusion. I might not expect them to know of Cyrus Scofield (1823–1921), editor of the celebrated *Scofield Reference Bible*, which was much revered in the South because it was annotated along Dispensationalist lines. But surely it is a scandal that virtually no one recognizes the founder of Methodism. After one of my Methodist pastor-friends kept quoting Wesley in his sermons, his wife overheard two parishioners discussing the matter: "Who is this Wesley fellow?" asked one of the Methodist ladies. "I don't know," replied the other; "it must be a friend of his." A Baylor colleague began a class by asking if his students were aware of that particular day's special significance. No one had noticed that it was Yom Kippur. Yet these students were ignorant not only about the timing but also about the meaning of the day. When my professor-friend then explained what happens on the Day of Atonement, they were still largely oblivious to its connection with Christianity.

Still another friend tells of the shock she received upon attending a Christmas party for her university's computer technology staff. When the time came to sing carols, she quickly discovered that most of the technicians did not know even the most basic songs of the season. I also recall a memorial service, held in the chapel of my former university, for three students who had been run down by a reckless driver. Asked to repeat the 23rd Psalm, most of the audience could not do so. If these pieces of anecdotal evidence are indicative, as I believe they are, they reveal that even our Christian colleges and universities are in danger of producing what C. S. Lewis called "trousered apes"[1] and other critics have described as "barbarians with clean fingernails." We may be in dire peril of graduating professionally well-trained people who are almost wholly ignorant of their own intellectual and religious traditions.

Such litanies of Christian illiteracy could be multiplied endlessly. Lest I be found guilty of my own smug self-congratulation, let one final example suffice. Our own formerly Baptist minister, journalist, and presidential adviser Bill Moyers helped John Kennedy gain the American presidency in 1960 by writing a celebrated speech wherein Kennedy assured a meeting of Houston pastors that his Catholicism would not prejudice his presidency. Moyers was rightly commended for having helped Baptists and many other Protestants to overcome their anti-Catholicism, for in his speech Kennedy pointed to both the Constitution's Bill of Rights and the Virginia Statute of Religious Freedom as protections against the denial of elected office to anyone because of their religious convictions.

Yet virtually no one bothered to question why Moyers should have had Kennedy stress that his "views on religion are his own private affair." "What kind of church I believe in," Moyers had Kennedy declare, "should be important only to me." The one thing that mattered, he added, was "what kind of America I believe in." Kennedy also insisted that the fulfillment of his presidential office would not be "limited or conditioned by any religious oath, ritual, or obligation." This is an astonishing claim to be made by any Christian who, as in Kennedy's case, has vowed in his baptism to abjure the devil and all his pomps, in the sacramental Supper to die with Christ rather than forsake the faith, and in reciting the creeds to give first and last fealty to none other than the triune God. Moyer's speech had Kennedy appeal, instead, for Protestants and Catholics and Jews to "promote instead the American ideal of brotherhood."[2] Perhaps Kennedy would not have been elected if Moyers had written a speech urging Baptists and other Protestants to vote for Kennedy only if his religion *would indeed* shape his policies and decisions as president, since Christian faith is not chiefly a private but a public matter, and since the church has a rich and complex tradition of teaching about the right relation of the church and the state. But perhaps we might also have been spared the horror of Vietnam.

Civilization vs. Culture

Our task is to ask what we might do about this crisis of Christian culture in church-affiliated colleges and universities. I will argue in the following chapter that we should seek vigorously and diligently to create a Christian educational culture of our own. But such a prescription must follow a prior description of what I conceive to be our massive educational malaise.

We would do well to begin with a definition of terms. The word "culture" has immensely complex origins and uses, many of them contradictory. Suffice it to say that the Latin *cultura* was linked to the cultivation of crops and to the husbandry of animals. Not until the sixteenth century was the word extended to the domain of human growth and development. By the eighteenth and nineteenth centuries, *culture* had become a virtual synonym for *civilization*. Yet a huge shift had occurred. The term "civilization" pointed to life in the *civitas*—to the truly human state or city wherever it is found, not only in Athens or Rome or Constantinople. Civilization entailed a set of restrictions and limitations no less than a host of virtues and possibilities. To be civilized meant that human character is to be shaped by received communal traditions and *mores*, that citizens are formed by values and virtues which they do not choose for themselves, but which they receive almost through the pores of their skin, via the very atmosphere of their homes and schools, their holy places and their cities.[3]

It is true that the word "culture" seeks to retain the old meaning of civilization as a particular way of life. Hence Max Weber's definition of culture as the "web of significance," the matrix with reference to which everything else makes sense.[4] The anthropologist Clifford Geertz defines culture in similar terms as "an historically transmitted pattern of meanings embodied in symbols."[5] But the prominence now given to "culture" represents a decisive novelty. As with the old Latin *cultura* and its link to agriculture, so does our modern word "culture" imply what "civilization" never connoted—namely, growth and development and progress. From the Enlightenment forward, culture came to mean an advance upward from barbaric savagery—first into the domestication of wanderers and gatherers, then slowly into the social existence of mature human societies, and finally into the life of free and autonomous beings. Unlike civilization, culture in its modern sense does not seek to shape us toward definite pre-determined ends, so much as it liberates and improves us according to ends, whether personal or social, that we freely choose for ourselves. No ancient Greek or Roman or medieval Christian could have conceived of freedom in this fashion—as lying in what the

Declaration of Independence calls our own "pursuit of happiness." For our ancient forebears, by contrast, happiness was a derivative by-product of civilized life in the well-ordered *polis*. It is not surprising, then, that the word "civilization" gradually became linked with stagnating and calcifying institutions which were thought to work against the aims of freedom-enabling culture.

Two Kinds of Multiculturalism

There is neither world enough nor time to trace out the radical implications of this seismic shift in emphasis from civilization to culture. The most obvious result is the contemporary notion that there is not one but many cultural ways of seeking our liberty and pursuing our happiness. It has become a commonplace, therefore, to call ours a multicultural age. If we mean by this claim that ours is increasingly a world of multiple races and ethnicities and religions, then the truism is surely true. It is often observed that there are now more Muslims than Episcopalians and Presbyterians in the U.S., and that there are more Anglicans in Africa than in Britain. When my family lived in the London neighborhood of St. John's Wood in 1988, we noticed that the outstanding landmark in this elegant old section of the city was, even then, a soaring mosque. A huge new Hindu temple is now visible from the train that plies between London and the Heathrow Airport. San Francisco and Toronto and New York, like Houston and Washington and Los Angeles, have the feel not of western and Anglophone cities so much as multilingual and multicultural places. Most of our major urban centers, if the recent population statistics are reliable, will become ever more fully hybridized. Challenging the *de facto* reality of multiculturalism is rather like challenging the August heat in Texas.

Many educators believe that it is a good thing when our college campuses display a kindred diversity of cultures and ethnicities. If by this assertion they mean that Christian schools must welcome "all sorts and conditions of men," as the Book of Common Prayer puts it, then surely they are right. Yet it is another matter entirely for the Christian academy to embrace what Stanley Fish calls a "strong" multiculturalism. It values difference in and for itself, believing that we must honor the particular and substantial ways in which persons and cultures differ. These strong multiculturalists call us to nurture particularity and diversity through a tolerance that is understood as a first principle of both personal morality and public policy.

This multiculturalism of difference holds, as its central premise, that the greater the differences among us, the greater the good. Multiple viewpoints and multiple interests enlarge our comprehension of truth, whereas a singular culture and perspective shrink both knowledge and wisdom. Christians can find much truth in this assumption. Dialogical encounters with the "other" have been intrinsic to the Gospel at least since St. Paul's sermon on Mars Hill recorded in Acts 17. Yet the majority of Paul's pagan hearers turned away from his preaching when he mentioned Christ's scandalous resurrection from the dead, revealing the limits of even the Apostle's irenic attempt at engagement.

Fish declares that such an impasse will always come, not only for confessing Christians, but for serious multiculturalists as well: the time when a particular religious and cultural tradition will reveal itself to be intolerant at the core:

> The distinctiveness that marks it as unique and self-defining will resist the appeal of moderation or incorporation into a larger whole. Confronted with a demand that it surrender its view point or enlarge it to include the practices of its natural enemies—other religions, other races, other genders, other classes—a beleaguered culture will fight back with everything from discriminatory legislation to violence.[6]

Fish cites, as an obvious example, the death sentence handed down by the Ayatollah Khomeini against author Salman Rushdie for his alleged slurs against Mohammed in his novel entitled *The Satanic Verses*. The dilemma for serious multiculturalists quickly becomes evident. They must stretch their tolerance to include the intolerance of a group that they abhor, thus rejecting tolerance as their first principle; or else they must condemn the intolerance, in which case they no longer advocate multiculturalism at the very point where it is most obviously at stake. In a very real sense, one must conclude, there is no such thing as a thoroughgoing multiculturalism, either epistemically or morally. At bottom we are all willy-nilly particularists, for we all privilege the practices and institutions of one social order over others.

Over against the multiculturalism of difference Fish poses what he calls a "boutique" multiculturalism, a trendy admiration of nearly every other culture than one's own: "Boutique multiculturalism is the multiculturalism of ethnic restaurants, weekend festivals, and high-profile flirtations with the other in the manner satirized by Tom Wolfe under the rubric of 'radical chic.'"[7] Boutique multiculturalism cannot finally value the central affirmations of other traditions, because it sees them not as basic and definitive, but as mere accessories to a standard model of universal humanity as defined by the boutiquers own Enlightenment rationalism. Boutique multiculturalism thus limits itself to a superficial respect of other ways of life, unable to regard radical cultural particularity as any other than "icing on a basically homogeneous cake."

There is much that is fashionably anti-American and anti-Western in the boutique multiculturalists. They often invest so-called "indigenous" cultures with highly idealized qualities that they want American society to make its own: peacefulness, non-competition, care for the environment, sexual liberation, and the like. Yet while deploring the ruination of pristine native cultures by the spread of dreaded "McWorld" values, they have no desire to import the Chinese custom of female infanticide, the Indian system of caste, the practice of clitorectomy among certain African Muslims, etc. Already in 1965 the philosopher-scientist Michael Polanyi had given an apt name to the force that undergirds boutique multiculturalism. It is a "moral nihilism charged with moral fury," declared Polanyi, that should be properly called "*moral inversion*."[8]

The enmeshment of cultures is altogether as likely to divide as to unite—indeed, to produce war and permanent strife, as Ireland, Israel-Palestine, the Balkans, and sub-Saharan Africa all attest. Ortega y Gasset thus insisted that cultural and ethnic differences are beneficial only when a civilization is imbued with a common purpose and mission that unifies deep cultural disparities.[9] Without commonality of vision and virtue, I would add, only inexhaustible wealth and unlimited consumption can serve to bond a culture. Perhaps such materialist glue is the real substance that makes twenty-first-century American culture cohere. If this is indeed the case, then Christian education has an even more radical call—namely, to help remedy a malaise that is devastating the church and the academy alike.

The Post-Modern Character of the Church and the Academy

Just as there are two kinds of multiculturalisms, so are there at least two varieties of post-modernism. The multiculturalism of difference holds, as we have seen, that there are no value-neutral distinctions to be made among cultures and civilizations: we see by way of the blinders and binoculars of our own time and place. Such strong multiculturalism, at least in this regard, is closely allied to post-modernism. They both deny the Enlightenment assumption that it is possible to stand above the flux of history and to view things *sub specie aeternitatis*. This modernist and foundationalist premise holds that all people of good will and right mind can agree upon the basic moral rules that are essential for human existence. The American Founders are perhaps the most obvious exemplars of the notion that we can sacralize certain virtues—indeed, that we can build a new world order on them—without much regard either for their dependence upon particular historical communities or their rootage in particular narrative traditions and religious practices.

It is precisely this modernist premise that post-modernism denies. There is no vision without glasses, the post-modernists insist, since we all wear lenses of one culture or another. To stand outside time and space is the ultimate Enlightenment delusion, for it ignores our locatedness, and thus the historical character of all our knowledge and truth. This radical post-modern premise can be taken in opposite directions, one destructive and nihilistic, the other constructive and redemptive. Post-modernists such as Richard Rorty conclude that, since all of our seeing is a lensed seeing, we cannot declare any single perspective superior to another. There is nothing outside ourselves that can command our obedience. "'Post-modern' philosophers," Rorty writes, "are willing to respect reality as presenting us with problems to be dealt with, but not as an authority to be obeyed."[10] Given such a view of "reality," it follows that we must choose whatever way of life conduces to our own private happiness, so long as it doesn't harm others: "[. . .] the only test for a political proposal is its ability to gain assent from people who retain radically diverse ideas about the point and meaning of human life, about the path to private perfection."[11] The substance and content of this curious "assent" remains open and undefined, for Rorty embraces what he calls "the Whitmanesque and Whiteheadian romance of unpredictable change." The preferences of individual agents must always have supremacy. Hence Rorty's utopian confession of "the need to create new ways of being human, and a new heaven and a new earth for these new humans to inhabit, over the desire for stability, security and order."[12]

Rorty's kind of perspectivism offers a philosophically rigorous case for multiculturalism, denying the naive notion that we can occupy a hypothetical eyrie outside the cosmos. Yet Rorty honestly admits, as many multiculturalists do not, that this very inability to transcend ourselves makes the preference for Martin Luther King over Charles Manson largely personal. One of Rorty's advocates, James Edwards, willingly embraces the nihilistic implications of a Rortian aestheticism as it is practiced in ordinary American life:

> In air-conditioned comfort one can stroll from life to life, from world to world, complete with appropriate sound effects (beeping computers; roar-

ing lions). Laid out before one are whole lives that one can, if one has the necessary credit line, freely choose to inhabit: devout Christian; high-tech yuppie; Down East guide; great white hunter. This striking transforma- tion of life into lifestyle, the way in which the tools, garments, and atti- tudes specific to particular times and places become commodities to be marketed to anonymous and rootless consumers: they are the natural (if also banal) expressions of our normal nihilism.[13]

The life of self-construction is not likely to produce a somebody but an *any- body* having almost anything at its onion-like center. As Charles Taylor makes clear, an anybody is also a *nobody*: "This democratized self which has no necessary social identity can then be anything, can assume any role or take any point of view, because it *is* in and for itself nothing."[14]

Jeremy Bottum claims that Christians should not be panicked by the post-modernists. On the contrary, we are agreed with them that "knowledge depends on the existence of God." Truly to know a thing is to grasp what it is for, to know its ultimate cause and end—namely, God. "To the medieval eye," Bottum argues, "beings disclose their purposes precisely as they imitate God. God moves things as their final cause: the aim of their growth and motion, the object of their desire. Everything is thus an image of God [. . .]." Post-modernists deny such truthful knowledge, of course, but they are to be praised also for denying the false modernist claims to an unblinkered ratio- nality that is neutral and value-free when in fact it masks an unbridled will- to-power. So can we also reject the modernist reading of Aquinas and Anselm, among other medievals, as having sought to master the knowable God with their proofs for his existence. The post-modernists help us to read them as offering intellectual praise and worship for the God who can never be categorized. Hence Bottum's call for Christians to seize the post-mod- ernist moment:

> The collapse of modernity may allow believers to speak once again about God without defensiveness or self-consciousness, may allow believers both to escape political categorization as liberal or conservative and to escape the modern view that sees political categories as fundamental. [. . .] The [postmodernist] critique of modernity offers the possibility of reclaiming a long history of belief, the possibility of critically reading medieval authors without supposing them to be involved in the attempt to master God.[15]

Stanley Hauerwas, James Wm. McClendon, and John Milbank are among the most prominent Christian theologians who have sought to answer the post-modernism challenge. Rather than having first to establish the philosophical or moral grounds on which the Christ can be credited—thus making the Gospel a subset of some allegedly larger reality—they insist that the church is once again free to proclaim the Gospel as the unique and radical thing that it is: as the Truth which has no other foundation than the God revealed in Israel and Jesus Christ. Against the charge that this makes the Gospel irrelevant to the world's clamant questions and needs, leaving it isolated in its own little ghetto, the church seeks to demonstrate its universality by its own narratives and doctrines and practices. For these storied ways of living and believing answer the profoundest religious questions and meet the deepest human needs, not by offering one therapy among others, but by redefining these questions and needs in the light of God's self-declared will for the world in Israel and Christ.

To deny that truth can be known or faith embraced apart from narratively constituted communities—and thus to affirm that Christians know the truth about themselves and the world only through the story of Jesus as it is celebrated in the church and enacted in the world—is not to claim that there is no common humanity, no capitalized Truth, no singular Gospel declaring Jesus Christ to be "the way, the truth, and the life" (John 10:10). Much less does a radical Christian particularism condemn all cultures and religions to a Hobbesian war of all against all. Hauerwas summons the church to confess, for example, that Christians have been given the truth provisionally and thus that we must invite others to it peaceably. This narrow path of repentance and conversion distinguishes the church's way from the wide road of worldly coercion. Grandiose notions of natural and universal rights often serve, ironically, to justify military violence and political oppression.

Our churches and our universities have usually failed to offer a vigorous witness to the world by way of either Christian practices or Christian thinking. Thus have we become what we have heard Stanley Fish calling "boutique" post-modernists and multiculturalists. We have done it largely unawares, spreading before our people a set of autonomous and unencumbered choices as if such preferences constituted true freedom. Baptist theologian Barry Harvey describes this new kind of church as "simply another vendor of goods and services."[16] It is noteworthy that, seeking to commodify even the Gospel, many contemporary congregations have abandoned the old cruciform shape of suffering in their architecture and accoutrements, lest anyone be threatened with a reminder that they are called to reshape their lives in imitation of Golgotha. These churches are designed, instead, to resemble theaters and shopping centers: a gymnasium here, an exercise room there, a grief-counseling or weight-loss room elsewhere. So have worship services been transformed into an assortment of religious entertainments that serve to cheer and comfort us in largely therapeutic ways. Thus have we lost the real purpose of worship—namely, to re-define and transform our needs in light of the Gospel.[17]

Yet the academy has done little better than the church. Christian colleges and universities have also spread a bazaar of options before our students and told them to pick and choose rather as much as they wish. Our curricula are in great disarray, lacking anything other than the most minimal educational coherence. We have surrendered the conviction that educators know what things are requisite for serious learning, whether these requirements derive from general human wisdom or the specifically Christian tradition. We have come to believe that the curriculum should cater to what students prefer— as if we were to send a child sick with asthma to the medicine cabinet, telling him to choose whatever remedy he likes, even if he likes the sticky sweet cough drops.

We no longer hold, as our ancestors did, that young people are not yet capable of truly important choices. Their minds and characters must be formed, so our foreparents believed, before they know how rightly to decide about anything important. Mark Twain learned this lesson ruefully. By the time he was eighteen, Twain had discovered that his father was perhaps the most ignorant man on the planet. But by the time he reached twenty-five, Twain confessed, he could not believe how much his father had learned in just seven years! Ignoring the fundamentally unformed character of eighteen-year old minds, we teach them to make cafeteria choices about the most fundamental matters of religion, of morality—indeed, of truth itself. I believe that our task, quite to the contrary, is to help students shape their minds according to transcendent ends and purposes. The aim of education under the auspices of the church, I believe, is to teach students not to think for themselves, but to think in tandem with the rich complexity of the Christian tradition. For such thought to have both breadth and depth, we will need to engage other traditions, whether Greco-Roman, Eastern, African, or secular. Only then shall we succeed in not turning our students into mere sophisticated consumers—a lesson that our culture teaches them all too well—but into people of deep moral and religious conviction.

The Individualist Roots of our Cultural Malaise

The post-modern multiculturalism that now characterizes nearly every American university rests on the assumption that our universal humanity consists in our capacity for individual self-construction: "what makes a human being a human being is not the particular choices he or she makes but the capacity for choice itself."[18] Emerson sang this hymn in "Self-Reliance": "To believe your own thought, to believe that what is true for you in your private heart is true for all men,—that is genius." Yet Whitman was its true bard: "The whole theory of the universe is directed unerringly to one single individual—namely to You."[19] Against such brazen subjectivism, the conservatives rightly protest. They join the sociologist Robert Putnam in lamenting the loss of civic engagement in American life. A recent reviewer of Putnam's *Bowling Alone* offers this litany of community-oriented activities that have been largely lost:

> newspaper reading; TV news watching; attending political meetings; petition signing; running for public office; attending public meetings; serving as an officer in or committee member in any local clubs or organizations; writing letters to the editor; participating in local meetings of national organizations; attending religious services, socializing informally with friends, relatives or neighbors; attending club meetings; joining unions; entertaining friends at home; participating in picnics; eating the evening meal with the whole family; going out to bars, nightclubs, discos or taverns; playing cards; sending greeting cards; attending parties; playing sports; donating money as a percentage of income; working on community projects; giving blood.[20]

According to this individualist dream wished upon the star of nineteenth-century Romanticism, we can make up our identity out of whole cloth; we can strip away all of the bothersome particularities that locate us within concrete traditions; we can be free only as we rid ourselves of all the troublesome commitments and obligations that we have not chosen for ourselves.

Christians do not stand alone in questioning these assumptions. The notion that we are free only as we become autonomous selves who have been immunized from all moral and cultural obligations except those that we have independently elected is, after all, a notion of very recent vintage. As Alisdair MacIntyre has pointed out, traditional cultures regard the human self as irreducibly social. It is formed through a synthesis of communal roles and individual wills. The requirements of personal life are at once imposed from without and assumed from within. Character thus becomes a moral ideal legitimating certain modes of social existence. Wife, brother, cousin, household servant, village tribesman: these social roles are not *accidental* characteristics that must be sloughed off to disclose the "real self." They provide, on the contrary, the very framework for one's *essential* being:

They are part of my substance, defining partially at least and sometimes wholly my obligations and my duties. Individuals inherit a particular space within an interlocking set of social relationships; lacking that space, they are nobody, or at best a stranger or an outcast. To know oneself as such a social person is however not to occupy a static and fixed position. It is to find oneself placed within a certain point on a journey with set goals; to move through life is to make progress—or to fail to make progress—toward a given end. Thus a completed and fulfilled life is an achievement and death is the point at which one can be judged happy or unhappy. Hence the ancient Greek proverb: "Call no man happy until he is dead.[21]

Christians believe, it should be added, that the human journey is to a Life beyond life—toward either paradise or perdition—and that the quest for salvation has profound moral and social consequences. We become true persons only as we freely embrace the rightful obligations that have been laid upon us. Such responsibilities come to us less by our own choosing than through a thickly webbed network of shared friendships and familial ties and holy promises. Christians join their ancient forbears in believing that, in the very deepest sense, our "encumbrances" elect us before we elect them. We do not choose our convictions but rather, as the word suggests, we become *convinced* of them as the inexorable basis of our lives. There is no mythical free and self-originating person that exists apart from these communally produced convictions and ties. Nor do such ties bind us onerously, as many modernists believe, but blessedly, as the old Protestant hymn insists.

The Collapse of Culture Itself

To criticize contemporary individualism is not to call for the repristinization of some putative golden era that existed before our own wicked age dawned. On the contrary, nearly all of us are the blessed recipients of the political and religious liberalism that has made the modern world. My doctor-father, for instance, stood only two generations away from slavery. My own parents were first-generation college graduates, my grandparents were East Texas sharecroppers, and one of my uncles could neither read nor write. Except for those who came as bond-slaves, most Americans have found the United States to be an unexampled land of opportunity. An all-too-short litany of praise for the accomplishments of American liberalism would surely need to name at least the following: the ending of chattel slavery, the opening of economic prospects according to personal ability rather than inherited class, the education of the many rather than the few, the election of public officials and trial by a jury of one's peers, the liberation of women from stereotypical and submissive roles, and so on, lengthily, would the list go.

Walker Percy has joined others in warning that the Western cultural ship, having slipped both its humanist and its Christian moorings, is rapidly listing and foundering. Rather than bailing water, both conservatives and liberals continue adding cargo to the sinking vessel. Advocates of the political and religious right assume that the established forces of law and order form the matrix without which Christianity could not live. The church is thus called to maintain family values and personal morality because, if these collapse, so will the church and its institutions. The left holds, by contrast, that liberal democracy constitutes the *sine qua non* for all public life. The church has its right to exist only so long as it helps engender a social justice that is defined almost entirely as rights and entitlements. In both cases, the churches—and therefore their schools—are consigned to merely functional roles, serving some other ends than their own intrinsic purposes. They are enjoined to make their primarily private contribution to the larger public good. No wonder that Percy described the right and the left, as promoting a culture of choice, as mirror-image twins without knowing it. Percy's narrator, Dr. Thomas More, is both bored and bemused by their sameness:

> The scientists, who are most liberals and unbelievers, and the businessmen, who are mostly conservative and Christian, live side by side in Paradise Estates. Though the two make much of their differences—one speaking of "outworn dogmas and creeds," the other of "atheism and immorality," etcetera etcetera—to tell the truth, I do not notice a great deal of difference between the two. Both sorts are generally good fellows, good fathers and husbands who work hard all day, come home at five-thirty to their pretty homes, kiss their wives, toss their rosy babies in the air, light up their charcoal briquets, or perhaps mount their tiny tractor mowers. There are minor differences. When conservative Christian housewives drive to town to pick up their maids in the Hollow, the latter ride on the back seat in the old style. Liberal housewives make their maids ride on the front seat. On Sundays Christian businessmen dress up and take their families to church, whereas unbelieving scientists are apt to put on their best clothes and go bird-watching. As one of my behaviorist friends put it, "my cathedral is the blue sky and my pilgrimage is for the ivory-billed woodpecker [. . .]."[22]

There a similar sameness is at work within the academic right and left: we are *all* largely unaware that our entire culture is collapsing. Christopher Clausen argues, in *The Faded Mosaic*, that we are not witnessing the dawning of a new freedom-giving multiculturalism but rather the sunset of culture as such—if by culture we mean "a whole way of life." Clausen maintains that ours is a time and place of such drastic hybridizing and amalgamation that nearly all cultural distinctions are melting away. As a man of the left, Clausen doesn't believe that our cultural particularities are melting down into a pottage that is even minimally nourishing, much less progressive or improving. Rather is our much-vaunted diversity homogenizing us into very thin gruel indeed.

He cites the example of a Korean-American student to make his point. Though as a child she learned to use English better than Korean, she was placed in a bilingual elementary school because her parents were Korean-speaking. The result was that most of her early education was wasted. Now as a collegian, she must choose from among a plethora of majors. Her decision has been complicated by her need either to heed or to spurn her parents' desire that she embark upon a lucrative medical career. Though various members of her family have been Christians, Buddhists, and even militant atheists, this young woman has felt herself most at home among Jewish students whose parents have similarly high career expectations of their children. Such conflicts and confusions mean that her religious identity also hangs in the balance. It makes no sense, Clausen concludes, to describe this student as either bi-cultural *or* assimilated: she has received nothing normative from her Korean past which she might *embrace* alongside non-Korean values, nor anything sufficiently Western that would cause her to *reject* a Korean ethos.

When this coed describes herself as "American to the core," Clausen notes that she speaks more truly than she knows. She is creating her own identity by a series of individual choices that reduce all received traditions and cultures to mere personal preferences. In Clausen's view, therefore, "twentieth-century America is a graveyard of cultures." "Every tradition has been ruptured," he writes, "every institution open to question, if not by revolution then by changes that have undermined its authority. Whatever attitude one takes toward the religious, social, or political elements of one's own culture, one inevitably makes individual choices. There is no longer the possibility of spontaneous, unthinking acceptance beyond the age of childhood because there are simply too many options." The final result is frightening. We are witnessing the rise of what Clausen calls, in deliberately paradoxical terms, a "mass individualism, an individualism without much individuality."[23]

Once people have been urged to live according to their unencumbered individual choices, they will hardly be denied them—even when their choices enable them to assert their allegedly unique identities in nearly identical ways. Hence the exceedingly strange anomalies of our anti-cultural age. Constraint and variety have been simultaneously expunged, as we let go of the old taboos in order to be *freely and individually the same*. One of my former students sought to distinguish among her own students by making marginal notes in her gradebook, thus linking names with appearances. She soon discovered that, beside the name of nearly every coed, she had written the same words: "slender blonde, slender blonde, slender blonde." She well might have recalled the saying of Tom Wolfe in *The Bonfire of Vanities*: America is the country where no one can ever be too slender or too rich. No wonder that anorexia and bulimia have become major problems among well-off women who desperately seek to establish their collegiate individuality by appearing exactly alike.

Other anomalies abound. Whereas smoking was once almost universally approved and homosexuality almost universally condemned, the opposite now holds. Tobacco is seen as a threat to individual health, while sexual expression has become the key to individual happiness. To illustrate this sea-change in outlook, a theologian and ethicist at a major American university tells of the time he went to office late at night. After passing several signs that absolutely forbade all smoking, the professor came to a door with this student note scrawled on it: "Do Not Disturb: We're Having Sex." Thus has an ordinary vice been demonized while old-fashioned fornication has been transformed into a virtual right.

In a world where everything is acceptable so long as it is freely chosen, the old liberal-conservative barriers are collapsing: we have *all* become consumers within the marketplace of personal choices, no matter how contradictory. Thus do most Americans favor elective abortion while they also approve the teaching of young-earth creationism alongside evolutionary biology. All options and opinions become equal in a democracy where, as Kierkegaard wickedly said a century and a half ago, truth is determined by vote. Yet so fully have the political parties become indistinguishable purveyors of our consumption-driven culture that only fifty percent of the voting-eligible populace bothers to cast ballots at all, even in a presidential election. It would be vain and presumptuous to suggest that our Christian schools can entirely escape these massive multicultural and anticultural assumptions, but perhaps it is not entirely vain to suggest that we can offer an educational alternative to them.

A Personal Confession of Pedagogical Failure

Before doing so, it is important to make clear that we are not dealing with a mere theoretical problem. To demonstrate that the stakes are enormously high—indeed, that the consequences are matters of life and death—I confess to an egregious pedagogical failure of my own. It occurred during my very first year in the classroom. I was fresh out of graduate study at the University of Chicago Divinity School, and the lines of my life, as the psalmist says, had fallen in pleasant places. It was a lovely spring afternoon in 1972, when the North Carolina azaleas and dogwoods were blossoming, and the late April breeze was wafting into my office past the maple tree outside my open window. All seemed indeed right with the world.

The knock at my door came from one of my students in an introductory class called Theology and Modern Literature. Since he asked if he could bring his girlfriend in with him, I welcomed them both. Rather than indulging in empty chat, the student went straight to the core of his concern. He explained that they were on their way to the airport, where the girlfriend would take a plane for New York. *Roe v. Wade* had not yet been decided, and so the abortion she was seeking would also be a criminal act. My student was blunt: "We want to know what you have to say to us."

I had approached my first year of teaching believing that my chief task was to wipe the grins off fundamentalist faces. I wanted to sophisticate my students by rubbing their pious noses in the crusty snows of secularity, challenging what I assumed to be their firm but naïve faith by confronting them with the hard quandaries of modern unbelief. Thus had we read Ernest Hemingway and William Faulkner, James Joyce and D. H. Lawrence, Jean-Paul Sartre and Albert Camus. Our interpretive theological lens had been Paul Tillich's concept of "ultimate concern" as it is laid out in *Dynamics of Faith*. I had sought to show that, while none of these novelists was a professed Christian, they all address implicitly religious questions: the persistence of doubt, the problem of suffering and tragedy, the apparent meaninglessness of human existence, even the death of God.

It's an approach still worth taking, but I was made sharply aware of its limits on this fateful day. As my student made clear—and I soon discovered that he was altogether typical rather than exceptional—he and his girlfriend possessed so little faith that there was almost nothing to challenge, much less to overthrow. Their pregnancy had already posed to them an awful dilemma. What they needed was not sophistication, I can now see in retrospect, but edification and instruction of the most fundamental kind. What did I have to offer them, they wanted to know, in Christian judgment and succor?

In our class we had explored Camus's notion of human solidarity as a recourse against the world's evils. Yet this young couple was seeking something much more religiously rigorous than a deep personal identification with others. I suppose that I might have fleshed out the ethical implications of Tillich's claim that "the divine is characterized by the victory of the creative over the destructive possibility of the holy, and the demonic is characterized by the victory of the destructive over the creative possibility of the holy."[24] But such gassy abstractions clearly would not suffice. They wanted to know, as the student put it, whether their sin could be forgiven.

I wish there were a happy ending to this story—the good news that I persuaded them not to abort their baby, that I pointed them to a Christian community that would not be scandalized by illegitimacy, that I involved my own congregation in helping the young woman give birth to the child and then put it up for adoption, even that I convinced them to marry and nurture it themselves. But this was and is not the truth. Instead, I backed and filled and stammered and fumbled, making inane claims about God's grace and mercy. Having looked to me for the bread of life, this young man and woman received little more than a stone. I had been teaching as if it didn't matter, and when the time came for it really to matter, I was found wanting in the worst way.

My failure registered upon me with a magnitude that has remained unforgettable, now more than three decades later. I saw with devastating force that I had been utterly wrongheaded in my approach to teaching. My aim, as I discovered at considerable cost, is not to sophisticate my students with an experience of modern secularity, much less to belittle and bludgeon the faith that they bring to the classroom. Though most of them are Christians, they are often the products of churches that have already secularized them, albeit unawares, into our consumerist culture of comfort and convenience. Rather is my goal to build on whatever religious foundation they may have, seeking to challenge and deepen and enlarge it through an encounter with an unapologetic kind of Christian learning.

This is not to say that I teach texts that merely console and assure. On the contrary, Faulkner and Nietzsche, the Greek tragedians and the Stoics, all figure centrally in my courses, as does the darkest work in English literature—Shakespeare's *King Lear*. I also have recourse to theologians who possess a good deal more trenchancy than Tillich: Augustine and Luther, Calvin and Kierkegaard, Barth and von Balthasar. The literary artists whom I teach are equally unsentimental, often confronting more difficult challenges than the secular writers: Dante and Dostoevsky, Hopkins and O'Connor, Percy and Tolkien. Rather than trumping and trampling their opponents, they demonstrate that the way of the Cross is always past the worst of evils.

The main requisite for education of a distinctively Christian kind, I have come to believe, requires rigorous engagement—for teachers no less than students—with all that is entailed in thinking and living according to the bi-millennial Christian tradition in all of its wondrous variety and unplumbed depth. Yet such "training in Christianity," as Søren Kierkegaard called it, can occur only in communion with both the saints who have embodied the Faith most fully, and within the church which constitutes the worshipping and witnessing Body of Christ. If I had sufficiently schooled myself in the wisdom of the saints and doctors of the church, I would not have been so impoverished in the counsel I offered my student and his pregnant girlfriend. I would have known that the early Christians astonished their own culture by refusing to kill their "unwanted" babies. For then I might have pointed my young friends to a Christian community that would help them bring their child to life and eventually to faith. Then might we have been spared our common and terrible failure. Even had they rejected my teaching, I would not have been left halting and blundering about things that really matter. Even though it came by way of a guilt-laden lesson, I had received a summons of an ultimate kind, the kind that I could not refuse.

What I had yet to learn, however, is that neither the liberal nor the conservative solutions to my problem would suffice. I stood in need of a drastic theological alternative that would enable me to teach and live in faithfulness to the church and its Gospel. As I have suggested in the Introduction, I came gradually to understand that standard conservatism and standard liberalism would not suffice. What I had a much harder time comprehending, however, is their contemporary incarnatons in neo-conservatism and neo-liberalism. They seemed initially to have escaped the evils of their old-fashioned forbears, yet I found that they still didn't know quite what to make of the figure of Jesus Christ nor of his Body. Hence our need to examine with considerable care two of their most persuasive examplars: Russell Kirk and Peter Berger.

Chapter 2

A Neo-Conservative Alternative

In seeking to build a Christian educational culture, we must be careful to examine alternatives which seem to have a Christian cast but which in fact miss the mark. As we have learned from Walker Percy, opposites have a way of lapping the field and coinciding with each other, so that their differences turn out to be small rather than large. Two cases in point are Russell Kirk, a neo-conservative critic of culture, and Peter Berger, a neo-liberal sociologist of religion. The aim of this chapter and the next is to demonstrate that, though they stand at polar extremes from each other theologically, they share a similar outlook concerning the church and its institutions. Far from disqualifying their work for the task of constructing a Christian intellectual ethos, their insights are often acute and indispensable. Yet in their desire to make Christianity serve some allegedly larger good—even so large a good as Western culture—their work threatens to suborn the Gospel to what St. Paul called "a different gospel." The Apostle warns that the preaching of such an alien gospel deserves nothing less than anathema (Gal. 1:7–9).

Kirk the Cultural Conservative

Russell Kirk did not regard himself as a sterling Christian knight, but rather as a swordsman in the service of cultural conservatism. Yet he was not enlisted chiefly in the cause of right-wing politics, though he was a public advocate for Barry Goldwater, Richard Nixon, and Ronald Reagan. Kirk sought, instead, to conserve what he called "the permanent things": the fabric of common belief and general conviction and healthy prejudice that has been built up over the long run of human experience. Kirk's heroes were not stalwarts of action but writers and thinkers: Edmund Burke and Samuel Johnson, Walter Scott and John Henry Newman, Paul Elmer More and T. S. Eliot. They taught Kirk to wield the sword of imagination rather than the lance of power. Outward force is always coercive and thus secretly weak.

29

The imagination, by contrast, possesses true persuasive strength to raise up "images of truth and terror in the mind." Hence the awesome might of the written word, as Kirk learned from the poet John Taylor:

> Pens are most dangerous tools, more sharp by odds
> Than swords, and cut more keen than whips or rods.[1]

The Sword of Imagination: Memoirs of a Half-Century of Literary Conflict is Russell Kirk's autobiography, completed in his seventy-sixth year, not long before his death in 1994. It is a sprightly and spiritually invigorating book. Kirk's Victorian stateliness of style, his lavish quotations and citations from his prodigious reading, his puckish use of archaisms, even his decision to narrate his life-story in the third person—all of these old-fashioned devices ring right. They serve to create a winsome distance between Kirk and his own persona. They are signs of a courtesy and decorum that are all the more welcome in this age of in-your-face, tell-it-all publicity. From Kirk's eloquently formal account of his own life and work we can learn much about the nature of civilization, about the relation of Christian faith to political ideology and, perhaps most importantly, about the means of maintaining good cheer amidst the gloom of an anti-cultural age. Kirk even quotes Ambrose Bierce's celebrated definition of a conservative in his *Devil's Dictionary*: "Conservative, *n*. A statesman who is enamored of existing evils, as distinguished from the Liberal, who wishes to replace them with others."[2]

Though he loved the great houses and families of his ancestral Scotland, Russell Kirk was a product of the working-class. His father was a railroad man in Plymouth, Michigan. Kirk studied at Michigan State University in East Lansing, where as an undergraduate he began to turn out essays so incisive that they were published in leading literary quarterlies, whose editors mistook the collegian for a professor. Kirk wrote his master's thesis at Duke on a political figure of the Old South, John Randolph of Roanoke. Later to be published as an important book, this work led not to a career in history, as Kirk's teachers had hoped, but to a doctorate in the arts from St. Andrews University in Scotland. There for his dissertation Kirk drafted the book that would launch his career as a man of letters, *The Conservative Mind*.

When the book was published by Henry Regnery in 1953, it seemed unlikely to get a hearing. Only three years earlier the literary critic Lionel Trilling had declared, in *The Liberal Imagination*, that "In the United States at this time liberalism is not only the dominant but even the sole intellectual tradition. For it is a plain fact that nowadays there are no conservative or reactionary ideas in general circulation." Trilling offered his magisterial judgment not boastfully but regretfully. He complained that, in its prosaic desire to enlarge human freedom through a rational organization of life, liberalism neglects the poetic "imagination of variousness and possibility, which implies the awareness of complexity and difficulty." Liberals often forget, Trilling warned, that "the world is a complex and unexpected and terrible place which is not always to be understood by the mind as we use it in our everyday tasks."[3]

Wrestling with the World's Mystery and Complexity

Russell Kirk answered Trilling's summons to wrestle hard with the world's mystery and complexity. In his thirty books, as well as his countless reviews, essays, and lectures, he gave lasting witness that the world is both laden with wonder and full of wolves. Kirk's first work made him the godfather of the paleo-conservatives—those original rightward-turning thinkers who were not converted and disillusioned ex-liberals like Irving Kristol and other neo-conservatives who got "mugged by reality," as they like to say. Together with the sociologist Robert Nisbet and the philosopher Richard Weaver, Kirk helped inaugurate an American conservative resurgence that would produce, among other things, William Buckley's *National Review* and the election of Ronald Reagan. Yet it was not chiefly journalistic and political change that Kirk sought; he wanted to make a radical revaluation of the entire Enlightenment project. Long before the post-modernists, Kirk was already aware of its limits and fallacies. While serving as a soldier in the Utah desert during the Second War, Kirk came to discern his fundamental misgivings about modernity:

> His was no Enlightenment mind, Kirk now became aware: it was a Gothic mind, medieval in its temper and structure. He did not love cold harmony and perfect regularity of organization; what he sought was a complex of variety, mystery, tradition, the venerable, the awful. He despised sophisters and calculators; he was groping for faith, honor, and prescriptive loyalties. He would have given any number of neoclassical pediments for one poor battered gargoyle. The men of the Enlightenment had cold hearts and smug heads; now their successors, as the middle of the twentieth century loomed up, were in the process of imposing upon all the world a dreary conformity, with Efficiency and Progress and Equality for their watchwords—abstractions preferred to all those fascinating and lovable peculiarities of human nature and human society that are the products of prescription and tradition.[4]

Few folks still share the nineteenth-century hope that mechanical effi-
ciency would produce inevitable social progress, but even fewer share Kirk's
love of prescription and his scorn for equality. Hence the need to fathom
what he means by his outrageous defense of prejudice and hierarchy. Jaroslav
Pelikan distinguishes between *tradition* as the living faith of the dead and *traditionalism* as the dead faith of the living. For Kirk, prescription and tradition are virtual synonyms. Prescription refers to those vital beliefs that
undergird our civilization because, as the word indicates, they have been
"written before." Prescriptive loyalties are not individual values devised for
one's own benefit; they are communal allegiances received and affirmed
through ancient custom and immemorial use. To exalt prescription is, in
Chesterton's celebrated aphorism, to enfranchise our ancestors, giving the
vote to the great silent majority. Prescription and tradition are ways of breaking bread with the dead. We have lost vital communion with the past, Kirk
claims, "because history gives up its meaning only in the perspective of eternity."[5] Yet even when belief in God dies, the past continues to haunt us with
its unmanageable otherness. "Only the past is knowable," Kirk asserts, "even
though history is an art, not a science. Through a fuller understanding of
vanished civilizations, modern men might do something to postpone or
avert their own destruction."[6] Thus does Kirk commend the saying of
Gustave Le Bon that "the dead alone give us energy."[7]

Against the egalitarian grain of our age, Kirk asserts that hierarchy is the
primary way to insure excellence. As one who insists that human liberty is
linked with merit, Kirk opposes all attempts to level human diversity into a
bland uniformity. Without higher and lower, greater and lesser, everyone is
condemned to mediocrity. A necessary insolence inheres in all greatness. He
quotes Burke: "They will never love where they ought to love who do not
hate where they ought to hate."[8] Kirk doubts, therefore, that universal suf-
frage is an unmixed blessing. Nor will he abide the democratic dogma that
all exemptions and exclusions are evil, nor the notion that "one man is as
good as another, or maybe a little better." Kirk also denies the banal idea that
poverty is the chief source of violence, and that prosperity will cure it.
Barbarity and fraud have increased, Kirk argues, with the burgeoning of the
welfare state.

> To the student of history, as contrasted with the doctrinaire positivis-
> tic reformer, it seems that people are decent, when they are decent, chiefly
> out of habit. They fall into habits of decent conduct by religious instruc-
> tion, by settled family life, by assuming private responsibilities, by the old
> incentives of gain and advancement in rewards for decent conduct. When

the individual seems to run no risks; when food, shelter, and even comforts are guaranteed by the state, no matter what one's conduct may be; when the state arrogates to itself a complex of responsibilities that formerly were undertaken by church, family, voluntary associations, and the private person—why, then the old habits of decency are weakened, and the police [. . .] are required to maintain precariously by compulsion what was once taken for granted.[9]

Civilization as Necessarily Hierarchical

Civilization, for Kirk, is the slow habituation of humanity to the proper hierarchies of law and custom, of reverence and honor, of authority and consent. He rejects the now-popular view that these conventions are mere social constructs devised by the powerful to dominate the weak. Kirk insists, on the contrary, that such received patterns of behavior are grounded in what he calls the Permanent Things—in transcendent moral and spiritual reality. Civilization enables human beings not to live like dogs, from day to day, but to transcend the provinciality and the ephemerality of place and class and time. It is not the *servile* arts that Kirk exalts—not those skills which provide us food and shelter and clothing—but the *liberal* arts: the music and literature, the history and science, the philosophy and theology that allow humankind to look up from the trough of survival and to espy the horizon and to ask questions of ultimate order and meaning. Though it is the hard-won product of centuries, civilized life is an exceedingly fragile thing that can be torn down in a trice. Beneath its surface Hell always lurks. Kirk agrees with Thomas Hobbes that brutishness, not peace and equality, is our native state. "Order, justice, and freedom are garden plants," Kirk writes; "the natural condition of humankind is that of the jungle." The barbarous heart of human darkness can be subdued only by consent, never by coercion: "Not by force of arms are civilizations held together, but by the threads of moral and intellectual belief."[10]

The fundamental belief of Western civilization, Kirk argues, is the doctrine of the soul. Though first formulated by Plato and the Greeks, this foundational principle was confirmed and enlarged by the Christian doctrine of the resurrection of the dead. "Men and women are made for eternity," Kirk maintains, because they are souls.[11] The human drama is not only historical; it is also transhistorical. Human self-transcendence means that our race cannot be understood by the strict canons of logic, much less in economic terms, but only in theological and poetic categories. "The world is governed, in any age, not by rationality but by faith: by love, loyalty, and imagination."[12] Kirk insists against all literalism that high truths are never matters of fact but always rooted in symbols. Hence the centrality of imagination for the moral and political no less than for the spiritual and aesthetic life. Kirk agrees with Coleridge that imagination is the faculty for discerning the transcendent in the temporal. It enables us to experience what T. S. Eliot described as "the still point of the turning world," those mystical moments when the timeless intersects time. Kirk calls them "our best evidence of eternity."[13] Even the most unlettered soul can cultivate such an imaginative life:

> Those men and women who fail to perceive timeless moments are the prisoners of time and circumstance. Only by transcending the ravenous ego, and sharing their joys with others, do mortals come to know their true enduring selves, and to put on immortality. What Hell symbolizes is imprisonment within the ego [. . . .][14]

A Heterodox Christian Humanist

Kirk's Christian humanism makes him a heterodox conservative, far more akin to Hilaire Belloc and G. K. Chesterton than to Milton Friedman and Friedrich von Hayek. In fact, he scorns Hayek's worship of the perfectly free market economy, even as he makes mincemeat of Ayn Rand's cold-hearted individualism. Though he praises Henry Ford for establishing Greenfield Village as a place that would preserve the past and unite the humane with the technological, Kirk decries the triumph of "the automobile [as] a mechanical Jacobin, [. . .] breaking the cake of custom, running over oldfangled manners and morals, making the very air difficult to breathe."[15] Against conservatives who genuflect before the shrine of capitalism, Kirk regards avarice as the mortal sin of our century. He also denies that the multinational corporations conserve anything other than their stockholders' investments, and he admits that wealthy people are rarely "given to reading serious books and to taking long views."[16] Such lack of imagination was the main failing of Gerald Ford and George Bush, Kirk declares, and he blasts the elder Bush for the carpet bombing of Iraq, not so much because 50,000 lives were destroyed, but because Iraq is the cradle of civilization.

Kirk praises Richard Nixon for having been the first American president to ask, disturbingly, whether "America might be decadent."[17] When Nixon asked Kirk to recommend a single book dealing with the question of cultural decadence, expecting him to name one of his own works, Kirk suggested instead T. S. Eliot's *Notes towards the Definition of Culture*. (At about the same time, William Buckley was urging Mr. Nixon to read, mark, learn, and inwardly digest a quite different kind of book, Walker Percy's apocalyptic novel of 1971, *Love in the Ruins*.) One wonders what, if he ever read Eliot's book, President Nixon might have made of Eliot's claim that the link between behavior and belief should deeply discomfit us. This inseparable connection between faith and ethics, writes Kirk, "gives an importance to our most trivial pursuits, to the occupation of our every minute, which we cannot contemplate long without the horror of nightmare."[18] Neither does Kirk have high regard for Dwight Eisenhower. As a Taft Republican, he tartly observes that Eisenhower succeeded in paving America with "gigantic highways, ruinous to the railways."[19] Yet Kirk curiously fails to report his own witty retort to Robert Welch, founder of the John Birch Society, when Welch accused President Eisenhower of being a Communist. With wicked bifrontal irony, Kirk responded by saying that Ike was not a Communist but a golfer.[20]

Kirk the self-confessed contrarian was a nay-sayer with positive purposes. He cut and thrust with the sword of his imagination in order to preserve freedom and excellence against all shibboleths—whether global capitalism on the right or multicultural diversity on the left. Kirk assented deeply to John Henry Newman's definition of Toryism as "loyalty to persons." Ideology is its opposite. It seeks to submerge persons within the mass. It offers to improve their lives by rational planning, centralized power, and abstract schemes for "betterment." Kirk cites the testimony of the novelist Wyndham Lewis about the Communists' actual regard for the down and out: they "treated the real poor, when they were encountered, with [. . .] overweening contempt, and even derision."[21] He also observes that "the fell spirit of totalist collectivism [. . .] detests equally the conservative and the liberal understanding of social order."[22] Kirk the conservative thus voices ungrudging praise for the integrity of such liberals as Norman Thomas and Eugene McCarthy, Dick Gregory and Arthur Schlesinger, Jr. It becomes evident that Kirk was no reactionary scold but a man of thoughtful moderation: "The worst enemy of genuine civil rights is the fanatic who demands exclusive and unlawful privileges for his faction, who asks the impossible, and so receives nothing worth possessing."[23]

As a good-humored and charitable conservative, Kirk was also an old-fashioned romantic in the largesse of his spirit. With consummate courtliness, he wooed and won the hand of a strikingly lovely woman half his age, Annette Courtemanche. At Piety Hill, his restored ancestral home located at Mecosta in central Michigan, the Kirks and their four daughters gave sanctuary to all sorts of strangers and friends: "scholars and waifs, flotsam and jetsam of the twentieth century's disorders. [. . .] There were Scots, American

Indians, Italians, poets, wayward young folk, professors deprived of academic posts, students [. . .], musicians, painters [. . .], folk of three or four colors. The place seemed rather like Samuel Johnson's house in Gough Square, where the garret had been inhabited by Scots laboring away at the Dictionary, as well as pensioners who otherwise might have begged on the street."[24] This all-welcoming refuge was a house of true civility and diversity. For the Kirk menagerie was united by the shared belief that our prime need is to recover permanence and stability in this time of tempestuous change and disorder.

The Theological Limits of Cultural Conservatism

Kirk's cultural conservatism reveals weaknesses that are both political and theological. Kirk argued in his early writings that the American founding—insofar as it sought protection for life, liberty, and property elsewhere than in the British Constitution—was inspired by the same Enlightenment atheism that prompted the French Revolution. Kirk's attempt to radicalize the American Enlightenment is wrong-headed. Weak as they may have been, Christian churches of eighteenth-century America served to check and harness the rationalist self-sufficiency of the French *philosophes*. James Madison, for example, was a man whose political vision was moderate in temperament, tolerant of opponents, and even reluctant to assume the powers of office. Ignoring such distinctions, Kirk virtually equated the freedom-giving patriotism of Washington and Jefferson with the death-dealing fanaticism of Danton and Robespierre. Such a bizarre reading of the American Revolution prompted Harry Jaffa to comment acidly that "when Paul Revere called out 'The British are coming' he meant that they were coming to rescue us from French philosophy."[25]

Stung perhaps by Jaffa's criticisms, Kirk declines to repeat his strange case that the Declaration of Independence is "not conspicuously American in its ideas or its phrases." Yet he remains steadfast in his denial, against Leo Strauss and the Straussians, that human rights are grounded in what Jaffa calls "the more fundamental laws of nature." In fact, Kirk joins Alisdair MacIntyre in spurning the language of rights and values. He speaks instead of virtues and vices, insisting that their source and criterion is not a Lockean notion of Nature and Nature's god, but rather the true God of Christian revelation. He also contends that human freedom produces a demonic despotism when it is neither rooted in nor restrained by divine liberty and justice. What many conservatives and liberals fail to understand, Kirk argues, is that the loss of truly ultimate norms has led to the contemporary despotism of sensate pleasures and possessions.

Yet Kirk has difficulty translating these large moral concerns into practical politics, especially when he assesses the presidencies of Richard Nixon and Ronald Reagan. He blames the Watergate disaster on Mr. Nixon's unscrupulous and unimaginative subordinates, concluding that "[I]t was from lack of imagination that the Nixon administration fell." He quickly explains that a greater intimacy with great poetry might have made Nixon "shrewder [. . .] in concerns of state and judgments of character."[26] Kirk never asks whether the president's own moral deficiencies—none of which were likely to be addressed by the preachers invited to Mr. Nixon's White House worship services—led him to have high regard for the "pragmatic" men who surrounded him. Much to his own praise, however, Kirk refused all presidential offers to become a cultural bureaucrat. He knew that he was not called to be a man of affairs but a critic of American culture. His liberty of judgment depended upon his independence of life. Hence also his refusal to accept any permanent academic appointment. Such free discernment enabled Kirk to trace the academic disease of the 1960s—a sickness whose fevers still rage—not so much to theoretical mistakes of pedagogy and philosophy, but to academic flaccidity and superficiality, the dread producers of Giant Boredom.

> By its nature, the college is a place for academic leisure and reflection, not for action; a place for preparation, not for domination [. . . .] Had Karl Marx spent his years parading around Trafalgar Square with a sandwich board on which he had inscribed the legend "Off the pigs!" rather than burrowing in the British Museum, he would have been altogether ineffectual [. . . .] [The] college and university are places for the acquiring of academic disciplines, for sober meditation and inquiry and pleasant discourse. But this comes to pass only when courses of study offer something for the mind, and when professors are something better than dry sticks or frustrated soap box orators. When the Academy ceases to be boring, the student will cease to wave the bloody shirt.[27]

While Kirk wields the sword of criticism with considerable *éclat*, he joins many other conservatives in having a functionalist understanding of Christian faith: it serves to undergird Western civilization with moral and spiritual restraint as well as moral and spiritual motivation. In Kirk's view this faith provides the religious basis for Western life, just as other civilizations have their own religious grounding. Thus does Kirk speak in generic terms about morality and divinity and religion, as Edward Ericson unintentionally reveals in quoting Kirk's credo from *The Conservative Mind*:

> "Conservatives believe that a divine intent rules society as well as conscience, forging an eternal chain of right and duty which links great and obscure, living and dead." *The Politics of Prudence*, Kirk's late-in-life summation of the principles of conservatism, lists as the first principle, "The conservative believes that there exists an enduring moral order. That order is made for man, and man is made for it: human nature is constant, and moral truths are permanent." A conservatism that seeks "the restoration of the ethical system and the religious sanction upon which any life worth living is founded," Kirk has said, "is conservatism at its highest."[28]

Laudable as these claims may seem, it must be noted that there is nothing distinctively Christian about them. They could apply to any civilization or religion.

Kirk's attempt to transcend particular convictional traditions by speaking in generic religious terms has its roots in the Enlightenment, despite his scorn for it. The rationalists of the seventeenth and eighteenth centuries sought, like Kirk, to identify universal principles of morality that would bypass the doctrinal disputes of the various Christian denominations. Benjamin Franklin famously developed his twelve-point program for personal perfection in generic moral terms, the last injunction being to "imitate Jesus and Socrates." So did the deist Lord Herbert of Cherbury deny the authority of the church and the creeds, arguing in *De Veritate* that God had created man as a reasoning being who should not be confined to the pronouncements of so-called revelation. Like Franklin, Lord Herbert worked out five reasonable propositions concerning God and morality that any intelligent person should be able to accept as a substitute for the conflicting beliefs of conventional Christianity. These common notions have held true among all people in all times and places, without regard to their race or religion, except when they have been obscured by distortions and excretions: (1) that God exists; (2) that He ought to be worshipped; (3) that virtue and piety are the chief part of worship; (4) that there must be repentance for crimes and vices; (5) that there are rewards and punishments hereafter, according to how we have acquitted ourselves in this earthly life.[29]

C. S. Lewis is another cultural conservative who joins Kirk in embracing the Enlightenment assumption that it is possible to stand above the flux of history and to view things *sub specie aeternitatis*. Lewis attempts, therefore, to discern the commonalities shared by the various world religions and to exalt their most enduring values.[30] Like Kirk, Lewis is a foundationalist who assumes that all people of good will and right mind can agree upon the basic moral rules that are essential for human existence. The American Founders are perhaps the most obvious examples of this notion that we can elevate certain virtues as normative, without regard either to their dependence upon particular historical communities, or to their rootage in particular narrative traditions and religious practices. Lewis stands at a very far remove from Thomas Jefferson; yet there is a Jeffersonian quality to his doctrine of Objective Value and his formulation of the Tao in *The Abolition of Man*. Lewis and Kirk both fail to recognize that, though we indeed share a common human nature that is divinely shaped, it takes radically different forms within the world's civilizations and religions, and that they conflict no less than converge.

Alasdair MacIntyre points out, for example, that suicide was regarded as one of the highest moral virtues among both the Roman Stoics and the Japanese Samurai, while Christians have held self-murder to be a deadly sin—perhaps even the unforgivable sin. We know, moreover, that the Aztecs, though they had highly advanced civilization, made human sacrifice central to their religion. Infanticide was so widely practiced throughout the Greco-Roman world that Christians became known as the weird people who did not kill their so-called "unwanted" babies. We should also note, glaringly obvious though it is, that every human society has made *war* its central means of self-preservation, even if not of self-aggrandizement. In the central Christian tradition, by contrast, war is sanctioned only as the last and worst of alternatives and, in sizable Christian groups, it is prohibited even for self-defense.

The Scandal of Particularity Made Unscandalous

Ignoring such important distinctions, Kirk honored biblical faith as a specific instance, indeed the noblest, of the larger phenomenon called religion. His first loyalty was not to the church but to what he called "the body social." He described it as "a kind of spiritual corporation, comparable to the church; it may even be called a community of souls."[31] He rightly roots his understanding of the soul in Plato and Christian doctrine, insisting that "Men and women are made for eternity."[32] Yet Kirk does not regard the church as the community of God which exists to preserve the preciousness of every human being from the depredations of ancient and modern evils—including those evils stemming from the various civilizations. For him, the wisdom of the human race provides our essential guard and stay:

"The individual is foolish, but the species is wise," Burke declared. In politics we do well to abide by precedent and precept and even prejudice, for "the great mysterious incorporation of the human race" has acquired habits, customs, and conventions of remote origin which are woven into the fabric of our social being; the innovator, in Santayana's phrase, never knows how near to the taproot of the tree he is hacking.[33]

Such uncritical confidence in the unfailing rightness of tradition sometimes blinds Kirk to the truth about pagan religion. Nor does he seem aware that Christianity itself can be conscripted for pagan purposes. I confess to being chilled, for example, by his admiration for the Valley of the Fallen, Generalissimo Franco's mountainous mausoleum in honor of the Fascist heroes of the Spanish Civil War.[34] Kirk fails to notice that this monstrously impressive monument puts Catholic faith in a terrible thralldom to the political despotism he elsewhere decries. It is a shrine that frightfully memorializes death as the ultimate good, not as the true way to eternal life. Kirk's enthusiasm for seances, spiritualism, and the occult is also troubling. He confuses the preternatural with the supernatural, the spooky with the revelatory. This high regard for the magical is also linked, I suspect, with his naïve contention that Christian faith will be wondrously reborn if the Shroud of Turin proves authentic.

Kirk's desire to vindicate Christianity against its cultured despisers and uncultured deniers was prompted by a desire to shore up faltering western civilization. It was a desire shared by T. S. Eliot, whose prophecy from 1931 Kirk was fond of quoting:

The World is trying the experiment of attempting to form a civilized but non-Christian mentality. The experiment will fail; but we must be very patient in awaiting its collapse; meanwhile redeeming the time: so that the Faith may be preserved alive through the dark ages before us; to renew and rebuild civilization, and save the World from suicide.[35]

The preservation of civilization is the first and fundamental requisite. The Gospel serves, in this view, as our culture's transcendent religious support rather than the church's one source of life and thus the world's radical critic and transformer. For Kirk, God is hidden within human hopes and decencies more than he is operative within the church's own life. Just as our culture's decadence is religious, so must its restoration take religious shape, though once again Kirk remains curiously generic in his call for "the renewal of our awareness of a transcendent order, of the presence of an Other":

What ails modern civilization? Fundamentally, our society's affliction is the decay of religious belief. If a culture is to survive and flourish, it must not be severed from the religious vision out of which it arose. The high necessity of reflective men and women, then, is to labor for the restoration of religious teachings as a credible body of doctrine.[36]

Kirk's primary concern for the renewal of civilization may account for the unexplained delay of his baptism. Though he began his instruction in the Catholic faith as early as 1953, he was not received into the church until 1964, on the eve of marriage to his Catholic fiancée. Kirk confesses that his conversion was almost entirely intellectual. He came to believe as much in an authoritative system of Christian ideas as in the incarnate God whom such ideas imperfectly reflect. Perhaps this accounts for Kirk's wry confession to a friend at Hillsdale College, where he held periodic lectureships, that he was a buttress—indeed, a *flying* buttress!—rather than a pillar of the church. As one who fleetingly bolsters more than he permanently undergirds, Kirk sometimes misunderstands important Christian doctrines. He extols the Augustinian understanding of original sin, for example, while making it a virtual synonym for our generic fallibility. There is no deep sense of either human bondage or divine deliverance in this Kirkean description of Last Things that might have been borrowed, albeit unconsciously, from Milton's Satan:

> Hell [. . .] is a state of being in which all the evil one has done is eternally present—and there is no escape from it. So it is that human creatures make their own destiny, their own Heaven and their own Hell. [. . .] If people firmly believed this doctrine—that our every decision for good or evil, here below, is eternal, and determines our eternal state—why, how differently most folks would live![37]

Yet it would be churlish to conclude an assessment of the life and work of Russell Kirk on a sour note. Unlike Malcolm Muggeridge and Paul Johnson and Walker Percy, Kirk is to be praised for having largely avoided the biliousness that afflicts so many critics of modernity. His gladness of heart was rooted in an ardent love for European culture in both its particularity and impermanence. Kirk had no mere theoretical regard for the glories of our civilization, having spent much of his life taking walking tours to our chief cultural monuments, especially the neglected ones. Rambling among the Roman ruins of Tunisia, wondering whether contemporary American culture will create such ghosts once it is gone, Kirk ponders the One Thing truly permanent:

No strong political power endures forever. In those times, when Roman emperors were bred up in the Province of Africa, no man expected that all this splendor would become the abomination of desolation. Only after Alaric's barbarian Goths had taken Rome did Saint Augustine see that Roman might, too, was a vanity that must pass; and he wrote *The City of God*, about the community of souls that endures when the cities of this world have been given up to fire and sword.[38]

Such faith enabled Russell Kirk to transcend, at least occasionally, the limits of his cultural conservatism. Though in appearance he resembled both the Buddha and a bulldog, Kirk was no doleful man-at-arms tilting testily at liberal windmills. He was a knight of cheerful countenance defending the best traditions of the West, even if he failed to see that, while often rooted in Christian faith, they are not identical with it.

Chapter 3

A Neo-Liberal Alternative

For more than four decades Peter Berger has served as our chief American sociologist of religion. He stands in the grand tradition of his master Max Weber, who was among the first to teach that religion—like every other human institution—is a social construction. Berger has played interesting variations off this persistent theme throughout an impressive career. Though chiefly descriptive and analytical, Berger's work also seeks to construct new alternatives to old ways of conceiving and practicing the Christian religion. For him, the phenomenon of pluralism has produced a major crisis of faith. He is convinced that Christians must wrestle hard with this pluralism—neither ignoring nor succumbing to it. If we do not, our faith is already dead, even if not yet buried. Alongside his theoretical and empirical studies, therefore, Berger has sought to erect his own constructive alternative, a theology possessing enough steel to withstand the corrosions of modernity. Having begun this daunting task with *A Rumor of Angels* and continued it in *The Heretical Imperative*, Berger offers a provisional summation of his efforts in two more recent books: *A Far Glory: The Quest for Faith in an Age of Credulity* and *Redeeming Laughter: The Comic Dimension of Human Experience.*

Despite its thorough-going consistency, Berger's theological project has often been misunderstood. Because he has joined his friend Richard John Neuhaus on the conservative side of social and political issues, because he is an unapologetic proponent of capitalism, because he seeks to recover a sense of the supernatural, because he was an author and signatory to the 1975 Hartford Appeal with its Thirteen Theses against bourgeois-style liberalism in the mainline churches, Berger is often regarded as a theological right-winger. Though seemingly correct, this popular estimate of Berger is profoundly wrong. He is not a neo-conservative but a reconstructed liberal. His entire theological effort, as he makes especially evident in *A Far Glory*, is to carry out the liberal Protestant program that runs from Kant and

Schleiermacher to Troeltsch and Tillich—i.e., to correlate the content of Christian faith with the best insights of the Euro-American Enlightenment. In a time when multiculturalism has put the Enlightenment under great suspicion, Berger's theology of transcendence seeks to restore the universalism which lay at the core of its enterprise. Yet I will argue that Berger, the liberal, forms an almost perfect mirror image of a conservative such as Russell Kirk. For they both seek a universality that, however noble, makes the Church and the Gospel subservient to an allegedly larger good—namely, to a generic faith that is not specifiably Christian.

Modernity as Pluralism Incarnate

Berger is at his best when offering the fruits of his work as a sociologist. He has spent his entire career contending that pluralism is the defining mark of modernity. Pluralism derives, Berger argues, from the central sociological discovery that not only religion but the whole of human reality is socially constructed. Unlike other creatures, we humans build our own world. The domain of dogs and mice and horses is given instinctively at birth. Their prefabricated worlds are closed to radical alteration or development: "each animal lives in an environment that is specific to its particular species."[1] The human organism, by contrast, is precariously unfinished at birth, leaving the world that we make for ourselves open to many possible constructions. What must be said of human beings can be said of no other animals: we are more cultured than natured.

Our uniquely human world is fashioned by means of a dialectical endeavor that Berger describes as *externalization* (the imposition of a human order, via language and symbols, on the flux of our experience and the chaos of our extra-organismic environment), *objectification* (the recognition that our social conventions have authority over the subjective desires of individuals), and *internalization* (the harmonizing of the objective social world with the subjective personal world). This open-ended process produces as many cultures as there are social groups who can be held together by a particular set of commonalities. Such commonalities differ radically according to the experiences and situations of the groups. Not only do they vary; they are often incompatible. The social world of Hindus is quite incommensurate, for example, with that of Muslims, just as Nazi culture cannot be reconciled with that of the Quakers. The problem of plurality and conflict among social and religious worlds is compounded by their perilous instability. The delicate equipoise that constitutes culture is perennially tipping toward one or the other of its polarities. The objective social norms become too rigid and authoritarian to accommodate the legitimate aspirations of particular individuals, or else the internalized values of a culture prove unable to redeem the countervailing social realities of war, famine, pestilence, and death. Hence the constant human need to shore up the fragile social balance; i.e., to produce and reproduce culture.

Religion, as Berger understands it, is the chief means for preserving this tenuous thing called culture. Religion legitimates culture by giving it transcendent plausibility, by erecting a sacred canopy over the world, by rooting social reality in cosmic reality. Religion is nothing less, therefore, than "the audacious attempt to conceive of the entire universe as being humanly significant."[2] Whether in questions sexual or social, whether in matters familial or agricultural, religion enables the human order to manifest the holy order. It makes the microcosm of everyday life reflect the macrocosm of ultimate power and mystery: "Everything 'here below' has its analogue 'up above.' By participating in the institutional order [we humans], *ipso facto*, participate in the divine cosmos."[3] Within such a mythically ordered world, there is no clear boundary between self and society: "The individual self," says Berger, "is embedded in a continuity of being that extends from the human community through what we today call nature to the realm of the gods or other sacred entities."[4] Indigenous religions and archaic cultures fix individual identity according to society membership, not according to personal will:

> [One's] life and relation to reality are a matter of destiny, not choice. So is [one's] relation to the gods of one's community. Can such an individual be said to *believe* in these gods? Hardly. The gods here are part and parcel of taken-for-granted reality. Their existence and specific traits are assumed, indeed "known." No act of faith is required to believe in them.[5]

The Total Transcendence of God

Here precisely is the rub: Berger believes that the socially constructed self which Alasdair MacIntyre, Charles Taylor, Stanley Hauerwas, and other communitarians want to reclaim is no longer available. He contends that, at two definitive moments, Western culture turned irreversibly away from this archaic notion of selfhood. Following the lead of Mircea Eliade and Eric Voegelin, Berger contends that, in ancient Israel and ancient Greece, the seamless fabric that knitted self and society and divinity was shredded. Once Israel discovered that God is not many but One, and once Greece discovered that something cannot be both A and not-A, religion and reason made a

decisive and irreversible turn. "The principle of monotheism and the principle of contradiction loom powerfully," Berger declares, "over the entire
development of the Western mind."[6] No longer can the Holy be identified
with nature and society: it radically transcends them.

For perhaps the first time in history, Berger argues, the possibility of a
radically individual and faithful self emerged. This new self cannot readily be
grounded in social and religious convention. It must be formed in relation
to the transcendent God. Berger regards both Abraham and Paul as figures
who, for all their imbeddedness in the world of ancient Near Eastern culture
and religion, acted as solitary individuals in answering their call to believe in
the transcendent God. Both men were summoned to make a radical break
with the secure tribal and religious worlds wherein they had previously
found their identity. Their lives were no longer socially fated but individually chosen. And while both the synagogue and the church were to remain
covenanted communities of faith for Jews and Christians, the way to radical
individualism was now irreversibly opened. Conversion, the total redirection
of the will in relation to a Reality not discerned in the social or natural order,
is the unprecedented call issued in the Jews and Jesus:

> The faith of ancient Israel constituted one of the great historic breaks out
> of archaic community, and the faith of the early Church further radical-
> ized this break in separating the owning of the covenant from the accident
> of an individual's birth. Even when the Church instituted the baptism of
> infants, the liturgy surrounding this ceremony maintained the fiction
> (empirically speaking) that the infant chose to be baptized.[7]

Once religion is chosen rather than bequeathed, once faith is elected
rather than inherited, then it becomes open to skepticism: what can be
believed can also be doubted. Religion is no longer a matter of knowledge,
Berger insists, but of faith. The archaic world, as we have seen, has no real
experience of either faith or doubt: there the gods are directly apprehended
through ritual and myth. The invisible and transcendent God of Israel and
Christ cannot thus be known. To identify the earthly with the divine is idolatry: the deadliest misperception of both God and the world. Even in the
true act of faith, Berger avers, we experience what God is *not* far more than
we experience what God *is*. As the advocate of an utterly transcendent God,
Berger is drawn to the ancient apophatic tradition. Rudolf Otto, the nineteenth-century historian of religion, also spoke of the encounter with the
"totally other" as the essence of religious experience. For Berger, this same
quality of divine otherness lies at the heart of transcendence: "the divine,

wherever it manifests itself, goes beyond anything that human beings are familiar with."[8]

In Berger's view, such a necessary negativity about the divine nature has remained a minority position through most of Christian history. It is exceedingly hard, Berger admits, to maintain this discomfiting division between the human and the heavenly realms that the church and the synagogue are founded upon. Biblical faith promises not a secure life in the ritual round that discerns the sacred in the patterns of nature and culture, but rather a perilous pilgrimage through time and space into the Eternal and the Infinite. Hence the frequent defections from biblical faith, the repeated returns of both Israel and the church to a pagan identification of God with chthonic forces and political movements and ethnic identities. The fate of the prophets and the martyrs reveals how rare and difficult it is for a people to put its trust in God alone.

It was the Protestant Reformers, Berger contends, who recovered the radical biblical message: the call of Abraham and Paul to faith in the God who is not many (and thus resident in the powers of the cosmos) but One (and thus transcendent over all such powers). If only gradually, Protestants ended all identification of God and world, self and society, church and state, birth and faith. Berger believes that the Reformation's stress upon faith as individual decision served to strengthen the democratizing and capitalistic forces that were already at work in the Renaissance—even if the Reformers looked backward to St. Augustine and the Bible more than they anticipated Hobbes and Locke. New political and economic freedoms were being unleashed at the same time ecclesiastical liberties were opening up. These radical changes combined to effect a profound alteration in church and culture alike. In the seventeenth century, Berger contends, life in the West shifted from the archaic to the modern—from life understood as destiny to life understood as decision.[9]

For both good and ill, Berger insists, human existence in the modern West has gradually come to depend on personal choices, not on the repetition of impersonal, pre-established patterns. The Protestant refusal to identify God with any such patterns—Paul Tillich called it the Protestant principle—has served as the religious foundation for the central modern tenet called pluralism. Berger defines the term succinctly. It is the acknowledgement of multiple world-views and thus the recognition of multiple moral and religious options—not only Protestant and Catholic and Jewish, nor even Muslim and Hindu and Buddhist, but also animist and atheist and New Age.

When religious tradition can no longer be taken for granted—and tradition means, for Berger, the theological and cultural assumptions that are ingrained and inherited rather than argued and chosen—secularism becomes the inevitable threat. People are now free to live without benefit of clergy, so to speak. Many do, as the recrudescence of modern paganism and atheism attests. Even those who seek to remain faithfully Christian face a formidable task. We, too, must confront the pluralistic fact that the ways of construing the world are multiple rather than single. Even if for us the truth revealed in Christ is the final and unsurpassable truth, we know that there are alternative truths. Berger's chief thesis is that *haeresis*, the taking of a choice, is no longer an act of lamentable apostasy, as it is in the New Testament. Quite to the contrary, "heresy"—the making of religious decisions—is the unavoidable modern imperative:

> *In premodern situations there is a world of religious certainty occasionally ruptured by heretical deviations. By contrast, the modern situation is a world of religious uncertainty occasionally staved off by more or less precarious constructions of religious affirmation.* Indeed, one could put this change even more sharply: *For premodern man, heresy is a possibility—usually a rather remote one: for modern man, heresy typically becomes a necessity. Or again, modernity creates a new situation in which picking and choosing becomes an imperative.*[10]

The Homeless Mind

Berger is no uncritical apologist for modernity. In *The Homeless Mind*, he and his wife Brigitte make a searing indictment of the *anomie* that attends life in a radically pluralized world. The solitary self, whether in the factory or the bureaucracy, does its work largely in isolation from other selves. The individual is often devoured by the monstrous mechanisms of industry and society. The state treats its citizens as instances of abstract categories, even of such ethical categories as equality, without regard to individual circumstances and needs. The result is what the Bergers call a "moralized anonymity."[11] It comes as no surprise that many people regard the governmental bureaucracy as an impersonal power system of rules and regulations, and thus not as their friend but their enemy. The inner and outer spheres are thus riven, as individuals seek compensation in their private lives (often by way of narcotic stimulants and the sundry nostrums of self-help) for the frustrations they experience in the public world. That government agencies steadfastly seek to name the nature of the good, and thus to refuse religion a central role in public life, is especially annoying to most Americans. Since research has shown only India to be a more religiously devout nation than the United States, and since Sweden is notorious for being the most secular, Berger has famously said that America is a nation of Indians governed by a bureaucracy of Swedes.

The upshot is that millions of Americans suffer from a terrible anxiety and rage, a feeling of emptiness and impotence, an utter homelessness in the world. This sense of abandonment has occurred, ironically, in spite of Max Weber's fond hope that the sociology of knowledge would make us at home in the world, demystifying our lives of all supernatural fears and other-worldly terrors. Far from making us satisfied worldlings, the acids of modernity have corroded our one remaining source of transcendent consolation: religion. Though it once had the singular power to knit the outer and inner worlds into a wondrous unity, religious life is now rendered irreparably multiple. It has become a consumerist choice like all others. Amidst a welter of world-views, reality itself threatens to splinter, to shatter into an ever-increasing plurality of perspectives. Even if Christian faith envisions the world as a unified whole—as the biblical doctrine of creation most certainly attests—it is not the same unity and the same wholeness that other faiths discern. To concede this pluralist point is to suffer what Berger calls a dizzying "vertigo of relativity."

Berger understands that his own sociological relativism is religiously subversive and destructive. He confesses that the pitiless constructionism of *The Sacred Canopy* often makes it read "like a treatise on atheism."[12] For if (as he argues with Thomas Luckmann) all cultures and religions are socially created "plausibility structures," then human beings become the makers of their own meaning. The sociology of knowledge offers but a slender Kantian hope against such reduction of religion to its social function: it relativizes the relativizers. Modern pluralism must itself be understood as a cultural construction, one among many. Berger insists that such healthy historical skepticism precludes any apodictic statements about what modern people "can no longer believe."[13]

To negate the negativists is to offer the thinnest of affirmations. Hence Berger's search for deliverance from the vortex of a relativizing socio-historical analysis, for while he is most certainly a relativist, Berger is not a nihilist. He does not believe, with Feuerbach and Nietzsche, that we project human needs and desires onto the blank face of an empty cosmos. There is an inherent link between mind and world, Berger insists, an intrinsic connection between religious belief and transcendent reality. We are makers of ideas and doctrines because we have ourselves been made. "There is a fundamental affinity," says Berger, "between the structures of human consciousness and

the structures of the empirical world. Projection and reflection are movements within the same encompassing reality." Hence Berger's modest
Kantian hope:

> The same may be true of the projections of man's religious imagination.
> [. . .] The theological decision will have to be that "in, with, and under"
> the immense array of human projections, there are indicators of a reality
> that is truly "other" and that the religious imagination of man ultimately
> reflects.[14]

Yet because the indicators of ultimate reality are ever so hard to descry,
we are left whirling in a maelstrom of relativism. "History posits the problem of relativity *as a fact*," Berger likes to say, "the sociology of knowledge *as
a necessity of our condition*."[15] This means that the pluralist acknowledgment
of competing world-views is not a mistaken development that could have
been avoided; it is the inexorable conclusion inherent in modern culture
itself. For if all culture is socially constructed—albeit within a dialectical process of discovery and creation—then religion is bound to be multiple rather
than solitary. Abraham's call to leave his Aramaean home and to follow the
path of Yahweh, like Jesus's claim to be the one true Way, must be regarded
as one among other life-routes, none of them leading necessarily to the
Truth. Even when we exclude what we believe to be false paths, we must still
acknowledge their existence. Berger concludes, therefore, that Jews and
Christians have the distinction of being the first to discover and the first to
confront the unavoidable reality of religious pluralism.

Berger's Liberal Project

Given such a radical and uncompromising sociological accounting of
religion, we must ask what is the nature of Berger's own constructive theological project? As he has repeatedly iterated, he stands in the line of
Schleiermacher and his fellow liberals—neither with their nineteenth-
century scholastic heirs nor with twentieth-century Barthians. It is the liberals, Berger believes, who have wrestled most seriously with the challenge of
modern historical consciousness. They are to be saluted for their courage, he
declares, in giving "birth to modern biblical scholarship, thus producing the
historically unheard-of case of scholars officially credited as representatives of
a religious tradition turning a sharply critical cognitive apparatus against the
sacred scriptures of that same tradition."[16]

Liberal Protestants such as Troeltsch went even further. They were the
first to see Christian faith itself as a human construction, and thus as one

among many religious possibilities. A self-revealing God who uniquely discloses his nature and will through a particular people and person and book is, for Berger the liberal, quite literally incredible. Against Barth, therefore, Berger insists that Christian faith does not kerygmatically "posit itself." Like all other faiths, it must be chosen as a single option to be credited against others. Even then, Christian faith must be seen as having profound similarities to Pure Land Buddhism and especially to Islam. According to Berger, even the most drastic Calvinist version of Christian uniqueness reveals an uncanny resemblance to the call that resounds from the minaret:

> God's revelation, as contained in the Koran, confronts the individual as an unshakable objective fact. Before this fact the individual can do nothing but submit, and it is from this submission ('*aslama*, in Arabic) that Islam derives its name. And, as in the case of Calvinism, the Muslim view is that God, in his infinite wisdom, has predestined who will make this submission and who will not. In the words of the Koran, "Had your Lord pleased, all the people of the earth would have believed in Him. [. . .] None can have faith except by the will of Allah." [. . .] There is a road to Mecca as there is a road to Calvary, and the first step on either road (at least for modern man) is in the nature of a "leap of faith."[17]

Such theocentric pluralism, with its emphasis on the sheer transcendence of God, would seem to make Berger an enthusiast for contemporary religious liberalism. Yet it does not. Berger is convinced that most liberals, especially of the Protestant stripe, have abandoned their own tradition. Hence his scorching critique of the religious and political left. He has greater contempt for fashionable liberalism, in fact, than for nostalgic conservatism. Whereas Barth seeks to deduce faith from a pristine revelation that largely ignores Christian kinship to other religions, Protestant liberals reduce Christianity to mere ethics or psychology or politics. Just as many liberals scorn Berger for endorsing the excessive individualism of modernity, he in turn reviles them for becoming rampant communitarians. As wags have said, they may soon demand that the old Christmas carol be renamed: "O Little Community of Bethlehem." Communitarian sauce for the church becomes communitarian gravy for society. "The same communal embrace," Berger laments. "is available in secular versions—black brotherhood, feminist sisterhood, revolutionary comradeship, and so on."[18]

Berger remains decidedly unimpressed with the longing for *ersatz* community. He criticizes secular Jews, for example, who convert to orthodox Judaism and who thus "discover" their Jewishness. In a community based on birth rather than choice, "the individual who undergoes this conversion knows all the time that it was he as an individual who chose to identify with this alleged destiny, in specific actions that he can remember well, and he also knows that it is within his power to reverse those actions."[19] Yet Berger reserves his most vitriolic satire for communitarian Christians. He is exceeding wroth with liturgical revisionists who have decreed that the officiant at the sacramental Supper shall no longer face the altar and thus represent the people to the high and holy God, but that he must face the congregation from behind the altar, looking out at them not so much like a priest as a bartender. "This new position makes wonderfully clear," Berger declares, "that the sacred being that is worshiped exists not outside the gathered community but rather inside it. There is a strong suggestion that what is happening here is a community worshiping itself. [. . .] From a biblical point of view, what is happening is a form of idolatry."[20]

Berger the liberal is angry at liberalism's idolatrous denial of God's radical mystery and wonder. Instead of nourishing the human hunger for the Holy with the bread and wine of transcendence, liberal Christianity offers up the stone of communitarianism. Rather than opening windows onto the world of our divine Origin and End, it encloses us within a cosmos which is finally no larger than our own mundane questions and pragmatic answers. Such relevance-mad religion serves to endorse our culture's contempt for the metaphysical. It accommodates when it should be resisting what Berger calls "the triumph of triviality." His diatribes against the crudities and credulities of religious liberalism often cause Berger to be labeled a theological conservative. Again, it is not so. He remains a liberal from beginning to end. "Starting With Man" is a chapter title in *A Rumor of Angels*, as Berger makes ever so clear the anthropological—not the Christological—source of his vision. Against all theologies of divine self-disclosure, he asserts that "the human [is] the only possible starting point for theological reflection." He rejects "any external authority (be it scriptural, ecclesiastical, or traditional) that would impose itself on such reflection."[21] For Peter Berger, the reality of God is not first of all discerned within biblical proclamation or ecclesial tradition, but in the allegedly universal human encounter with the Holy.

The heart of Berger's theological project is to discern the sacred within the secular, to locate signals of transcendence amidst the mundane realm of everyday experience, to detect the flutter of angel wings among the cold, silent spaces that Pascal found so frightening. He wants, in sum, to demonstrate that our impulse to give cosmic scope to our cultural constructions is not a human-all-too-human act of self-delusion. We create worlds of transcendent order and meaning, as we have seen, because we ourselves have been created. Our penchant for world-building "implies not only that human order in some way corresponds to an order that transcends it, but that this transcendent order is of such a character that man can trust himself and his destiny to it."[22]

Berger proves himself most clearly a liberal in his conviction that there are universal experiences of the Holy that all religions seek to identify and express—though not all equally—in their particular symbols and sacraments. In *A Rumor of Angels*, he identifies five human experiences that he believes to be common to all cultures and that might thus serve as the basis for a universal theology of transcendence: (1) the human propensity for order, (2) the human playfulness about such order, (3) the human capacity for hope despite death, (4) the human encounter with evil so radical that it demands damnation, and (5) the human love for laughter that leaps beyond the bounds of the world. Each of these proclivities requires the ultimate entrustment of oneself and one's destiny to the Transcendent.

Laughter as Self-Transcendence

It's the last of these, the self-transcending power of the comic, that Berger marks as the most religious. He argues that man the knower is also man the laugher: "*homo sapiens* is always *homo ridens*."[23] Ours is the uniquely laughing species. Other animals play and perhaps even smile, but only human beings laugh. The comic sense is common to all cultures, Berger maintains, even if its local expressions remain hard to transfer from one time and place to another. Berger understands that this is always the relation of the universal and the particular, the divine and the human: "In acts of projection, man reaches out toward the infinite. But he is only capable of doing this because the infinite reached out to him first. Put succinctly, man is the *projector* because ultimately he is himself a projectile. The symbolizer is himself the symbol."[24]

Laughter is universal because human life is universally incongruous. Berger agrees with theologian Blaise Pascal and anthropologist Helmuth Plessner that we are creatures caught between incongruous realms: between the subatomic particles and the starry spaces, between nothingness and infinity. We are neither apes nor angels but frail reeds with self-transcending minds. Like other animals, we *are* our bodies, behaving instinctively; but unlike the animals, we also *have* our bodies, acting intentionally. To maintain perfect equilibrium between these contrary worlds is impossible. Being both finite and fallen, we walk life's tightwire ever so tipsily. When the balancing act fails, we collapse either into laughter or tears. Tragedy declares the ultimate triumph of the dense and ponderous requirements of everyday life, giving finality to groans and sighs. Comedy is the deeper response, Berger argues. It points to another reality than the empirical world with its necessary compromises and conformities: to a free and redeeming realm where death and destruction do not finally reign, but where mirth and glee ultimately obtain. Far from being merely subjective and idiosyncratic, therefore, laughter yields objective truth about nature and nature's God: they are not malificent but beneficent, even joyful and comic.

Berger specifies not only the cultural and anthropological sources of comedy but also its five basic kinds and functions. The benign *humor* of P. G. Wodehouse and Will Rogers holds back the darkness by returning us to the innocent childlike world of laughter for its own sake. The grinning- grimacing *tragicomedy* of Sholem Aleichem and Isaac Bashevis Singer—both of them Yiddish writers who knew the emarginated and tormented life of Jews—consoles us even amidst our tears; its laughter sublimates horrors that must not be erased from memory. Hence the tragicomic joke that God rewarded his Chosen People by giving them the only Middle Eastern country that has no oil. The sheer intellectual *wit* of Oscar Wilde and H. L. Mencken makes playful use of paradox and irony in order to cultivate a sardonic detachment—often with malice aforethought—from the madding crowd and suffering world. Wilde thus observed that living morally is like washing one's clean linen in public.

Berger argues that two greatest forms of comedy seek far more than escape from sadness and consolation for pain. *Satire* turns laughter into a weapon for moral reform rather than a toy for indulgent pleasure. It combats corruption and injustice, stupidity and delusion, by means of a militant irony. Berger cites the work of the Viennese satirist Karl Kraus, though the fiction of Walker Percy might have better illustrated a satire that often avoids Kraus's bitter probity. Berger regards *folly* as the distinctively religious kind of comedy. It turns the grim ordinary world—even the grim religious world—upside down. This foolish inversion discloses the extraordinary world of the sacred, where tears are redeemed in joy and lament is replaced with laughter. Berger dares to suggest that the French absurdists and surrealists open the way to such holy folly by pointing up the madness that often passes as ordinary reason. They enable us to see Christ as the ultimate Fool who surrenders his infinite majesty by taking the form of a mocked and murdered man, the crucified Clown whom God raises in victory over the world's sober-sided pride.

Here we find yet another of Berger's many variations on his perennial theme: the Holy is the transcendent dimension of life. Human beings, especially in their comic moments, encounter an invisible sacred world lying beyond and behind mundane reality. These universal glimpses of the unknown God enable individuals to make comic leaps of faith despite the seeming godlessness of the world. For Berger, the redeeming power of comedy to overthrow the deadly certainties of ordinary existence can be descried in all the world's religions: in Isaiah's perambulating without clothes or shoes for three years, in Jeremiah's collaring himself with a wooden yoke, in Ezekiel's being commanded to eat excrement, in Jesus's entering Jerusalem on a donkey, but also in the Tibetan Buddhist "figure of Kali Durga, the goddess of destruction, depicted as a woman of monstrous appearance dancing on a mountain of skulls."[25]

For Berger himself, the transcendent experience of redeeming surprises to be found at work everywhere in the world is best expressed and identified through the story of Jesus Christ: "the reality it alleges fits with my own experiences of what is real about the world, about the human condition, and about my own life."[26] Berger's language is deliberately subjective and suppositional ("alleges") because his theology is irreducibly individualist and hypothetical. Indeed, he perceives all true acts of faith to have a lonely "as if" quality. In a radically pluralistic world of endless personal choices, ecclesial Christianity seems dead for him. Like a latter-day Kierkegaard, Berger believes that Western selfhood now derives its being from the life of solitude lived before the solitary God. The key religious word for him is not *credimus* but *credo*. "To say 'I believe' is to set myself off as an individual against other individuals who do not. [. . .] In the classical sense, it is a *confessional* statement." He adds the rather portentous warning that "in Christian history, confession was very often the prelude to martyrdom."[27] Speaking much more like a market capitalist than a sociologist of religion, Berger concludes that free selfhood is born whenever individuals take their lonely stand in the face of the ultimate reality who is God, often against the grain of their own communities. "*Freedom presupposes solitariness*," he emphatically declares. "*Thus it is only the solitary individual who can engage in an act of believing.*"[28]

A Critique of Berger's Enlightenment Liberalism

This equation of faith and freedom with individual solitude is an astonishing claim for a sociologist to make. It is stranger still for a Christian to speak in this fashion. Suffice it to say, all too briefly, that Berger's Enlightenment liberalism sets him on a collision course with the Gospel as it is lived in the Church. Beginning with supposedly universal human experiences of the sacred, Berger ends by putting his confidence in solitary acts of self-transcendence. Berger's understanding of faith has a gnostic quality about it, having no necessary location in particular places and times, certainly not at Jerusalem in A.D. 34. Nor is it surprising that he should quote his fellow liberal Reinhold Niebuhr on the generic rather than the specific character of faith: "Faith is the only possible response to the ultimate incongruities of existence which threaten the very meaning of our life."[29] Such a generalized faith is focused on an unknown and unknowable God, not on the self-identifying God of Israel and Christ and the church:

> God's dealings with mankind can be seen as a cosmic game of hide-and-seek. We catch a glimpse of Him and then He promptly disappears. His absence is a central feature of our existence, and the ultimate source of our anxieties. Religious faith is the hope that He will eventually reappear, providing that ultimate relief, which, precisely, is redemption.[30]

Which, precisely, is *not* redemption in a distinctively Christian sense. God's absence is indeed an agonizing reality, but it is to be encountered precisely in his presence, most notably in Christ's agony at Gethsemane and on Golgotha. He hides himself from Isaiah the better to make known his will for Israel. Thus is he the seek-and-find God who has searched out and formed his own elect people. They dwell not in lonely and lip-gnawing anxiety so much as they struggle toward the gradual transformation of their lives into the image of God within a community of judgment and forgiveness. Their suffering derives less from individual misery than from the world's anger at them for bearing scandalous witness to the true and living God. Their hope is that the Christ who is coming is the Christ who has come, that the church militant already knows his reconciling communal love, and that the church triumphant will enjoy full communion with the triune God and all the saints.

The doctrine of the Trinity is indispensable for Christian faith, as it is not for Berger, because it makes God's inner identity (the immanent Trinity) inseparable from his outward will for the world (the economic Trinity). Far from being an abstruse distinction made by what Berger calls the "grim theologians," this trinitarian claim arises out of God's own self-disclosure, not from the projections of a universal religious longing for transcendence. Being a communal God himself, he is known in his community called the church. Berger's solitary God, by contrast, all too greatly resembles solitary modern man: a deity trapped in his own oneness, a lonely and secluded divinity standing at a remote remove from any communal life. Nor is this unknown God able to transform the world by doing a new thing. Surely it was the conviction that God had summoned them to something radically and positively new—namely, to be the blessing and redemption of all the nations—that drove Abraham out of Aramaea and that struck Paul blind on the Damascus Road.

In electing Israel to be his unique people and in calling the church to be his unique community, God seeks to make the entire world into a singular society that participates in his own triune and communal life. This means, among many other things, that the God of Jesus Christ deals with the world not through the private decisions of isolated individuals, but through the worship and service, the witness and the tradition, of his irreducibly social people. The real offense of Christ's cross and resurrection is that they create a community which makes God disturbingly near at hand rather than unrecognizably far off. As Paul discovered in the great multicultural city of Athens, the stone of particularist revelation will always offend, causing religious pluralists to stumble.

Peter Berger is to be honored for his keen insight into the nature of religion, for his prophetic assault on the apostasy at work in much of contemporary Christianity, and for his passionate summons to recover the sense of divine transcendence in our age of idolatrous self-worship. To his credit, he wants to preserve the scandal of the Gospel. Yet Berger cannot resist the itch to generalize it into a species belonging a larger class called religion. Thus does he make Jesus into a disturber of our safe and sanitized lives because his message has no specifiable content except that God remains impalpable: "this savior proclaimed in the Gospel is one who breaks into human reality like an intruder—unexpected, unrecognized, indeed unappealing. In this, the savior actually authenticates his divine provenance: the divine always manifests itself as that which is alien, not human, not part of ordinary reality."[31]

What Berger fails sufficiently to comprehend is that the God of the Gospel offends, not because he is alien and far off and unknowable, but because he has made himself strangely known and uncomfortably close at hand. The scandalous life and death and resurrection of Jesus Christ serve to create a community that, even more scandalously, both demands and enables our transformation into God's own likeness. This is no generic faith. It is the radically particularized faith of Abraham, Isaac, and Jacob. It is the concrete faith of the church: the faith *of* and *in* Jesus Christ. It was Israel's own attempt to generalize faith in Yahweh by amalgamating it with the surrounding religions that drew the wrath of God, just as Paul's own anger is kindled against the Galatians because of their desire to give it another focus than its drastically specific point. The glory of Jesus Christ is to be found, therefore, in his often scrofulous Body no less than his immaculate Head. The glory of all absconding gods, by contrast, is forever receding because they are forever unreal. "What therefore you worship as unknown, this I proclaim to you" (Acts 17:23). This summons to hear and heed the incarnate Lord is one that evangelical Christians claim to have answered, and so our next task is to examine the adequacy of their engagement with contemporary culture.

Chapter 4

The Inadequacy of the Evangelical Engagement with Culture

Since my own religious and institutional identity is linked to evangelical Christianity, and since a goodly portion of the book's readership will consist of evangelicals, I believe that we would do well to begin by examining the current status of evangelicalism as it has been formulated by Mark Noll, while also looking backward to three nineteenth-century writers who were marked, for both good and ill, by the evangelical piety of their day—Abraham Lincoln, Mark Twain, and Emily Dickinson. However much we may applaud or lament, the fact remains that much of vital Christianity in the United States is decidedly evangelical in its expression. Hence my concern to offer both affirmations and criticisms of the kind of Christianity in which I myself have been nourished. My aim is to make the witness of evangelical churches more faithful to the Gospel, and also to enrich their life with other forms of Christian witness, especially Roman Catholic.

The Essential Marks of Evangelicalism

Evangelicalism, as Noll concedes, is notoriously difficult to define. What Wittgenstein said about the aroma of coffee can also be said of evangelicalism: everyone knows it exists, but no one can precisely describe it. Wags have declared that an evangelical is anyone who likes Billy Graham. Noll, far more helpfully, pares the leading evangelical characteristics down to three: a radically life-reorienting experience before God, an unabashed priority given to the Bible—especially its cross-centered gospel—as the one authoritative rule for faith and practice, and an adaptive engagement with the environing culture. It's this last ambiguous item that creates difficulty, since it produces things both helpful and harmful to Christ's cause. Its adaptiveness gives evangelicalism—especially in its Pentecostal expression—a vitality that makes it the most rapidly expanding form of Christianity today. Yet these same cultural adaptations bring compromises and corruptions that threaten the integrity of the faith which evangelicals so ardently advocate.

Together with Nathan Hatch and many other historians, secular and Christian alike, Noll has insisted for many years that there has never been any such thing as a Christian America. He reiterates the point that the American Founding was a notably secular event. It was accomplished—for the most part, and contrary to conservative myth—by deistic Episcopalians who believed neither in original sin nor in Israel and Christ as God's unique provisions for the world's salvation. Benjamin Franklin's celebrated motion for prayer at the climax of the Constitutional Convention was in fact not passed, and the orison itself not prayed, at least not in public. Nor did the cultural hegemony of evangelicals begin with the Great Awakening of the 1740s. As Noll crisply notes, this infusion of religious fervor into American life "was more successful at ending Puritanism than inaugurating evangelicalism."[1]

It was the frontier revivals of the 1770s and 1780s, Noll demonstrates, that marked the real emergence of the voluntarist, individualist, and sectarian kind of Protestantism that we know as evangelicalism. These new and distinctively American Christians did indeed embrace and adopt—though they did not inaugurate and inspire—the essential qualities of the Founding: "the democratic, republican, commonsensical, liberal, and providential conceptions by which the founders had defined America."[2] The result, for the first six decades of the nineteenth century, was a thoroughgoing alignment of American Protestantism with the American political project. A country once ruled by Congregationalists, Episcopalians, and Presbyterians was now dominated, at least religiously, by Methodists and Baptists.

The moralistic zeal of their revivalism seemed to find its perfect echo in the ethical excellence required by democratic principles. Non-Christian politicians such as Thomas Jefferson had seen, in turn, that republican government could not flourish without citizens of sterling character. Church-state separation in politics thus made for church-state symbiosis in religion. Government provided the liberty and space for evangelical Christians to express what Noll calls their "strong communal sense [. . .] through voluntary organization of churches and parachurch special-purpose agencies"— i.e., Sunday schools, aid endeavors for the poor, missionary enterprises, publishing houses, etc.[3] Noll cites the massive involvement of evangelicals in the sectional antagonisms prior to the Civil War as proof that they had learned to make public use of their state-granted freedom of religion. Yet such engagement with American culture proved, all too predictably, to have sectional as well as religious motivation. Evangelical loyalties to region shaped evangelical responses to slavery, as adaptability yet again revealed its bicephalous nature.

The Evangelical Revolution in Images

The ambiguous adaptability of evangelicalism is revealed in all its complexity by David Morgan in his excellent study entitled *Protestants and Pictures*. He demonstrates that—contrary to the assumption that American Protestantism has been essentially verbal—it was once driven by a powerful visual piety. By the early part of the nineteenth century, the ready availability of printed material had given rise to our first mass culture. It was made possible, Morgan reveals, by a convergence of several forces: national aspiration, mass migration, and an economy based more on consumption than production. It was also prompted by drastic new means of communication: "mail order, a reliable postal system, uniform currency, widespread literacy, and dependable transportation via an ever-expanding infrastructure of roads, railroads, canals, and steam-powered river vessels [. . . .]"[4] The standard way of reading this revolution in mass culture is to see it as having an inexorably secularizing effect. Morgan argues, quite to the contrary, that Protestant evangelicals so decisively shaped the new print-culture that they were able to set their stamp on the entire national ethos, creating "a fundamentally visual culture."[5]

The chief agencies driving this cultural and religious revolution were the American Tract Society and the American Sunday School Union. Morgan contends that the founding of the ATS was a decisive moment in American religious history. It meant that the Protestant churches came to share the new national urgency about education and literacy. They believed that a reading citizenry is at once the most readily evangelized and also the most likely to uphold republican ideals. Just as printed advertisements had proved immensely effective in commercial life, so could tracts "sell" this combined republican-Christian message. (Even though evangelistic revivals were not centered on the printed and illustrated Word, they partook of this same commodifying ethos, as the saving decision for Christ became analogous to the consumer's personal choice.) Yet evangelism was no longer limited to garnering souls for heaven. The mission of the church was also to be realized on earth. Far from being alien to the social gospel, evangelical tracts promoted moral reform, philanthropic giving, benevolent agencies, and especially the mother-tended home. The aim of this first mass propagation of the

Gospel was to make the postmillennial Kingdom dawn first on these democratic shores and then to illumine the entire world. As the one nation that combined perfect religious and political liberty, the United States would serve as the flagship of western Protestant civilization.

This conflation of national and religious aims would have lasting consequences. At first the Protestant tract-movement seemed radical in its ethical rigor. Its early advocates sought, for example, to end both slavery and war. But these drastic demands were soon subordinated to the more convenient and easily realized aims of the young Protestant republic. Native Americans were depicted not as noble savages but as barbarians who blighted our Christian civilization. Slaves were limned as happy Christian simpletons whose masters were guilty not of sinfully shackling their fellow creatures but of politically disrupting our national unity. Roman Catholics were shown as drunken louts and superstitious heathens who needed amalgamating as well as converting. The impoverished working classes were displayed as intemperate and wayward souls whose improvidence proved a burden to taxpayers. The ideal American Protestant culture was envisioned, by contrast, as a tranquil rural affair presided over by mothers who instilled in their children the Christian virtues of thrift and honesty and abstinence from worldly vices.

During the latter half of the century, Morgan argues, American visual piety underwent a seismic though gradual shift. From having had primarily a didactic purpose—to illustrate the truth of God's biblical Word—Protestant pictorial efforts sought increasingly to prompt personal piety, especially among children. If children could be reached for the Gospel, so could their parents. Children, in turn, could best be influenced through sentimental images of pity and comfort on the one hand, fear and shame on the other. Hence the birth of the chalk-talk, where pastors and others sought to overcome the limits of the catechism by sketching biblical stories on blackboards. Entertainment and amusement became essential tools in the marketing of evangelical faith, as American commerce and American Protestantism were ever more fully entwined.

For a nation and a religion increasingly at ease with each other, there seemed but little need for the venerable Puritan—and the more recent revivalist—demand for radical conversion and conscious submission to the will of God. These extravagant practices among old-style evangelicals gradually gave way to a new-style liberalism built on the idea of Christian nurture. Horace Bushnell, its most famous advocate, held that the organic development of character may best be assured through wholesome images and unconscious influences rather than doctrinal inculcation. The most wholesome of all images is surely that of history's most influential figure, Jesus himself. "It is the grandeur of his character," wrote Bushnell, "which constitutes the chief power of his ministry, not his miracles or teachings apart from his character."[6] Devotional images of a haloed and idealized Jesus—concentrating especially upon his face—thus came into immense vogue. Warner Sallman's *Head of Christ* and Heinrich Hofmann's *Christ in Gethsemane* were but the most popular among many hundreds of such sentimental images of the Savior. There also arose a concomitant interest in Jesus's childhood. Just as the boy-Christ underwent his own development of faith, so did the new graded and illustrated Sunday School lessons seek to insure full spiritual consciousness at the end of adolescence—so great was the confidence that the faith formed during one's youth would last through adulthood without great change.

Morgan concludes his magisterial survey of nineteenth- and early twentieth-century American visual piety by noting that the triumph of the suggestive image over the illustrated text constitutes a decidedly modern and post-Enlightenment turn. It moves from the rational to the affectional, from clearly conveyed knowledge to nonrationally evoked feelings. The outcome was decisive. Whereas the didactic images of the early nineteenth century sought to create a culture of character that "endorsed moderation, self-restraint, even self-denial,"[7] the devotional images that emerged in the latter half of the century produced a culture of personality if not celebrity. This new kind of visual piety that had begun with "effeminate" images of a suffering Christ ended by depicting a strong Personality who exuded energy and self-fulfillment, competition and self-expression, masculinity and self-assertion. Bruce Barton's *The Man Nobody Knows* was its literary expression. Yet if Barton's sentimentalizing of the Gospel reveals evangelicalism at its weakest, we need only to turn to another American figure to witness its paradoxical power.

The Case of Abraham Lincoln

Though not a professed Christian, Abraham Lincoln was shaped by the evangelicalism of his youth. In *Abraham Lincoln: Redeemer President*, Allen C. Guelzo argues that Lincoln was a Whig liberal whose heroes were Hobbes and Locke and Paine, Mill and Bentham and Adam Smith. He hated the farm life that he had known as a raw Kentucky youth. The romantic myth that he was a rough-hewn log-splitter who brought the wisdom of the land to the nation is entirely a figment. On the contrary, Lincoln thought the future of America lay in its cities, and in the economic opportunities that they brought for individuals to better themselves by way of wage labor. Farm life, by contrast, sank its inhabitants into a cruel dependency on the vagaries of the markets and the weather, on the exhaustibility of the land, and thus on a perpetual indebtedness.

Lincoln's chief ideological enemy was Thomas Jefferson and his vision of America as an aggregate of small communities made up largely of yeomen/tradesmen and farmers needing no strong central government or national financial system, but instead depending on each other in closely communal ways. Thus did the federal bureaucracy increase under Lincoln as under no other president, and he had no aversion to using the patronage system for his own political ends. Whereas Jefferson wanted a strict division between the sacred and secular realms, Lincoln shared the Whig and evangelical notion that state and religion were to be allied for deeply shared purposes—the chief of which was a strong sense of the nation as transcending all other goods, uniting men and women in common freedoms (chiefly economic), and thus not allowing the states to go their separate ways when they disagreed about even the most fundamental matters. For Lincoln, therefore, the Civil War was fought first of all on nationalist grounds. He issued the Emancipation Proclamation and made the defeat of slavery the war's main aim only when he saw that it could not be won any other way.

Both the Jeffersonian and Lincolnian visions, Guelzo shows, were equally inspired by the Enlightenment, even as they were equally secular in their aims, though Lincoln's outlook had an authentially religious underpinning as Jefferson's did not. Lincoln valued reason above all things, and he despised the Democrats' exaltation of the passions, especially as exhibited so crudely during Andrew Jackson's presidency. Lincoln's Baptist upbringing in Kentucky also gave him deep Calvinist sympathies that linked his radical sense of divine sovereignty with his radical devotion to national sovereignty. Lincoln's God was not Thomas Jefferson's impersonal deity who distantly oversees his creation. Lincoln's divinity was the omnipotent personal Judge who governs the events of history by his own incalculable and implacable will. And so while Lincoln thought that individuals were inflexibly determined by their own largely selfish interests—hence utterly incapable of changing their natures as self-interested animals—he believed that the grand events of history were undetermined in their outcome. Lincoln's political decisions were governed, therefore, by a strange reliance on divine providence as he discerned it mysteriously at work in history.

Despite the evangelical piety of his Baptist youth, Lincoln never thought of himself as a subject of redemption—since human beings are but rational animals—and he never professed a distinctively Christian faith. Like Emily Dickinson, he may have drawn back from the evangelical insistence on a sudden and emotional conversion. Even so, he thought that God's own redemptive purposes were indeed operative in the fundamental movements of peoples and nations. Most remarkable of all was Lincoln's refusal, derived it seems from his evangelical rearing, to make a moralistic reading of history. He did not believe that God rewards good and punishes evil according to any kind of human calculus. Thus did he refuse to make the winning of the Civil War a vindication of Northerners and a condemnation of Southerners. Both sides were equally responsible for the original institution of slavery, and there were good and evil men fighting on both sides, indeed within Mary Todd Lincoln's own Kentucky family. Unlike nearly everyone else defending either the South or the North, therefore, Lincoln could have charity toward all, malice toward none. It was not courageous Northern righteousness that ended slavery, in Lincoln's view, but God's own mysterious willing and ending of the War. Hence the gigantic irony that Allen Guelzo has uncovered: the Lincoln who never considered himself a candidate for redemption has been exalted into a virtual savior, our one "Redeemer President of These States," as Walt Whitman called him.[8] And it happened because Lincoln both rejected and appropriated his ambiguous evangelical past.

Mark Twain and the Death of the "No-God"

It is not unreasonable to suggest that many who, like Lincoln, were raised as evangelicals turned away from the faith of their youth because of its unwillingness to countenance the doubt that, as we shall see, characterizes Scripture itself and that has made itself strongly felt in modern life. Nearly every careful observer of the American scene has noted the disappearance of God from our literature. There seems to have been a great collapse, not only on the pages of our poems and novels, but also in the very courts of heaven. The welkin that once rang with the music of the spheres now seems silent. Writers openly scoff at the God whom earlier ages took for granted. "Old Nobodaddy" is the nasty name William Blake gave to the God who was once addressed as the Heavenly Father. "Our nada who art in nada, nada be thy name," declares one of Ernest Hemingway's characters in scornful parody of the Lord's Prayer. "It is not unbelief that is dangerous to our society," George Bernard Shaw wrote in his preface to *Androcles and the Lion*; "it is belief."[9] Unlike our foreparents who regarded religious faith as the very fundament of society, Shaw saw it as the chief enemy of the people. At a time when genocidal religious wars continue to let the blood of our planet, we may be tempted to agree with Shaw that belief is indeed a deadly thing. Yet our best artists have also noticed the fearful consequences of the divine death. Dostoevsky's Ivan Karamazov thus declares that, if there is no God, then everything is permitted; there are no moral constraints whatever. Like the monsters of the deep, as King Lear says, we are left to devour each other.

Who is the God whom many modern literary artists have declared dead? Evangelical critic D. Bruce Lockerbie believes that it is the God of biblical revelation and orthodox Christian faith. In his *Dismissing God: Modern Writers' Struggle Against Religion*, Lockerbie chides such writers for their unbelief. He argues that the preponderance of nineteenth- and twentieth-century authors "have forsaken belief altogether and chosen the vacuum of unbelief; still others, more aggressively, seem obsessed by a warring spirit against belief that compels them to challenge God's supremacy. In a manner of speaking, they seem to have wished to battle God on equal terms."[10] Lockerbie cites Mark Twain as a case in point when, in *Huckleberry Finn*, he has Huck make fun of Miss Watson's God. She had taught Huck to pray in the assurance that God will grant whatever he asks. But Huck has tried Miss Watson's notion of petitionary prayer and found it false:

> "[I]t warn't so. I tried it. Once I got a fish-line, but no hooks. It warn't any good to me without hooks. I tried for the hooks three or four times, but somehow I couldn't make it work. By-and-by, one day, I asked Miss Watson to try for me, but she said I was a fool. She never told me why, and I couldn't make it out no way."[11]

Miss Watson cannot satisfy Huck's demand that he be told why he is a fool. Twain suggests that Huck is, in fact, no fool at all but an uncannily wise youth who has penetrated the façade of a false deity. If such a Supreme Being—existing on a plane with us, only at a higher level—were in fact directing the universe like a master chess player, then he could indeed provide hooks as well as fish-line. Christians have not traditionally understood miracles to contravene the natural order as Huck has been taught. In the earliest gospel, the Markan Jesus guards against such a sensationalist conception of his powers: he abjures those whom he heals or raises to retain strict secrecy about these matters. The Fourth Gospel eschews the word "miracle" altogether. As David Garland points out, the mighty works of the Johannine Jesus are called "signs" because they always point to the Kingdom whose presence they manifest; they never demonstrate Jesus' arbitrary power over ordinary causality. The sentimental notion that miracles are God's willful violation of nature for our own selfish benefit is mainly a modern notion.

William Placher observes that, from Augustine through Aquinas to Luther and Calvin, the chief thinkers of the Christian West have a virtually unanimous estimate of miracles as God's working *in* and *through* the natural order for his own purposes. As Augustine said, the whole of creation is at once natural *and* miraculous. Aquinas described miracles as those events which, because their natural causes are hidden from us, excite *admiratio*, the *wonder* which existentially and etymologically lies at the root of the word *miracle*, as Placher explains:

> [I]n a world where God sustains everything at every moment, what distinguishes miracles is our inability to understand their causes and the wonder that results, not the fact that God acts in them but not elsewhere.
>
> Calvin likewise refused to set aside one class of events as uniquely miraculous. "For there are as many miracles of divine power," he wrote, "as there are kinds of things in the universe, indeed as there are things either great or small." Each human being contains "enough miracles to occupy our minds, if only we were not irked at paying attention to them."[12]

Though appropriately ignorant of such a thoughtful theology, Huck faithfully and wittily persists in his questioning of the Widow Douglas's false deity who jumps in and out of his creation as if he had one life and the cosmos another—as if he were our heavenly hireling, a divine factotum and sacred Santa Claus who brings us what we want when we prove ourselves not naughty but nice by praying aright:

> I says to myself, if a body can get anything they pray for, why don't Deacon Winn get back the money he lost on pork? Why can't the widow get back her silver snuff box that was stole? Why can't Miss Watson fat up? No, I says to myself, there ain't nothing in it. I went and told the widow about it, and she said the thing a body could get by praying for it was "spiritual gifts." This was too [much] for me, but she told me what she meant—I must help other people, and do everything I could for other people, and look out for them all the time, and never think about myself. This was including Miss Watson, as I took it. I went out in the woods and turned it over in my mind a long time, but I couldn't see no advantage about it—except for the other people—so at last I reckoned I wouldn't worry about it any more, but just let it go.[13]

Lockerbie interprets this passage as revealing not only Huck Finn's "cynicism toward religious profession,"[14] but also as reflecting an unbelief that pervades all of Twain's work. Not at all am I offering up Samuel Langhorne

Clemens as an orthodox Christian writer. Twain paid an awful price indeed for denying the wonder of petitionary prayer—for dismissing, out of hand, the unfathomable mystery that the God who does not need our prayers strangely uses them to accomplish not our own will but his. Twain's contempt for false Christianity robbed him of any deep appreciation for true faith. It cost him a bitter final cynicism, not only about his daughter's death, but also about God and the world in general.

Yet Twain was right, I believe, to deny the gimcrack god of Miss Watson and the Widow Douglas, even if he was wrong also to deny the true God who has become flesh and who thus, in forming for himself a new people, fills them with spiritual gifts that cannot be confused with bland ethical injunctions. Huck needs no Creator-Redeemer to look out for others instead of himself, as the Widow Douglas enjoins him to do. If he so wanted, Huck could accomplish such humanly possible things, such Boy Scoutish good deeds, by his own powers. W. H. Auden gave the lie to the widow's moralistic pietism when he confessed that we all know that we were all put here to serve others, but what the others were put here for, only God must know. Against Lockerbie's reading of Huck and his authorial creator as religious cynics, therefore, I believe that Huck is a far better theologian than his tutors.

The Supreme Being of popular piety—worshipped by many other Christians than nineteenth-century evangelicals!—is a Zeus-like autocrat. John of Damascus was the first Christian thinker to distinguish between this false deity and the true God of Christian faith. He insisted that all human categories collapse in the attempt to name God. *Deus non est in genere*, declared this eighth-century theologian: "God does not belong to the class of existing things, not that God has not existence but that God is above all existing things, no even about existence itself." Paul Tillich helpfully expands this ancient Christian contention:

> The being of God cannot be understood as the existence of a being alongside others or above others. If God is a being, he is subject to the categories of finitude, especially to space and substance. Even if he is called the "highest being" in the sense of the "most perfect" and "most powerful" being, this situation is not changed. When applied to God, superlatives become diminutives.[15]

Karl Barth is even more vehement in his denunciation of what he calls the No-God of spurious faith. Barth regards this pseudo-divinity as the most pernicious of all human inventions because it stanches any radical transformation of either individuals or their institutions. Such a god confirms "the course of the world and of men as it is."[16] This comforting and consoling deity, as Barth makes clear, is ever so difficult to surrender:

> We suppose that we know what we are saying when we say 'God'. We assign to Him the highest place in our world: and in so doing we place Him on fundamentally one line with ourselves and with things. We assume that He *needs something*: and so we assume that we are able to arrange our relation to Him as we arrange other relationships. We press ourselves into proximity with Him: and so, all unthinking, we make Him nigh unto ourselves. We allow ourselves an ordinary communication with Him, we permit ourselves to reckon with Him as though this were not extraordinary behaviour on our part. We dare to deck ourselves out as his companions, patrons, advisers, and commissioners. We confound time with eternity.[17]

If such a Supreme Being—whom Lockerbie likens to "the heavyweight champion of the universe"[18]—were in fact directing the universe like a master chess player, then he could indeed provide Huck with hooks as well as fish-line, and so could Miss Watson "fat up." God does not so act, and Huck is no atheist for denying the efficacy of selfish prayers made to him. "The cry of revolt against such a god," writes Karl Barth, "is nearer the truth than is the sophistry with which men attempt to justify him."[19]

The Salutary Doubt of Emily Dickinson

Along with Lincoln and Twain, Emily Dickinson is a third nineteenth-century American writer who found herself unable fully to embrace the evangelical piety of her age. Unlike Lockerbie his fellow evangelical, Roger Lundin in *Emily Dickinson and the Art of Belief* refuses to dismiss Dickinson's work because it falls outside the prescribed Christian lines of her time. During her single year of college life at the Mount Holyoke Female Seminary, the seventeen-year old Dickinson was tutored by the school's founder, the redoubtable Mary Lyon. Like other Whig evangelicals of her day, Lyon envisioned Christianity as forming a powerful tandem with science and education for bringing about a moral revolution of the entire planet. The Kingdom of heaven was soon to come on earth—if not in the nineteenth then surely in the twentieth century, which would so certainly be the Christian Century that a still-thriving journal was thus named. In an 1842 address setting forth this confident evangelicalism, Lyon envisioned a time rapidly approaching when all people would "act according to the principles of reason and religion," when "all that now goes into the war channel, will then be consecrated to the service of knowledge and benevolence."[20]

The key to such moral transformation lay in the act of becoming a Christian by way of a drastic and emotional conversion experience. Such a dramatic rebirth was public proof that one had personally appropriated the gift of grace. A miraculous conversion was the spiritual equivalent of the physical violations of nature that were said to be miraculous evidences of God's existence. "In working toward the conversion of her students at Mount Holyoke," Lundin writes, "Lyon divided them each year into three groups." The "Christians" were those who could testify to the certainty of their salvation experience. The "Hopers" believed themselves on the verge of conversion. The "No-Hopers," by contrast, could attest to no drastic emotional reversal that proved their faith in Christ.[21] What had begun in the seventeenth century with the Puritan practice of the examined conscience, whereby one sought human evidence of divine election, thus led in the nineteenth century to a radical spiritual subjectivism. Salvation was located not in public and communal acknowledgement of Jesus Christ's objectively accomplished act at Calvary, but rather in the solitary self, whose traumatic conversion experience alone could attest to the efficacy of Christ's work.

Emily Dickinson was numbered on the short list of souls called the No-Hopers. They were the special targets of fervent evangelical attention at Mount Holyoke and Amherst alike. Dickinson remained one of the few holdouts. "How lonely this world is growing," she wrote in the spring of 1850. "Christ is calling everyone here [. . .], and I am standing alone in rebellion, and growing very careless."[22] To her friend Abiah Root, Dickinson confessed that "I have perfect confidence in God & his promises and yet I know not why, I feel that the world holds a predominant place in my affections. I do not feel that I could give up all for Christ, were I called to die."[23] That Dickinson declined to make a public profession of faith does not mean, as Lundin makes clear, that she was an atheist scoffer at all things Christian. On the contrary, Dickinson admitted "that I shall never be happy without I love Christ." Yet if the love of Christ were signified by an overwhelmingly subjective conversion, Dickinson knew that she lacked it. To her friend Root, she thus explained her refusal to attend the Amherst revival meetings of 1850: "I felt that I was so easily excited that I might again be deceived and I dared not trust myself."[24]

Lockerbie seizes upon such confessions to interpret Dickinson as a woman who would not submit herself "to the sovereign authority of God and the lordship of Jesus Christ." Dickinson "deprived herself of [. . .]

grace," Lockerbie maintains; she abdicated true belief and thus minimized "the scope of her soul's experience."[25] Lundin is theologically much more astute. He contends that the same Protestant individualism which failed to convert Dickinson succeeded in teaching her to worship at the shrine of her own inviolate self. She came thus to conceive of her poetic integrity as something she would have to surrender if she became a professed Christian. Given this awful (even if wrongly posed) dichotomy, surely Dickinson was *right* to refuse such a heroic act of will, such a denial of the world's goodness, such excited enthusiasm requiring ever-new infusions of emotion. We should commend rather than condemn Dickinson for daring not trust herself to such subjective notions. In rejecting the No-God of nineteenth-century Protestant piety, she did not minimize her soul's experience so much as she expanded it. Indeed, Dickinson became our most important American religious poet, rather than another dreary and virtually unreadable Victorian pietist.

A poem at once sprightly and re-readable, precisely because it is at once troubling and edifying, is Number 501. Here Dickinson sets forth what I believe to be the right relation between faith and doubt:

This World is not Conclusion.
A Species stands beyond—
Invisible, as Music—
But positive, as Sound—
It beckons, and it baffles—
Philosophy—don't know—
And through a Riddle, at the last—
Sagacity, must go—
To guess it, puzzles scholars—
To gain it, Men have borne
Contempt of Generations
And Crucifixion, shown—
Faith slips—and laughs, and rallies—
Blushes, if any see—
Plucks at a twig of Evidence—
And asks a Vane, the way—
Much Gesture, from the Pulpit—
Strong Hallelujahs roll—
Narcotics cannot still the Tooth
That nibbles at the soul—

The No-God who can be known within worldly categories offers his disciples the blessings of finite faith, the comforts of mundane assurance. The true God, by contrast, dwells within the world while standing beyond it, a Reality as unseen as music yet as real as sound. This unknown God who alone can make himself known both attracts and repels. He is what Rudolf Otto called the *mysterium tremendum et fascinans*: the Mystery who at once frightens and captivates. Philosophy, with its knowledge of things visible and intelligible, can fathom nearly everything but this Mystery who is the real God. Eluding all confining categories, he prompts an agnostic "don't know." The world's wisdom, even at best, is but a set of riddles and conundrums. Airy academics, with their dry distinctions, can only speculate about this Species who stands beyond all species. Those who actually gain Reality must lose their lives in grappling with the unobvious God, either dying to themselves in daily martyrdom or else suffering the contempt of both the cultured and uncultured despisers of doubt-filled faith.

Such faith always entails radical risk. It is never something as clear and certain as a proposition. It's an affair of slipping and sliding, of losing and rallying, of laughing and weeping. So shy of self-confidence is true faith that it blushes when asked to expound its own piety. Calvin himself would say no more than that he had come to evangelical faith *subita conversione*—by means of a sudden reversal of his life's path. Believers know that their evidence is as slender as a twig, their ecclesial direction as uncertain as the cock atop the Puritan church. Though it announces the Resurrection, it also blows with every wind of doctrine, even as it perhaps also crows with erotic energy. Despite the flailing of perfervid preachers and the praise-songs of easy believers, true faith is never free from the toothache of doubt. The feel-good pharmacists of the No-God offer vain narcotics to ease the pain sent by the true God. The real Lord will not anesthetize shallow souls with worldly conclusions, even of the most "spiritual" sort. Instead, He implants the molar of doubt no less than the tusk of truth, and they both nibble at the soul like a mouse at cheese. For this God is not the Old Nobodaddy whose death we ought rightly to celebrate. This is the God whose Son was himself wracked by doubt as he mounted the bloody tree from which he would rule the world.

The Witness of Black Churches and the
Failure of White Accommodation

Insofar as nineteenth-century evangelicalism held to belief in an autocratic Supreme Being, together with a moralizing confidence about human history, it often led such thoughtful figures as Lincoln and Twain and Dickinson to seek religious refuge outside its confines. One happy exception to this unhappy rule is to be found in the black churches and among black artists. That they have remained on the margins of evangelical existence is a fact both ironic and sad. Noll's statistics reveal that most black Protestants are imbued with the same warm-hearted, Bible-centered, culturally adaptive faith that characterizes other evangelicals. Fifty-two percent of them give at least a tithe to their churches, eighty-six percent believe that miracles still occur, and eighty-three percent pray at least once daily. Though these figures are higher than those registered among white Christians of all kinds, black evangelicals have remained largely segregated because of white social attitudes and religious customs, and thus largely unable to teach their counterparts the most salutary of lessons. Noll states the truth simply and clearly: "black Christians are the ones who have experienced the cross most dramatically in American history."[26] This experience of radically undeserved suffering also informs Negro spirituals, making them a permanent and powerful legacy to global Christianity.

The enslavement of black Christians, both before and after manumission, taught them not to confine their piety to the space allowed by the sovereign social system. Because they had learned that true liberty comes from God chiefly and from government only secondarily, they also learned that such liberty must also be public and social, not merely personal and private. Negro spirituals such as "Swing Low, Sweet Chariot" were not only affirmations of eschatological hope, but also appeals for worldly rescue via the Underground Railroad. So was the civil rights movement in the 1960s imbued with the same theology of this-worldly and other-worldly transformation, as Martin Luther King's final speech attests. Black churches were thus able to ally their moral power with the legal power of the state, yet without giving religious sanction to the nation or reducing the Gospel to the cause of racial equality. One might add, as Noll does not, that much of the vigor has been drained from the black equality movement since, in the intervening half-century, it has sought a mainly secular rather than a centrally ecclesial forum.

Noll catches the vitality of black Christianity in his fine chapter on evangelical hymns. As he points out, there is no color or class or gender line running through a gospel song such as Thomas A. Dorsey's "Precious Lord." To sing Dorsey's immortal spiritual is to discover the gargantuan difference—both public and private—between wandering and following, falling and standing; between storm and calm, darkness and daylight; between weariness and renewal; between dwelling in an alien place and coming home. William B. McClain makes much the same point about the theology of gospel songs. It is not, he says,

[. . .] the theology of the academy or the university, not formalistic theology or the theology of the seminary, but a *theology of experience*—the theology of a God who sends the sunshine and the rain, the theology of a God who is very much alive and active and who has not forsaken those who are poor and oppressed and unemployed. It is a *theology of imagination*—it grew out of the fire shut up in the bones, of words painted on the canvas of the mind. Fear is turned to hope in the sanctuaries and storefronts, and bursts forth in songs of celebration. It is a *theology of grace* that allows the faithful to see the sunshine of His face—even through their tears. Even the words of an ex-slave trader [John Newton] became a song of liberation and an expression of God's amazing grace. It is a *theology of survival* that allows a people to celebrate the ability to continue the journey in spite of the insidious tentacles of racism and oppression and to sing, "It's another day's journey, and I'm glad about it!"[27]

During his brief stay in this country, Dietrich Bonhoeffer discerned the power of the original Reformation at work in such gospel songs, which he called "the most influential contribution made by the Negro to American Christianity."[28] Yet he lamented the fervent singing of these spirituals by whites who at the same time denied blacks the most basic privileges and amenities of American life.

While the black church and the art it inspired both flourished during the early years of the last century, white evangelicalism suffered a decline. With the failure of William Jennings Bryan to garner a national political majority, and especially with the public ignominy he brought on his cause at the Scopes trial of 1925, white evangelicals became politically quiescent until the 1970s. Their influence in American public life was largely muted by the fundamentalist controversy in theology and the anti-evolutionist animus in education. Yet Noll is at considerable pains to show that evangelicals have not been simpletons, at least until recently, about either science or theology. From Cotton Mather in the seventeenth century to Charles Hodge and B. B. Warfield in the nineteenth, most evangelical theologians were enthusiasts for science. They understood it largely as "a methodological commitment to observation, induction, rigorous principles of falsification, and a scorn for speculative hypotheses."[29] These theologians sought to use science in order to defend the veracity of the Bible and to establish a Christian world-view. Thus did they regard both Nature and Scripture as great storehouses of unvarnished empirical facts. Any fair-minded observer, employing the disinterested powers of reason, could ascertain these facts, and then assemble them into a coherent order that proved the truth of the Christian religion.

Yet this alliance of science and religion ultimately backfired. Historical critics of Scripture soon began to dispute the factuality of many biblical events, even as scientists began to make totalizing anti-religious claims concerning the naturalist and materialist character of the universe. Noll laments the resulting "wars of science and religion," especially as they have been fought by proof-texting creationists on the right and by evolutionist imperialists on the left. He names Carl Sagan and Stephen Jay Gould as the chief offenders among the latter sort. By contrast, Noll praises the historical efforts of Ronald Numbers and David Livingstone, as well as the scientific work of Michael Behe and William Dembski, for challenging the standard secular accounts of evolution. Noll hails postmodernist thinkers of whatever stripe who acknowledge the context-dependent character of both science and religion: "they have succeeded in showing as clearly as humanly possible that no capital-S science and no capital-R religion exist beyond the bounds of space and time or the boundaries of personal and communal existence."[30]

Noll strikes a similarly mediating stance in his assessment of Billy Graham. Until recently, Graham was the sole evangelical to gain large public attention. Noll lauds him for preaching nothing other than the central conversionist doctrine of redemption through the cross and resurrection of Christ alone. Not only has Graham avoided the sexual and monetary scandals that have often brought shame upon the evangelical cause; he also has shrewdly "traded angularity for access." By condemning generic rather than specific sin, Graham has been able to address men and women of every kind and condition with the glad tidings of the Gospel. Thus did Graham become, in Noll's estimate, "one of the most powerful forces for Christian ecumenicity ever seen."[31]

The Dangers of a Mediating Evangelicalism

It is not surprising that, in his constructive chapters, Noll urges evangelicals to adopt a mediating political theology that lapses into "neither a world-denying pessimism nor a redemption-denying immanentism." Noll's own theological "realism" has a decidedly Niebuhrian cast. Not within this world can "Christian ideals" ever be fully realized, so inveterately ingrained is the human bent toward sinfulness. It behooves evangelicals neither to demonize their political enemies nor to divinize their own political pronouncements. The paradoxical double-sidedness of nearly every Christian doctrine indicates, for Noll, that all political judgments must be at once local and universal and unavoidably complex. He therefore praises the mediating spirit of Canadian evangelicals for leavening their culture with the yeast of Christianity: "where in Canada evangelical connections with politics have often moderated extremes, in the United States they have more regularly exacerbated extremes."[32]

Mark Noll's confession that twentieth-century evangelicals have been guilty of intellectual malfeasance,[33] together with his own fair-minded and non-extremist scholarship, have won him a well-honored place in the pluralist public square. Yet his inclusion there risks a scandal of its own—the scandal, namely, of muting the Gospel's offensiveness, its necessary disjunction with all cultures and nations. It is a fair question, I believe, to ask whether evangelicals have made a costly error in adapting Christian faith to the basic American assumption that to be free is to be a sovereign individual unencumbered by any aims or attachments that we have not elected for ourselves, nor by obligations to any communities that we have not autonomously chosen to join. These voluntarist notions often cause us to violate the radically obediential and communal character of Christian faith. Thus did Dietrich Bonhoeffer complain in the fateful year of 1939 that, despite their admirable "multiplicity of Christian insights and communities," American Protestant churches suffer from a lack of Reformation in the upper case. He feared that the churches' acceptance of the private sphere allotted to them by the state had robbed them of their power to give public embodiment to the often offensive truth of the Gospel. Perhaps, if Bonhoeffer were living today, he would add the adjective "evangelical" to his stark warning that "denominations are not Confessing Churches."[34]

To be a confessing church is to have a drastically unadaptive allegiance to the God of Israel and Jesus Christ. As the Barmen Declaration makes clear, it is to reject all "other events and powers, figures and truths, as [if they were] God's revelation." Thus do evangelicals need to make a sharp critique of such sub-Reformation adaptations as Billy Graham's three baptisms, his virtual adulation of Ronald Reagan, his immunity to real religious doubt, and especially his decisionist and non-sacramental brand of revivalism. It will also be necessary, I believe, for evangelicals to confess that, even if the advocates of Design Theology eventually prove that nature operates not by an unsponsored and undirected evolutionary process, but by an intelligent Shaper, their discovery would still constitute a far-off echo of the scandalously self-identifying and kingdom-creating God of Abraham, Isaac, Jacob, and Jesus Christ.

Noll rightly praises evangelicals such as Charles Colson, J. I. Packer, and George Carey for seeking doctrinal solidarity with Roman Catholics. Yet there is much that evangelicals have also to learn from the patristic tradition. Evangelicals such as Robert Webber and Daniel Williams have demonstrated our need to recover the church's witness during the first five centuries.[35] I believe that evangelicals must also begin asking hard questions about the need for authoritative ecclesial offices and social teachings. The encyclicals of Pope John Paul II, for example, have served—like nothing possessing similar authority within the evangelical world—to help Catholics resist the demands of our consumerist culture of convenience as well as the omnicompetent nation-state that undergirds it.

In a more recent work, *The Old Religion in a New World*, Noll has shown both the bane and the blessing of the adaptations that have characterized American Christianity. Unlike anything known in Europe, the churches in the United States have benefited from not being identified with the conservative order of the *ancien regime*—its public creeds and codified morals, its traditional class stratifications and inherited ecclesial benefits.[36] The absence of government-allied religion has infused American churches with the revolutionary spirit of voluntarism. They have established schools and hospitals and charitable agencies that are the veritable wonder of Christendom. Thus have they put populist individualism, the democratizing spirit, and mass-marketing strategies to many good uses. Classic liberal principles of autonomy and self-determination have also succeeded in the secular realm as well, offering Christians and Jews and millions of other believers and unbelievers an unprecedented economic and educational and political freedom.

Yet a massive confusion and a subtle subversion have also been the result of this alliance of the American churches with the Enlightenment understanding of freedom. As H. G. Wells observed early in the twentieth century, the labels "right-wing" and "left-wing" are but "different species of [American] liberalism."[37] As we have noted in the Introduction, so-called conservative and liberal Christians often regard each other as dire enemies, when they both embrace an individualist and voluntarist understanding of Christian existence. So are Jews plagued by the same paradox. It was articulated to me many years ago by Rabbi Manfred Vogel: "While America has been good for Jews," said Vogel, "it has been bad for Judaism." Jews have been freed, on the whole, from the persecutions they often faced under the old regimes of Europe, and thus have they come to participate fully in the political and social life of the nation. Yet Judaism is not a religion meant to govern one's activities merely in the private and so-called religious sphere. To live by Torah is to have the rule of Yahweh prevail in every aspect of public life, from governmental regulations to Sabbath observances, all the way down to dietary restrictions and sexual practices. These things being impossible in a pluralist polity such as obtains in the United States, a truncated Judaism is the result.

Noll argues that, in the face of a freedom-granting American liberalism that requires drastic church compromises and adaptations, the only way to maintain traditional orthodoxy of both belief and practice is a radical way indeed: "to become sectarian—that is, to actively oppose marketplace reasoning; to refuse to abide by the democratic will of majorities; to insist upon higher authorities than the *vox populi*; and to privilege ancestral, traditional, or hierarchical will over individual choice."[38] Noll argues that such drastic church resistance to the American individualist ethos has never been successful, for it entails—in Noll's Niebuhrian view—a separation of the church from the profoundest concerns of politics and learning and family life. It is this seemingly obvious truth that this book seeks to resist. I will be arguing, therefore, that the church can best engage its individualist American culture precisely by seeking to remain uncompromisingly faithful to the community-centered Gospel.

Evangelical and Catholic at the Same Time

In a response to my review of Noll's *American Evangelical Christianity*, the associate editor of *First Things* chided me for excessive evangelical self-criticism.[39] I confess that academics are often prone to the more-sinful-than-thou syndrome. We often find perverse pleasure in the failings of our own ilk. But if James Nuechterlein had daily encounters with young evangelicals, as I do, he might be less sanguine about our often (though not always) privatized, individualistic, and non-ecclesial kind of Christianity. That he failed to mention my protest against Billy Graham's three baptisms is revealing. Neither do many of my fellow evangelicals protest, for they too believe that baptism is a mere personal affirmation of faith—or else a declaration of membership in a particular denomination rather than the one unrepeatable act of initiation into Christian faith. Thus do they repeat it as often as they desire, especially on trips to the Holy Land (as most evangelicals still call Israel), even though the shallowness of the Jordan River militates against the notion that Jesus himself was baptized by immersion.

Nuechterlein also complains that I want an impossibly pure evangelicalism. He fears that if we evangelicals adopt the virtues of other Christians, especially Catholics and other liturgical churches, we will lose the convincing particularity of our own witness. If he means that we should not abandon our missionary impulse, our emphasis on personal piety, our devotion to the Lordship of Jesus, our stress on upright moral living, our belief in Scripture's final authority, and our conviction that the Gospel is not one among many ways to salvation, then he is surely right. But if he wants our revivalism to leave converts cut off from the sanctifying nurture of church, our decisionism to rest on sub-Christian notions of autonomy, our pietism to rob us of reverent worship, our devotionalism to lobotomize the life of the mind, our moralism to give us contempt for those who smoke tobacco and drink wine, our biblicism to make us ignorant of the bi-millennial Christian tradition, and our exclusivism to convince us that Roman Catholics are not Christians, then most surely he is wrong. To plead, as Nuechterlein does, that "all systems of thought, religious and otherwise, are partial," that they are "all package deals," that "their distinctive strengths come together with distinctive weaknesses"[40] is to remain content, I fear, with an evangelicalism that is neither *reformata* nor *semper reformanda*. It is to be invited, alas, out of the church catholic and Catholic. It is also to despair that the Body of Christ shall ever become one, as our Lord petitions in John 17:11. Surely our final hope is that we shall become both Evangelical and Catholic—not only together, but also at the same time.[41]

In his brief account of the twentieth-century Catholic intellectual revival, Noll himself provides a potential counter-argument to his own thesis about the necessary Niebuhrian compromises that the churches must make with American Enlightenment liberalism. From the late nineteenth century through the mid-60s, Noll shows, American Catholic culture experienced an unheralded renascence. This educational rebirth also had "many links to social action, missionary service, and liturgical renewal."[42] Noll asserts that there has been no comparable intellectual revitalization in the history of the American church except for the Puritan flowering of mind in the seventeenth century and the brief burst of theological creativity among Reformed theologians just prior to the Civil War. What made the renascence so surprising is that it occurred amidst an ethos that seemed ever so uninviting to an American renewal of the church. In 1899 Pope Leo XIII had issued *Testem Benevolentiae*, an encyclical roundly castigating "Americanism"— namely, "the mistaken desire for the church to conform to the shape of American culture, especially by introducing greater personal liberty in ecclesiastical affairs."[43] Again in 1907 Pius X had promulgated *Pascendi Dominici Gregis*, an encyclical condemning "modernism"—the equally mistaken desire to follow the attempt of Protestant liberalism to ground theology in subjective religious experience and in a historicizing kind of biblical criticism.

Yet it was exactly in the midst of this unwelcoming environment that the church was revitalized. From Dorothy Day and the Catholic Worker Movement, to Thomas Merton and the reinvigoration of Catholic monasticism and mysticism, to Bishop Sheen and his dissemination of popular apologetics, to J. F. Powers and Flannery O'Connor and Allen Tate with

their demonstration that Catholics can produce literary art of the highest
sort, to the scores of Catholic colleges whose neo-Thomism undergirded a
remarkable flowering of education—a vigorously theological kind of
Catholic Christianity proved to be a bracing religious alternative to the
bland American substitutes. Philip Gleason sums up the neo-Thomist ethos
that prevailed during these wondrous decades of the Catholic renascence:

> To learn more of God and God's creation was not merely to be called to
> apostolic action; it was to be drawn more powerfully to God as the object
> of contemplation, of worship, of prayer, of devotion, of the soul's desire
> for fulfillment. . . . The God-centeredness that was integral to Thomism,
> and the affective reactions it aroused, help us to understand how the
> philosophical dimensions of the Catholic revival—which seems, in retro-
> spect, so often dry and mechanical—nourished, and was in turn nour-
> ished by, the literary, aesthetic, and even mystical dimensions of the
> revival.[44]

Why, if the Catholic intellectual renascence was so vital, did it collapse
so quickly? Noll answers in fairly standard fashion—the influx of non- traditional students into Catholic colleges, aided by government assistance
given to myriads of World War II veterans; the secularizing pressures
brought on by the desire for status in American higher education; the new
prosperity of Catholics moving out of ethnic conclaves into the suburbs, and
thus wanting to enter the American mainstream; the cultural and political
upheavals of the 1960s that called all traditions into doubt; the internal critique of Catholic theologians who found the neo-Thomist synthesis inadequate; and "the unanticipated effects of the Second Vatican Council."[45] It's
the last of these reasons that I believe to be by far the most important. The
American Catholic renewal had, alas, been broader than it was deep. Some
of its advocates were imbued with a Jansenist and casuistic spirituality that
denigrated both the body and the world, while exalting moralistic law over
carefully cultivated virtue. Their neo-Thomism was sometimes characterized
by a brittle rationalism that failed to envision humanity and society in light
of the Gospel. Thus did the Council summons the church to recover a deeper sense of personal and contemplative participation in the eucharistic mystery embodied in the liturgy and lived in daily life. The first document of
Vatican II is devoted to worship, therefore, the decree on the church following rather than preceding it.

Most of the theologians whose work stood behind Vatican II—Karl
Rahner and Hans Urs von Balthasar, Jacques Maritain and Etienne Gilson,
Henri de Lubac and Jean Daniélou, Karl Adam and Karol Wojtyla himself—

intended its reforms to renew the life of the church in this deeply eucharistic way. Instead, the modifications often lurched leftward in destructive ways. The vernacular mass, for example, that the Council had *permitted* soon became *required*. Other losses of Catholic dignity and substance were multiplied countlessly: a dishabiting of many monks and nuns and priests, a sudden vogue for folk masses, a removal of traditional images from many sanctuaries, a naïve embrace of religious pluralism, an even greater gullibility in endorsing Marxist politics, and so on. Hence the frighteningly ironic effect of the Council's excellent work: it should have given the Catholic renascence the depth that it sometimes lacked, but instead destroyed it. Had Vatican II been allowed to accomplish its true ecclesial intentions, the twentieth-century Catholic renewal would surely be vitalizing the twenty-first-century Catholic church. Instead, the theologians listed above, who were regarded as liberals and visionaries prior to Vatican II, came to be dismissed as conservatives if not reactionaries.

I believe that something akin to the twentieth-century Catholic revival, as it might have been deepened by the Second Vatican Council, needs to occur among twenty-first-century evangelicals. There are signs of hope already manifest, especially in the evangelical enthusiasm for the Oxford Inklings—C. S. Lewis, J. R. R. Tolkien, Charles Williams, and their circle. Evangelicals have also shown considerable interest in the true grandfather of the Inklings, G. K. Chesterton, as well as the two mystery writers who followed in their train, Dorothy L. Sayers and P. D. James. Chesterton and Tolkien were actual Catholics, and the other four are essentially Catholic in their outlook. The Marion Wade Center, which serves as the international hub for the study of the Inklings and their friends, is located, quite remarkably, at evangelical Wheaton College in Illinois. So has the fiction of Flannery O'Connor and Walker Percy, two important Catholic novelists of the American South, been a source of theological vitality for evangelicals. Thousands of them have found, through Catholic figures such as these, that their own scholarly and churchly lives have been given theological rigor and depth.[46] It is such a Catholicized evangelicalism that I believe to be the clamant need of our time, if evangelicals are to produce a convincing religious culture of their own. Evangelical piety and morality linked with Catholic sacramentality could produce a scandalous and non-adaptive Christianity that will endure because it has sought what Bonhoeffer called a Reformation in the upper case. Our colleges and universities—Protestant and Catholic alike—stand in common need of such radical renewal, as I shall seek to show.

Chapter 5

The Challenge Facing the Church's Colleges

To analyze the state of Christian colleges and universities in contemporary America, there is no better place to begin than with two recent books. They offer such shocking alternative assessments, each right in its own way, that no one can take the pulse of Christian higher education in our time without recourse to them. James Tunstead Burtchaell's *The Dying of the Light: The Disengagement of Colleges and Universities from their Christian Churches* is a bear of a book. It's huge, it's hairy, and it's angry. It weighs in heftily at 860 pages of text and 1730 footnotes. It is thick-pelted with evidence hunted down during visits to the particular schools on which he has set his sight. And as with the Dylan Thomas poem which its title echoes, Burtchaell's book roars with the wrath of an educator who refuses to go gently into the dark academic night.[1] His thesis, starkly put, is that this country's Christian colleges and universities have squandered their patrimony. Having once sought to engage the life of the mind with the claims of the Gospel, they have now sold their rich Christian birthright for thin educational gruel. Yet it would be a deadly mistake to dismiss Burtchaell's bleak report as the embittered elegy of a disappointed man. Burtchaell's diatribe seethes not with the fury of personal pique but of holy anger. His rage against the dying of the educational light seeks to kindle and inspire, not to incinerate.

Robert Benne's *Quality with Soul: How Six Premier Colleges and Universities Keep Faith with Their Religious Traditions* is a kinder and gentler and shorter book. Benne contends that, while Burtchaell's jeremiad may accurately describe those Christian schools that have abandoned their religious identity, there are bright and shining exceptions amidst the encircling gloom. Benne seeks to declare the good things these counter-cultural colleges and universities have done to make their Christian character consonant with their academic excellence. To attend carefully both to Burtchaell's fiery lament and to Benne's warm tribute could spark something akin to a phoenix-flame in Christian schools of all sorts, both those that have very nearly incinerated their Christian identity and those that seek still to become a light unto the nations.

The Bartering of the Christian Birthright

Burtchaell's book extends the argument made in 1994 by George Marsden in *The Soul of the American University: From Protestant Establishment to Established Nonbelief.* There Marsden traced the nineteenth-century liberal Protestant attempt to make education non-sectarian, emphasizing common moral qualities rather than particular Christian doctrines. This effort to build up a unified American civilization—indeed, to usher in nothing less than a new Christian century—produced a huge unintended irony. The old-line universities where Protestant liberalism was once the established faith became so inclusive that they not only lost their Christian character but also excluded their own Protestant liberalism. Burtchaell documents, by way of mountainous data, the utter rightness of Marsden's claim. He shows how, by straining after acceptance in the secular marketplace, Christian colleges have broken the leash of their own basic commitments.

Yet Burtchaell supplements Marsden in two important ways. He provides detailed analyses of schools that Marsden does not assess, especially Catholic and Southern and black institutions. Burtchaell also traces a more recent retreat, even in smaller schools still ostensibly linked to their sponsoring churches, from Christian particularism into secular blandness and inanity. Yet Burtchaell does not proceed by way of historical survey; he offers, instead, detailed analyses of seventeen schools chosen from among the major denominations. By means of deft selection, he honors even the distinctive branches within each tradition. Congregationalists are thus represented by Dartmouth and Beloit; Presbyterians by Lafayette and Davidson; Methodists by Millsaps and Ohio Wesleyan; Baptists by Wake Forest, Virginia Union, and Linville; Lutherans by Gettysburg, St. Olaf, and Concordia at River Forest; Roman Catholics by Boston College, New Rochelle, and St. Mary's at Riverside; Evangelicals by Azusa Pacific and Dordt.

Having previously taught for twenty-six years at one of these universities (Wake Forest), I am astounded at Burtchaell's mastery of the school's history and character. Though I would quibble over a point or two—especially when he subjects my own anonymous assertions to scalding critique!—his analysis remains remarkably accurate. Burtchaell has immense gifts of discernment. As an outsider to all seventeen schools, he has read deeply in their defining documents. Campus visits have enabled him also to assess their ethos. The end-product is an enormous documentary history of Christian higher education in the United States. Burtchaell's work should become a standard reference guide, not only to the individual schools under scrutiny, but also for the denominational ventures in Christian education that they represent.

Despite its massive size and detailed documentation, Burtchaell's book is a delight to read. His prose is laced with racy metaphors that will offend only the thin-skinned. He declares an especially opaque mission statement to be "the prose equivalent of a Dali painting."[2] He worries that one college's droning declaration of purpose will induce comas rather than hives. He also notes that Clarence Darrow and H. L. Mencken could have signed still another putatively Christian document. Burtchaell describes Boston College's infamous Mary Daly—a feminist so determined to overcome patriarchy that she would not permit men in her classes—as "the Patty Hearst of Catholic theology."[3] Burtchaell also calls deism "the religious equivalent of safe sex,"[4] and describes Freemasonry as deism in drag. Here he wittily explains the three anathemas pronounced by evangelical moralism: Dancing "was traditionally condemned because men who went dancing didn't always come home with their wives. Cards were also condemned because men who gambled didn't always come home with their wages. Drinking was the third thing condemned because men who drank didn't always come home."[5]

The Retreat from Doctrine

About the homelessness of the nation's formerly Christian colleges and universities, Burtchaell is not at all amused. They have become alienated from their originating purposes by way of an all-too-predictable pattern. They often began as cohesive academic communities of confessing Christians gathered for worship and study. The personal piety and the rigorous morality of both their faculties and their students sustained their enterprise. It was rooted in common worship, the reliability of the Christian scriptures, and the truthfulness of Christian doctrine. The church's teaching on divine redemption and human sinfulness offered Christian colleges unique ways of approaching grand concerns about human nature and destiny, the order and purpose of the cosmos, public responsibility and private liberty, etc. Close ties to their sponsoring churches made them unashamed of their denominational identity. Indeed, it gave the best of them their vigor and distinctiveness. Thus were they pleased to call themselves

Baptist or Presbyterian, Methodist or Lutheran or Catholic, since such
adjectives described both their religious character and their academic
convictions.

Then, as denominational identity came to seem confining, Christian
schools began to substitute generic and moralizing language for specific
religious purpose. To be a Christian college or university—in this altered
view of their mission—was to serve common national ideals rather than
particular ecclesial concerns: to uphold general standards of conduct, to
observe the Golden Rule, to promote moral maturity and social advancement, to join the common search for knowledge, to create a caring
atmosphere. Just as the Gospel was said to produce the kingdom of heaven
on earth, so were Christian colleges supposed to make America into a new
Christian civilization. This transformation was conceived in vaguely ethical
rather than concretely theological terms. Increasingly vaporous claims about
character and citizenship and universal good will thus served to dissipate
distinctively Christian notions of the moral and spiritual life.

Almost without fail, dogma became the enemy of educational enlightenment. Thus in 1886 did Beloit College President Edward Dwight Eaton
declare the academic case against it:

> Christian education is not adequately given in forms of dogmatic asser-
> tion. The growing mind is sensitive and suspicious of mere authority. It
> dreads wearing a chain. If it submits itself for a time to the constraint of
> maturer minds, the reaction will be all the more pronounced when it
> emerges into the world of unbelief that is waiting to claim it. There is
> sometimes even an exalted feeling, as in the performance of high duty,
> when one abandons inherited convictions that seem to be invalidated by
> growth. [. . .] The hope of accomplishing this lies in cherishing a spirit of
> fearless investigation, teachers and taught seeking the truth in the love of
> truth; not paddling in the still water of tradition, but pushing out into the
> rapids of present thought.[6]

The Second Great Awakening—the enormous burst of revivalistic fervor
that swept the nation in the early years of the nineteenth century—was
largely responsible for this new-found suspicion of dogma and tradition. Its
pietistic and moralistic ardor help set fire beneath the frigid faith of the eighteenth century. Yet it also made inherited convictions seem inimical to the
life of the intellect. Revivalism, Burtchaell rightly argues, defeated deism at
a terrible price.

During the First Great Awakening, Jonathan Edwards had insisted that
Christian experience must have intrinsic relation to the workings of the

mind and thus to Christian doctrine. George Whitefield, the eighteenth-century itinerant Methodist evangelist, may not have been a theologian, but he believed that his theatrical preaching served to undergird rather than to subvert the Anglican Calvinism from which it sprang.[7] A century later, Charles Finney and Barton Stone were much less concerned about Christian thought. The schools sustained by revivalist experience exalted personal morality and devotion over hard Christian thinking. These two main evangelical gifts—the strangely warmed heart and the ethically straitened conscience—seemed to make the church colleges into mighty fortresses of Christian learning. Yet they proved to be houses made of cards. Burtchaell shows that, without rootage in Christian *thinking*—faith seeking understanding, the good of the intellect—Christian piety and morality eventually die, though they may thrive for a while.

The Golden Calves of Money and Success

Many Roman Catholics have followed the Protestant path of dalliance in matters ethical and religious. Catholic parents, seeing little need to imbue their sons and daughters with particular Catholic virtues and traditions, send them to formerly Protestant colleges, where they often constitute a plurality, sometimes even a majority. There these young Catholics join in ethical endeavors, group fellowships, and Bible studies that, even when sponsored by Catholic campus ministries, may have little Christian substance. Inclusiveness and diversity trump particularity and specificity. The result, in most cases, is massive Catholic illiteracy about distinctively Catholic things.

Whether Protestant or Catholic, the collegiate defections from distinctively Christian purposes have not always been sinister and deliberate. Burtchaell confesses that the exigencies of finance and enrollment have also loosened the ties that once were so blessedly binding. Church-sponsored colleges, often under-funded by their own denominations, have found it ever more difficult to compete with larger and less expensive state universities. And the schools themselves, fearful of religious backlash, have often backed away from the tough intellectual questions of their time. The demands of career-oriented education, as well as specialized faculties devoted to autonomous academic disciplines, have also served to dim the Christian light. Secular accrediting agencies and funding organizations—fearing right-wing fundamentalism while ignoring its left-wing counterpart—have set up standards of acceptance that not only encourage but often actually require colleges to take refuge in religious vacuity.

It is exceedingly hard, Burtchaell concedes, to resist the homogenizing pressures that cause so many formerly Christian schools to bow down before these latter-day Baals, these alien marketplace deities. Yet there has also been an *internal* surrender of Christian distinctiveness, as many church-related colleges have become embarrassed about the confessional foundations of their own enterprise. It need not and should not have happened. With self-perpetuating boards of trustees providing freedom from fundamentalist takeovers, and with generous alumni and philanthropic organizations proving strong financial support, it is a ripe moment for Christian academic excellence. There is also a sizable company of Christian scholars who, superbly trained in many of the disciplines, could be recruited to help create fine faculties. Yet in this moment ripe with promise, many Christian colleges and universities have succumbed to trendy secularization rather than seeking Christian invigoration. Not wanting to offend the pluralist establishment, they have trimmed and softened and silenced the very claims that give Christian education its unique purchase on the truth. Seeking diversity for its own sake, they have ended in a monolithic uniformity. Burtchaell thus notices the clay base beneath the most golden of our secular calves—"community." It is based on maximized individual preferences, than which there could be nothing more inimical to true community.

Burtchaell flags the 1960s as the era that marked the real failure of Christian nerve. Wanting rightly to enhance their academic life, denominational colleges wrongly measured such improvement by non-theological criteria. Christian schools came to define excellence in bare academic and professional terms. They undertook a laudable "quest for the best," but without asking whether there might be distinctively Christian notions of scholarly rigor and academic excellence. Prospective faculty now needed merely to support—perhaps only to be "comfortable" with merely or unopposed to—the school's often gossamer-worded mission statement. As a former provost at Notre Dame, Burtchaell is especially distraught that Catholic schools have sought secular acceptability at the price of Christian particularity. "In what sense can a college or university qualify itself as Catholic," he asks, "if being Catholic plays no part in the qualifications of its faculty?"[8]

Though most of the formerly Christian colleges have defected leftward, Burtchaell shows that a right-wing secularization can also occur. It happens chiefly at schools catering to the advantages of class and power that accrue to a prosperous clientele. Conservative Christian colleges may still speak the language of Zion, but the values of Wall Street and Hollywood are usually their sub-text. At many such schools, authoritarian administrators promote top-down reforms in the name of a Christian orthodoxy, when what they actually promote are personal power and academic mediocrity. On both the right and the left, Burtchaell discerns a pandemic loss of Christian luminosity, as church-affiliated schools grope in the same darkness that blinds their secular sisters. In shame over their own claims, Christian schools have blighted academic discourse with turgidity and opacity. Here, for example, is a Methodist version of the glutinous stuff Burtchaell has trudged through: "There is an intentionality in providing opportunity for perspective and introspection at a church-related school that is not always provided in other settings."[9] Lucky and Pozzo could not have said it better in Samuel Beckett's *Waiting for Godot*.

The Flight from Convictional Particularity

Burtchaell is especially apt at puncturing the by-words and buzzwords that have become academic surrogates for thought. "Tolerance," "openness," "sensitivity," "whole persons," "quality of life," and "values" all get their much-deserved deflation. The Aryan Nation, Burtchaell observes, can be said to have values. He also lets the air out of such a gassy phrase as "Judaeo-Christian." It is "a friendly term," he points out, "because it has no existing membership."[10] "All truth is from God"[11] remains, among Protestants, the favorite unguent to grease a multitude of academic sins. This single bromide has poisoned our ability to ask whether there are greater and lesser truths, whether there is a single incarnate Truth ordering all other truths, and thus whether there are counterfeits to be identified and opposed. "Finding God in everything"[12] is the Catholic chestnut of choice. Jesuit educators are especially fond of quoting Gerard Manley Hopkins's poetic claim that "The world is charged with the grandeur of God." Were they to honor the noble Jesuit's insistence that the world's inexhaustible glory is transcendently sustained, Catholic schools would root their life in the triune and incarnate God. For Hopkins ends his sonnet lamenting the human rape of the planet by honoring the hovering Spirit who, as in the creation of all things, still broods redemptively over the sin-bent world, renewing its ruinous life like a divine dove determined to bring the world's egg to birth.

> And for all this, nature is never spent;
> 　　There lives the dearest freshness deep down things;
> And thought the last lights off the black West went
> 　　Oh, morning, at the brown bring eastward springs—
> Because the Holy Ghost over the bent
> 　　World broods with warm breast and ah! bright wings.

Nowhere is the scholastic abdication among Christians made more evident than in the triumph of the generic word "religion." Colleges once built on the conviction that God in Christ is "reconciling the world to himself" (1 Cor. 5:19a) now regard religion largely as a human phenomenon. Religious Studies, as they are called, have become primarily a study of ourselves, Burtchaell argues, rather than inquiry into the self-identification that the real God has made in Israel and Jesus Christ. We approach religion largely as outsiders, as supposedly neutral observers, rather than as adherents and "professors" in the old sense—namely, as people who believe in the Word made flesh, and who thus believe that Logos and learning are deeply linked. Burtchaell points out that all other academic disciplines—except the one meant to wrestle with the Truth become incarnate—are premised on the truthfulness of their teaching. Biologists do not teach Biological Studies but Biology, nor do chemists profess anything other than Chemistry.

Burtchaell likens Religious Studies to the teaching of English by way of comparative linguistics. Just as there is no such thing as language in general, neither is there any generic religion. Religions are rooted in the particulars of time and space, have their own grammars and practices, and often diverge and even clash as much as they overlap and reinforce each other. There is no Archimedean point at which one can stand outside them and thus "privilege" one over the other. Religiously speaking, we are all located somewhere rather than nowhere.[13] Yet the regnant multiculturalism that Burtchaell laments assumes such a stance in mid-air. Religions whose campus adherents number no more than a few dozen receive virtually the same attention as the Faith ostensibly professed by the great preponderance of students. Even in officially Christian schools, few seem to care that the vast Christian majority remains largely illiterate about its own Christian traditions. And when Christianity is in fact taught, it is often reduced to such tame humanistic terms that it becomes a curiosity roughly akin to shamanism. "Proselytizing" and "indoctrination" are the scare words used to silence serious religious discourse. Burtchaell believes, by contrast, that if a subject is worth professing, then we ought to persuade our students of its truth. There is no artificial divide between how to think and what to think. Embarrassment over Christian truth-claims is the sure sign of the deeper disease infecting the whole of Christian higher education.

Robert Benne's Discernment of Hopeful Educational Signs

Burtchaell's disheartenment at the demise of Christian colleges and universities constitutes an implicit call for their renascence. Robert Benne has offered a salutary prescription for such a rebirth by describing how six Christian schools—Baylor, Calvin, Notre Dame, St. Olaf, Valparaiso, and Wheaton—have maintained both their religious identity and their academic standing. They have maintained what he regards as the three essentials necessary for Christian institutional identity: a clearly articulated vision, a fully embodied ethos, and a set of strongly committed trustees, administrators, faculty, and students. The first of these requires more than an articulate and unapologetic mission statement. Nor will a set of Bible or religion courses suffice to sustain a college's Christian vision. There must be a vigorous theology instantiated in all aspects of collegiate life:

> [T]heology would be amply employed by Christian colleges and universities to articulate their identity and mission, to stipulate the relation of revelation and reason in their particular tradition, to gather a theology department in which its members would gladly carry that vision on behalf of the school and the faculty, to construct a curriculum, to elaborate a public justification for the school's ethos, and to provide a Christian intellectual tradition with which the whole school in its many departments could engage.[14]

It is noteworthy that, of the six schools Benne surveys, Calvin and Wheaton have best succeeded in maintaining this clear sense of theological and academic vision. The results are quite remarkable. Wheaton has become one of the most selective colleges in the nation, having even more stringent matriculation requirements than the nearby (and far more prestigious) University of Chicago. Benne notes that Wheaton "enrolls more National Merit Scholars and sends more students to prestigious Ph.D. programs than all but a handful of the very best liberal arts colleges."[15] Calvin, in turn, has produced perhaps more internationally recognized scholars than any other school of comparable size in the nation. It has more than 100 philosophy majors within a student body of only 4300. Among its most notable products are Alvin Plantinga, Peter Kreeft, and Nicholas Wolterstorff in philosophy; George Marsden, Harry Stout, and James Bratt in history as well as Cornelius Plantinga in theology. Notre Dame has also reversed the usual pattern by developing larger departments of theology and philosophy than English and history. One evident result of an unabashedly Christian vision is that it enables the liberal arts to flourish as they often do not in more secular settings.

The Christian ethos of a college or university must constitute something a good deal more distinctive than "a caring atmosphere." Benne believes that a specifically Christian kind of education must be rooted in regular worship

and, more particularly, in Sunday services, in celebration of the liturgical seasons, and in baccalaureate exercises that embody a strong sense of the sacred.
The campus chaplain should have "cabinet" status,[16] and I would add that
the various campus religious organizations (such as InterVarsity Christian
Fellowship, Campus Crusade, as well as various denominational ministries)
should have their work coordinated by the chaplain. The ethos of a Christian
college must also be grounded in service projects for the poor and needy, in
music and art that give emotional life to Christian convictions, in a strong
emphasis on vocation as lifelong learning and discipleship rather than
careerist advancement, and thus in Christian moral practices that do not
center on sexuality and alcohol alone. Benne extols the "rector" system at
Notre Dame, which insures that a priest or nun or academic layperson lives
in every dormitory and thus becomes both a friend and mentor of the students.

The campus the

Benne concedes that rarely if ever are all of these requisites found in a
single college. He also laments the loss of Advent and Lent and Easter celebrations in favor of fall and spring breaks, and he warns against Christian
adoption of the spineless utilitarian morality that prevails in most secular
schools. They have recourse to a bland "public health ethic" whose most
stringent demand is to tell students that they should "consider the effects of
your behavior."[17] Yet Benne gives implicit praise to four of the six schools for
having prohibited Greek organizations on campus (Baylor and Valparaiso are
the exceptions), and to St. Olaf's for having instituted a restrictive car policy that helps keep students on the campus rather than the road. He also
commends the cohesion of faculty and students at Wheaton and Calvin,
where there is a common desire to create "a Christian counterculture that is
committed to the transformation of persons and society."[18]

The third essential quality for insuring a school's Christian identity is to
have a strong cadre of persons who articulate its vision and embody its ethos.
From the board of trustees or regents, to the president and chief administrators, on to the departmental chairs and holders of distinguished professor-
ships—all such key figures must be convinced and committed Christians, if
not necessarily communicants within the school's sponsoring religious tradition. Among these, the faculty is by far the most important. Although students like to think of themselves as the soul of their school, their teachers
actually transmit the alma mater's sustaining tradition. Vigorous recruitment
and retention of thoughtful Christian faculty—including forthright hiring
interviews and rigorous training seminars for new teachers—cannot be
underestimated. Yet denominational unanimity is no panacea for all academic ills. Benne notes the dangers that lurk even when a university's gov-

erning body is, for example, all Baptist or Reformed: "[T]he vast majority of trustees are there because they support the college with their expertise, prestige, and wealth. They are often characterized by the common lay opinion that religion and education, like religion and business, do not mix well. From this perspective, it is bad form to bring up religious matters in the practical running of a school."[19] Benne also cautions against university governance that becomes autocratic rather than shared, and he insists that churches must give generous financial support to their colleges if they want them to have more than a merely cosmetic Christian character.

Among the six institutions Benne treats, only Notre Dame and Baylor have a full panoply of professional schools and thus aspire to become major research centers, although he might well have considered Pepperdine, Georgetown, and Boston College as Christian schools which deserve this title. While undergraduate liberal arts programs can readily be given a Christian quality, it is much more difficult to integrate Christian concerns with advanced research in many of the sciences and the practical professions. Yet Benne does not despair at such an undertaking. He points out that Notre Dame has established "a remarkable number of centers, institutes, journals, and programs that engage Catholic interests and themes."[20] Baylor has been similarly successful in creating centers for Family and Community Ministries, Christian Ethics, Oral History, Jewish and American Studies, Biomedical Studies, and Religious Inquiry Across the Disciplines, while also sponsoring institutes of Church-State Studies as well as Faith and Learning. These centers and institutes seek to validate Benne's claim that, for a school to be seriously Christian in its scholarship, it must probe the methodological claims of all the disciplines, whether in the sciences or the humanities, in order to make clear their social and religious implications.

Four Types of Christian and Formerly Christian Schools

One of Benne's most helpful aids is found in his fourfold method for typecasting the various sorts of Christian and formerly Christian schools: orthodox, critical mass, intentionally pluralist, and accidentally pluralist. All six schools here treated belong in the first two categories, since a Christian vision is their organizing paradigm. Though Benne doesn't name schools that belong in the latter two categories, it may be worthwhile also to notice the essentially secular models for their existence, and to offer evaluations of the various types. Calvin and Wheaton clearly belong in the "orthodox" category. Their faculty and student bodies are entirely Christian, their mission is unabashedly evangelical, their statements of faith are required for everyone, their chapel services are mandatory, their theology departments are both large and privileged within the curriculum, their religion courses share a single Christian perspective, their campus ethos is derived from the overt piety of their sponsoring traditions, and they are both owned and governed by churches or their official representatives.

The scholarly benefits of such religious unity and coherence are evident, as we have noticed already: Wheaton and Calvin have produced an impressive contingent of first-rate Christian scholars, far out of proportion to their size. Yet the limits of such uniformity are also manifest. Despite the presence of the Marion Wade Center for the study of such Roman Catholics as G. K. Chesterton and J. R. R. Tolkien, and of such Anglo-Catholics as C. S. Lewis, Charles Williams, and Dorothy Sayers, Wheaton does not permit any non-evangelicals (i.e., Roman Catholics) to serve on its faculty. Calvin also requires its tenured faculty to be active members in the Christian Reformed Church or one of its allied denominations, thus constricting the ecclesial circle to an even smaller size than Wheaton's.

St. Olaf's, Valparaiso, and Notre Dame fall within the "critical mass" paradigm. Their faculties and student bodies are predominantly Christian, but with a noteworthy non-Christian minority. Christianity is given a privileged voice in the ongoing academic conversation at these schools, but other voices are also honored. Two or three religion and theology courses are required, but classes that seek to enter dialogue with non-Christian religions are also taught. Here chapel services, though often of a high quality and large attendance, are voluntary rather than mandatory. While the religious ethos of these campuses is imbued with the rituals and practices of their sponsoring churches, many of the students come from other Christian traditions. And though the majority of the governing board belongs to the founding denomination, the college or university itself is autonomously owned and governed.

Schools within the "critical mass" category have a large and inviting opportunity to engage the concerns of pluralist and even pagan America, thus avoiding the "hothouse" character of a sheltered Christian existence. Their scholarship is thus likely to reach a larger audience than the Christian world alone. Yet they are also threatened by a certain diffuseness of focus, and they can quickly lose their Christian patrimony to become schools of the "intentionally pluralist" type. Though Benne gives no examples, I would name Wake Forest, Stetson, and Richmond as formerly Baptist universities belonging to this category. There Christianity is given a nominal voice in the governance and ethos of the school, but it is regarded as the school's received heritage rather than its vital center. In their religion departments, non-Christian traditions are given a sizable place in the curriculum, and only a single course in religion is required. Chapel services are entirely voluntary and often poorly attended. Campus ministry still grants a privileged position to the Baptist tradition, but the student body has an ever-shrinking minority of Baptists, and the school atmosphere is predominantly secular.

Yet the academic benefits of such intentional pluralism are considerable. There is no danger of narrow-minded denominational control, so that major funding agencies (such as Olin and Ford) regard these schools as academically free and often endow them with large grants. The sciences also thrive under these conditions. And because there are still notable Christian faculty members—and even a divinity school at Wake Forest—students who carefully choose their professors and courses can still receive an education that is at once academically rigorous and seriously Christian. Yet I believe that the liabilities overwhelm the assets. In fear of fundamentalism from the right, these universities open themselves up to all sorts of fads and fashions deriving from the academic left, thus silencing rigorous conversation about the very subjects that most engross them: race, class, and gender. Because only a single "correct" viewpoint is permitted, a new sort of fundamentalism often reigns, albeit completely unrecognized as such.

It follows, as night follows day, that such formerly Christian universities in the Baptist tradition soon become, like Chicago and Brown, entirely secular and thus fall into Benne's fourth category: "accidentally pluralist." There the Christian vision is randomly present if at all, remaining little more than a vermiform appendix, an accidental leftover from the hereditary past. Religion is not a mandatory subject, but only an elective within a larger distribution requirement. The department of religion, in turn, treats Christianity as but one among the other religions, having no privileged authority whatsoever. Chapel services are confined to special occasions, while church financial support and governance are token matters at best. The Christian ethos of these campuses is thus reclusive, and the Baptist presence is felt hardly at all. But because there is no gainsaying the academic eminence of Chicago and Brown, some Baptists believe that we have done a noble thing in spawning such schools and then giving them over to secular aims. But for the purposes of serious Christian scholarship, as well as the shaping of student minds and lives by way of integrated faith and learning, it must be confessed (as Benne's category suggests) that these things are achieved almost entirely by accident.[21]

The Need for a Theological Core

Robert Benne believes that church-related colleges and schools must have serious theology at their core. Yet he laments the lack of a rigorous theological tradition to undergird such Baptist/evangelical schools as Baylor and Wheaton. Because they regard the Bible as their sole theological authority, they have produced Bible scholars of international standing. At Baylor, for example, the academic hall dominating the campus is significantly called the Tidwell Bible Building. Yet to make the Bible the sole conversation partner for academic study is to cut ourselves off, Benne argues, from the rich resources of the bi-millennial Christian tradition. It's as if we wanted to honor Christianity only in its infancy, not in the fully fledged thing it has gradually become. Hence Benne's call for recourse to theology as the true basis for education in the Christian tradition: "biblical knowledge and injunctions [. . . must be] modulated through theological reflection in order to supply the kind of comprehensive account needed for real engagement of faith and learning, let alone [their] integration."[22]

Benne is right to insist that an unapologetically Christian university must be "anchored in a specific tradition."[23] There is no such thing as generic Christianity: we believe and live out our faith only in specific churches having specific doctrines and specific practices. Yet it is a salient fact that ours is an increasingly post-denominational age. More than half of all Christians worshipping on Sundays in America are to be found in non-denominational churches. Here, I believe, a university such as Baylor can turn its debit into considerable credit. Having no well-developed theology of our own,[24] we are free to help engender the kind of ecumenical Christianity that is the clamant desideratum of our time. Despite his denominational commitments as a Lutheran, Benne himself stresses this point:

> [B]eing a Christian college or university means adhering to the general core of the Christian account before we get to our Christian differences. We are first of all catholic—meaning universal—Christians. We share so much of a common heritage of doctrine and practice that it is a mistake too eagerly to emphasize our differences, which do not amount to much when we compare them with secular approaches.[25]

At the heart of the universal Christian message lies its claim to unsurpassability. It is not one among many more or less equal truths, nor even the best of all the truths humanity has discovered, but rather the single name "under heaven given among men by which we must be saved" (Acts 4:12). To speak of the finality and absoluteness of the Baptist or the Methodist faith is demonstrably fatuous, and terribly unfaithful to boot. Our single centrifugal and centripetal core is what St. Paul calls quite simply "the gospel of God" (Rom. 1:1).

Benne admits that, unlike the other five schools he examines, Baylor cannot be easily typecast. It "stands midway between [the] orthodox and critical mass categories."[26] Baylor's faculty and administrators are required to be practicing Christians or Jews, and the Baylor regents have mandated that, if at all possible, at least half the faculty be Baptist. These requirements, rather than being oppressive, leave considerable space for an ecumenically Christian witness, especially when we also note that Baylor students are not required to be confessing Christians, though the overwhelming preponderance of them are. Such a strong denominational trunk—with branches grafted from the wider Christian and Jewish and even secular realms—could become an extraordinarily fruitful tree. It could produce a vigorous kind of academic ecumenism that has not yet been seen at any other Christian university. On the one hand, Christians of all sorts and stripes could enter into dialogue with each other in ways that fructify our common life as believers. On the other hand, the vital presence of Jews and other non-Christians in our midst prevents us from making easy and premature claims to Christian exclusivity and from trampling them with any sort of Christian triumphalism.

Remembering that the word "humility" is rooted in the Latin word for soil (humus) we would do well to bow low in the dirt to confess that we Christians have often made the words "dogmatic" and "sectarian" synonyms for oppression and close-mindedness. When our Protestant forbears spoke pejoratively of narrow creeds and confining doctrines, they were not targeting Catholics alone. They knew all too well that dogmas can lead to ossified dogmatism no less than to sanguinary strife. "Doctrines divide, ethics unite" was a slogan that, with good cause, had found wide acceptance already at the American founding. If dogmas shut off rigorous thought in favor of rote propositions, then even Christian learning must indeed seek another basis. Beloit's President Eaton was right to fear that a mind formed by dogmatic assertion rather than fearless investigation is a mind ripe for potential unbelief. It will not suffice to repeat the Baptist Faith and Message, the Baltimore or Heidelberg catechisms, nor even to master the *Summa Theologica* or the *Institutes of the Christian Religion* as sufficient answers to all academic questions.

Honest stock-taking would reveal that the academic cupboard is often bare because we Christians have failed to fill it. As Stanley Hauerwas often insists, our churches have not performed the radical set of practices called

Christianity that would result in a radical kind of scholarship called
Christian.[27] Our own thinkers have not generated Christian kinds of knowledge that would inform the various academic disciplines and thus challenge
the dominant secular assumptions. Critical inquiry—the search for truth in
its own right and for its own sake—has become the new basis for education
in ways that Christians cannot ignore. Much of the rich lore of the received
tradition has been lost with this seismic shift of foundations. Yet out of the
pluralist emphasis on a multiplicity of viewpoints, something good has also
come. Diversity need not always lead to flaccidity and fatuity. For Christians
are summoned, I believe, to create universities that offer true diversity—
namely, by providing radical exceptions to the secularizing rule.

My own ecumenical sort of education, although it occurred under secular auspices, may serve oddly to illustrate what is needed in our time. I happily confess, for example, that of all my teachers a Roman Catholic professor
whom I encountered at a state university shaped my own education in
Christianity most deeply. This professor widened and deepened my Baptist
faith by means of his theologically informed reading of Emerson and
Thoreau and Hawthorne, of Twain and Melville and Milton. He also introduced me to the great Catholic novelists of our century: Graham Greene and
Evelyn Waugh, George Bernanos and François Mauriac, Flannery O'Connor
and Walker Percy. I confess also that it would have been intellectually impov-
erishing to have missed the counter-witness of my atheist teachers. They
skewered what was sentimental and naïve in my provincial and small-
minded religiosity. They convinced me that any faith worthy of my (or their)
embrace would have to face up to Albert Camus and Samuel Beckett and
Jean-Paul Sartre, to Robert Frost and Ernest Hemingway and Eugene
O'Neill. Religiously pluralistic education, in this rather unexceptional case,
invigorated my own training in Christianity.

Yet it must also be confessed that the pluralism from which I so greatly
benefited—perhaps because Southern state schools did not feel any need to
be aggressively secular—has become a rare thing indeed. Diversity did not
mean then, as it usually does now, a fly-catching openness to anything and
everything. The pluralistic openness of the 1950s and early 1960s sought to
ground learning in solid moral and educational purposes. Instead of true
pluralism, most universities espouse a multiculturalism that admits no common core or center. The academic realm has fissiparated into the post-modernist tribalism of rival ethnicities, alternative gender groups, and
numberless other clamant causes.

Four Kinds of Christian Scholarship

Precisely in this ripened post-modernist moment, Burtchaell's choleric requiem and Benne's benign hymn to Christian quality could help inaugurate a veritable renascence of Christian learning. The elite research universities are splintering into ever more isolated divisions. At the same time, they are being made to question the modernist enterprise that served perniciously to marginalize religion by making it strictly a private matter. Christian colleges could offer an edifying alternative to errors of both the modernist and postmodernist sort. It will happen, if at all, only when we make careful distinctions concerning the enormous complexity of the task. Toward such an end, I offer four concentric definitions of Christian scholarship that could perhaps help to rekindle the dying light of Christian schools. They are not mutually exclusive but overlapping categories.

First, there is Christian scholarship that seeks to employ uniquely Christian warrants for evidence and methods of research. Scripture proofs, citations from the creeds and liturgies, and appeals to supernatural phenomena serve as the prime requisites. Bible colleges and extremely conservative Christian universities steep their students in Christian lore, largely in isolation from the insistent questions of modern intellectual life. They thus produce an education that seeks no approval from worldly accreditors. Rather than sneer at such folk, we would do well to notice how many secular intellectuals are former fundamentalists thus schooled. The Bible-college idea of Christian education is to be resisted only when it insists that there is a distinctively Christian chemistry or mathematics or even history. As W. H. Auden once observed, Christian poetry would be akin to Christian carpentry. Scholarship, like both poetry and carpentry, is measured by its own inherent excellences. The requirements of rigor and clarity and precision are universal rather than parochial; they belong to what Richard Neuhaus has taught us to call the open public square, where common intellectual protocols obtain.

Yet the Bible colleges are not alone in walling off scholarship into its own cozy ghetto. A strictly behaviorist psychology, for example, might be rigorous and clear and precise, while excluding any analysis of human action which does not adhere to the strict terms of operant conditioning. According to a psychology of this sort, the ascetic behavior of Francis of Assisi or Catherine of Siena is counted as aberrant. The rigid exclusion of teleology and design from much of modern physics and biology is yet another instance of such premature closings of the academic square. In the humanities, an ideologized neo-Marxist scholarship often silences all scholarly pluralism, as the new fundamentalism of the left comes to mirror the old one of the right.

Hence the need for a second idea of Christian scholarship, one whose circle reaches wider because its academic endeavors are prompted by a Christian vision of reality while embracing common intellectual standards. The indefinite article is crucial. There is no single Christian world-view but rather a cluster of cognate theologies which are sufficiently coherent to prompt serious scholarship. Here Burtchaell is especially instructive in calling for church-sponsored universities to retain their prickly particularity—for Baptist schools to remain distinctively Baptist; Catholic, Catholic. He insists that Christian scholarship should derive its identity from the churches' own confessional life, not from middle-class mores or national ideals or secular prosperity. Burtchaell wants Christian colleges to become unabashed "signs of contradiction"—schools willing to be "spoken against" for having rejected the destructively modernist or post-modernist suppositions of the so-called prestige universities.

Christian scholarship of this second sort—informed by the divine self-disclosure in the Jews and Jesus—finds its academic life in the intellectual love of God. Christian faith issuing in Christian mind: such is the integrative wisdom that Burtchaell proposes as a way of redeeming the terrible fragmentation of human knowledge in our time. It is not sufficient, he argues, to promise a Christian *context* when the real need is for Christian *content*. Such Christian substance cannot be provided by a single obligatory religion course, nor by service and mission projects, nor by individually pious professors. Christian thought and vision should suffuse the entire enterprise of Christian schools. Christian learning of this second kind will occur only when Christian campuses are populated with professors and students and administrators committed to the proposition that there is no such thing as freestanding truth. The enormous intellectual challenge of Christian thinking in our time is to determine whether all truth is strictly perspectival and historically contingent—so that Christian revelation remains one truth among others—or whether the Christian story is true because all human thinking and cultural achievement can be shown to have their value and significance within it. This latter vision gave intellectual vitality to Christian faith during its early centuries, when Christian thinkers sought "to bring all thoughts captive to Christ"—the motto also of the modern Calvinist such as Abraham Kuyper. Thus did our Christian forebears meet the Hellenistic world on its own intellectual terms, showing how Christian faith answered its deepest questions. They converted not only the simple and unlettered, but also many cultured and learned citizens of the ancient world.

A third kind of Christian scholarship takes Christian things as its central subject matter. Huge intellectual effort is required to master the huge body of art and worship, of devotion and thought, which two millennia of Christian history have built up. This is not only a matter of enfranchising our ancestors, as in Chesterton's celebrated definition of tradition as the democracy of the dead. Tradition "does not mean that the living are dead but that the dead are alive."[28] It therefore "refuses to submit to the small and arrogant oligarchy of those who merely happen to be walking about."[29] Without Christian studies, Christian culture itself soon vanishes, not only as historical memory but also as current practice. The church will surely die and the world will surely be impoverished if Christian colleges fail to provide a nurturing matrix for the preservation and promotion of Christian tradition. Scholarship devoted to Christian subject matter is most often undertaken by confessing Christians who see the world from a Christian angle of vision. Yet this is not always the case. Non-Christians are often our allies, as a personal example reveals. To my mind, a Jewish scholar at the University of Chicago has written the best single study of our greatest devotional poet, George Herbert.[30] Precisely because Richard Strier so finely enhances our understanding of this great seventeenth-century Christian poet would I welcome him to the faculty of my own Christian university—as I suspect James Burtchaell would have gladly added him to the Catholic faculties where he has taught.

A fourth notion of Christian education is defined by the communities it serves and the graduates it produces. Burtchaell is right to insist that Christian schools exist primarily to enhance the life of their sponsoring churches by forming, in both moral and intellectual ways, the lives of their students. To discharge this central task, Christian universities should be animated by theological purposes that help give their graduates a distinctively religious identity. Their lives and minds should be recognizably different than the products of secular schools. Here it is not only the curriculum that matters but also the ceremonial and ethical life of the university—its gathered worship, its parietal demands, its administrative practices, its faculty ethos. There is no doubt that a radically Christian kind of education will give offense to certain students and faculty alike. This should hardly surprise us. To be intellectually conformed to the cross is inexorably to make hard enemies rather than to win easy friends. G. K. Chesterton wisely noted that we are commanded by Christ to love our enemies, not to have none. Yet he also observed, all too discomfitingly, that "[t]he Bible tells us to love our neighbors, and also to love our enemies, probably because they are generally the same people."[31]

The task of moral and intellectual formation need not be narrowly con-strued. Christian education ought to make students self-critical citizens of the world as well as self-critical confessors of the Faith. For both efforts, we need Muslims and Hindus and Jews, indeed atheists and skeptics and other nonbelievers, in our midst. We will serve our non-Christian constituents not, however, by abandoning our distinctive Christian purposes for the sake of a tepid tolerance that accepts all points of view because it takes none of them seriously. Rather should we welcome non-Christians into our compa-ny as academic sparring partners. Surely our common hope is that, if non-Christians encounter an intellectually serious kind of Christianity at our colleges, they will become more intellectually serious about their own beliefs. The reverse is also true. We Christians who are engaged in serious intellec-tual exchange with non-Christian faculty and students should become more thoughtful and less complacent in our own convictions. Such intellectual engagements are centered upon dialogue and debate. Persuasion remains the only acceptable means of intellectual exchange. It appeals to universal war-rants for evidence and argument, even as it opens up the real possibility of conversion. Coercion, by contrast, is ruled out of academic court on both Christian and intellectual grounds.

Christian formation need not be centered on confessional claims alone. Yet our common academic endeavors would, in fact, require a common set of questions that faculty and students are willing to engage. How, for exam-ple, might Christian tradition—in its rich historical variousness—offer a framework for an academically rigorous set of core requirements that avoid the twin dangers of inflexible dogmatism and spongy relativism? What would constitute distinctively Christian responses to such matters as histor-ical causality and representation, the role of design and accident in the evo-lutionary process, the question of personal freedom and social determinism, the unrecognized ethical assumptions underlying scientific research, the pos-sibility of non-adversarial adjudication of legal conflicts, an altruistic con-ception of capitalism and international politics, not to mention the deadly allurements presented by ordinary life in a hedonistic democracy?

Such questions neither Burtchaell nor Benne had time or space to deal with. Even so, we stand hugely indebted to their books. Burtchaell disturbs the false peace that often lulls our Christian colleges and universities into a living death. Yet, almost in spite of himself, Burtchaell hints and nods and sometimes squints his way forward toward the light that might yet burn in our Christian colleges and universities. Benne, by contrast, provides an actu-al way out of our moribund condition into true newness of life by demon-strating that there are Christian schools that have retained and integrated both their Christian identity and their academic quality. For those of us who teach at such Christian universities, the task is never to rest at ease in any false Zion. Rather are we called to make them become true servants of the Gospel and the churches. Only then will they also become true bulwarks of scholarly and religious freedom in a world where such twin liberties are an increasing rarity. Only on such a firm foundation can we erect the Christian educational culture whose outlines I propose to sketch.

Chapter 6

Creating a Christian
Educational Culture

Given the problematic state of our Chrstian academies and the deadening academic effect of our pandemic anticulturalism, how can collegiate and graduate education in Christian schools even survive, much less flourish? What, specifically, might we Christian educators do to address our massive educational and cultural malaise? H. Richard Niebuhr once said that it is much easier to declare what we oppose than what we propose, and yet that the latter is far the more important task. It's easy enough to condemn and point out faults, but another thing entirely to remedy and to edify. Niebuhr was making a Christian no less than a common-sense claim. The Gospel is not fundamentally a word of negation, not even the negation of our own cultural sickness unto death. The Gospel is God's vehement No to the No of humanity's sinfulness, and thus God's great glad Yes to his whole creation. "Do I make my plans like a worldly man," asks St. Paul, "ready to say Yes and No at once? As sure as God is faithful, our word to you has not been Yes and No. For the Son of God, Jesus Christ, whom we preached among you, Silvanus and Timothy and I, was not Yes and No; but in him it is always Yes. For all the promises of God find their Yes in him. That is why we utter the Amen through him, to the glory of God" (2 Cor. 1:17b–20).

I believe that there are two principal ways in which we might re-create and develop afresh the great Yes which should lie at the heart of a Christian educational culture: by an increased emphasis on traditional texts and ideas through a greater attention to the past, both Christian and non-Christian; and by emphasizing the differences (rather than the likenesses) between Christian and other ways of construing the world. Rather than seeking to make the pagan Roman world operate according to Christian principles, notes Robert Wilken, the early church built "its own sense of community, and it let these communities be the leaven that would gradually transform

105

culture." Thus did the early Christians offer their world a radically new "way of life. The church was not something that spoke to its culture; it was itself a culture and created a new Christian culture." This way of life was built by meeting at regular times, by following a "distinctive calendar" of strong eucharistic worship in which preaching rehearsed Christian beliefs, by offering charity to their community, and also by having "clarity, and church discipline, regarding moral issues." All of these practices, says Wilken, served to "[make] up a wholesome community." Hence Wilken's prescription for our own time:

> Today I believe the most significant apologetic task is simply to tell people what we believe and do. We need to familiarize people with the stories of the Bible and to talk about the things that make Christianity distinctive. Many people are simply unaware of the basics of Christianity. They're rejecting something they don't know that much about. [. . .] We're really leading people to change their love. To love something different. Love is what draws and holds people.[1]

This radical summons to reorder both our minds and loves, our thinking and our ethics, applies to Christians no less than unbelievers, and it can be met, at least in part, by building an educational community of a specifically Christian kind.

The Perennial Newness of the Ancient Faith

The word "tradition" means to hand down or pass on—usually, to transmit something valuable from the past. The third verse of the Bible's shortest book, tiny little Jude, speaks therefore of "the faith which was once for all delivered to the saints." This "deposit of faith," as Roman Catholics call it, is not the dead and oppressive hand of the past, not a lump of knowledge to be packaged or marketed, not a set of power-arrangements that we can manipulate to our own selfish ends. That this *depositum fidei* has been delivered "to the saints" means that is intended for nothing less than saint-making. Catholics define saints as those who have been beatified and canonized by the church. Protestants regard *all* Christians as saints, however little evidence of sainthood we may display. As James Burtchaell rightly observes, Christians are not interested in religion but in faith of a radically challenging and life-restoring kind. He describes, in sketchy terms, how a Christian might respond to a humanist or pietist who is content to declare everyone brothers and sisters, calling no one teacher since we are all learners, since everything is summed up in love, since all things belong to God:

To someone who has absorbed the lore of Ananias and Sapphira, the martyrdom of Lawrence, Antony in the desert of Egypt, Augustine on grace, Gregory the Great on pastoral care, Bede on the conflict of Celtic and Anglo-Saxon Christianity, John Damascene's dialogue between a Christian and a Saracen, Maximos the Confessor on charity, Julian of Norwich on the divine love, besides some of Dante and Anne Hutchinson and Dean Swift and Berdyaev and Marx . . . to such a listener the pietist's [or humanist's] dense toss-off, "How could I own anything?" is enough to set her ears ringing and rearranging down the years. By contrast, to someone whose head is so empty as to make confusion impossible, for someone who is starting from an intellectual ground zero, the toss-off could be a quip that becomes the cornerstone of a new and lethally naïve *Weltanschauung*.[2]

To avoid reinforcing the notion that we occupy an intellectual ground zero, a Christian university must provide much more than a caring and supportive environment, indispensable though such an ethos surely is. An education centered upon the integration of Christian and academic learning, far from being tame and dull, should be explosive and disturbing, shaking faculty and students alike to their very foundations. When, by contrast, the Christian quality of our educational enterprise is made to consist almost entirely in nurturing relationships and individual care—good and necessary though these things surely are—then secular books and ideas quickly occupy the vacated intellectual ground. They alone seem interesting and vitalizing. As my Baylor philosopher-colleague Scott Moore points out, many of our critics assume that only strong secular minds can shatter religious complacency and overturn stodgy ways of thinking and living. In their view, to be Christian in outlook is to be provincial and small-minded, if not also cowardly and soft-headed. They fear that we will deaden our educational life if we seek to employ Christian faculty and to center our teaching and our research on the engagement of faith and reason. Thus do they call for us to recruit real disturbers of our educational peace, true provocateurs who will shock us out of our academic torpor.

They are utterly right for utterly the wrong reasons. What Christians must demonstrate, to the contrary, is that the deepest moral provocations and the most disturbing intellectual challenges come not from the secular but from the Christian world. There is nothing more intellectually rigorous and culturally encompassing than the Gospel of the One in whom all things cohere. For God "has made known to us in all wisdom and insight the mystery of his will, according to his purpose which he set forth in Christ as a plan for the fullness of time, to unite all things in him, things in heaven and things on earth" (Eph. 1:10). "He is before all things, and in him all things hold together. [. . .] For in him the fullness of God was pleased to dwell, and through him to reconcile to himself all things, whether on earth or in heaven, making peace by blood of his cross" (Col. 1: 17, 19).

That these are not mere high-sounding claims has been demonstrated by two millennia of Christian tradition that have enlarged and deepened and broadened the original "deposit of faith." Jaroslav Pelikan rightly defines this tradition as "the living faith of the dead." "Traditionalism," Pelikan adds by way of warning, "is the dead faith of the living." A faith which is alive is undergoing constant argument and redefinition as it engages the unique questions and problems of its own age. It is not a fixed and limited *quantity* but a vital and ever-enlarging *quality*. Yet the quality of Christian tradition is modified and increased not only in rigorous engagement with the great thinkers of the church but also in imitation of its great saints.

The Past as Our True Other

There is a very deep sense in which the past remains, like God, unalterably and objectively *other* to us. It calls us, in W. H. Auden's fine phrase, to break bread with the dead. When we speak glibly about "attending to the other," we ought perhaps to regard the past as our true other. We cannot undo it or make it something that it was not, however much we may seek to manage and manipulate history to our own ends. This is not to say that there is a single determinate reading of the past, but rather to confess that we cannot *entirely* construct it—though of course the Communists and the Holocaust-deniers have tried. The future, by contrast, is open to our endless reformulation, as Chesterton makes clear:

> It is utterly useless to talk about enlarging one's mind with visions of the future. The future does not enlarge one's mind in the least. The future is a blank wall on which I can paint my portrait as large as I like. If I am narrow I can make the future narrow; if I am mean I can make the future mean. I cannot make St. Catherine of Siena mean. I cannot make Plato narrow. In the past I have real antagonists, men certainly better, braver, or more brilliant than I. Among the dead I have living rivals. In the future all my rivals are dead because they are unborn. I know I could not write "Paradise Lost" but I could easily write a "Utopia" very favourable to the sort of poetry I can write. I know I might not die as bravely as thousands of Christian martyrs or mediaeval knights, but it is quite easy for me to say that future society will have eliminated Christian dogmatism or military peril. This explains almost the whole of the modern fascination for

the future, its scientific essays, its more credible romances. We are fleeing from the faces of our fathers, because they are faces. We are attracted to the future because it is what is called a soft job. In front of us lies an unknown or unreal world which we can mould according to every cowardice or triviality in our temperaments. But if we look back at our fathers, as they gather in the gate of history, we see it like the gate of Eden, described by one of them in verse which we cannot imitate: With dreadful faces thronged and fiery arms. . . .[3]

It is not surprising that we live in an age that is suspicious of history. We are suspicious of it because we are skeptical of the authoritarianism that it often ensconces. Yet we frequently confuse authority with authoritarianism, leading us to a dread heresy of our own. C. S. Lewis called it "chronological snobbery"—the false notion that the recent is always superior to the ancient. When we read the words "new and improved" on product labels, Lewis and others have wondered, why not ask, "What was wrong with the old?"

> A new book is still on trial and the amateur is not in a position to judge it. It has to be tested against the great body of Christian thought down the ages, and all its hidden implications (often unsuspected by the author himself) have to be brought to light. [. . .] The only safety is to have a standard of plain, central Christianity ("mere Christianity" as [Richard] Baxter called it) which puts the controversies of the moment in their proper perspective. Such a standard can be acquired only from the old books.[4]

Lewis concludes that, as a way of honoring the past and keeping "the clean sea breeze of the centuries blowing through our minds," we ought to read at least one old book for every three new ones. Old books give us remembrances of old things. Someone has wisely said that, while computers have memories, only human beings have remembrances. Ancient ideas and texts have the power to thrust us out of the imprisoning present, while also liberating us from the suffocating smallness of our self-made worlds into immensely larger and stranger worlds that are not of our own construction.

The Covenant between Church and Culture

Frank Lentricchia, a Duke professor of English who is also a former Deconstructionist literary critic, laments the imprisoning character of current assumptions regarding the nature of literature and language. He explains why he has undergone a deconversion from his former conviction that there is no essential covenant between word and world—that there is no possible adequation of *verba* to *res*. Lentricchia had once held, with his fellow Deconstructionists, that language is a purely interrelational play of differences. Like them, he assumed that language can communicate no determinate meaning or truth. Lentricchia's explains why he has surrendered this view—why, indeed, he has stopped perusing books of the kind that he himself once wrote:

> Over the last 10 years, I've pretty much stopped reading literary criticism, because most of it isn't literary. But criticism it is of a sort—the sort that stems from the sense that one is morally superior to the writers that one is supposedly describing. This posture of superiority is assumed when those writers accuse the major islands of Western literary tradition, the central cultural engine—so it goes—of racism, poverty, sexism, homophobia, and imperialism: a cesspool that literary critics would expose for mankind's benefit. Just what it would avail us to learn that Flaubert was a sexist is not clear. It is impossible, this much is clear, to exaggerate the heroic self-inflation of academic literary criticism.
>
> To be certified as an academic critic, you need to believe, and be willing to assert, that [. . .] despite what almost a century's worth of smart readers have concluded, Joseph Conrad's *Heart of Darkness* is a subtle celebration of the desolations of imperialism. My objection is not that literary study has been politicized, but that it proceeds in happy indifference to, often in unconscionable innocence of, the protocols of literary competence. [. . .]
>
> I've never believed that writers had to be superior in anything, except writing. The fundamental, if only implied, message of much literary criticism is self-righteous, and it takes this form: "T. S. Eliot is homophobic and I am not. Therefore, I am a better person than Eliot. Imitate me, not Eliot." To which the proper response is: "But T. S. Eliot could really write, and you can't. Tell us truly, is there no filth in your soul?" [. . .]
>
> When it's the real thing, literature enlarges us; strips the film of familiarity from the world; creates bonds of sympathy with all kinds, even with evil characters, who we learn are all in the family [. . . .][5]

Lentricchia's lament over the loss of intellectual rigor and humanistic excellence in our academic life applies not only to professors. It also accounts for the impoverished moral and spiritual lives of our students. I find this problem to be especially acute among my students who regard themselves as my fellow evangelicals. They love Jesus dearly, they are imbued with a deeply emotional piety, and they perform acts of volunteer service that put to shame a complacent faculty bookworm. Yet their faith often seems virtually void of theological substance. Our students, not unlike a goodly number of our faculty, live bifurcated lives. Many of them do hard study during the day but then, at their Bible study groups in the evenings and at their worship services on Sundays, they put aside all serious thought in order to enter a world of easy belief and belonging. There they receive—and here I seek not to judge too harshly—a religious version of the same therapeutic pabulum that is being hawked in the non-ecclesial world. Thus does their unecclesial kind of Christianity break the church's irrefragable covenant with the world.

Ken Myers—the able Episcopalian editor of the *Mars Hill Audio Journal*—has a devastating description of fellow evangelicals of this stripe. He says that they are *of* the world but not *in* it. So fully have we made the church reflect the ethos of the times that we have kept Christians from engaging the hard realities of tragedy and suffering and sin. Once these young Christians (who in fact remain naive worldlings) are shattered by the shocks that mortal flesh is heir to, their faith will perhaps collapse entirely—or else they will be forced to keep it permanently superficial, and thus immune to both doubt and depth. What they and we commonly lack is the religious and scholarly self-discipline that are required if we are to resuscitate our own moral and intellectual and spiritual lives, much less the life of our churches and their schools.

Surely someone will protest that the Christian college is not the Christian church, and that we thus seek not to indoctrinate but to educate. (One might ask, parenthetically, what is wrong with indoctrination—if it is dedicated, as the word suggests, to the inculcation of the church's own anciently contested and currently engaging doctrines?) Most Christian colleges do not require that students be Christians before they matriculate at our schools. Nor do we require that even our Christian students observe what John Calvin called the two marks of the church—namely, the hearing of the Gospel as it is truly preached and the receiving of the sacraments as they are rightly administered. Yet while Christian colleges and universities are never to be confused with the church, they can justify their existence only as they serve not only the world but also the church. We serve the church, among other ways, by enabling our students to understand the implications of Christian faith for the whole of their lives, not for their intellectual existence alone.

We are responsible, I believe, for deepening their emotional and spiritual lives, and thus for invigorating their engagement with the Gospel as it impinges on the world. Our students are often unable to think sharply or feel deeply for the simple reason that they have not worshipped truly. As William Willimon and Stanley Hauerwas have noted, "bad liturgy eventually leads to bad ethics."[6] Never to have encountered the aweful otherness-in-nearness of God in worship is never to have exercised either our hearts or our brains. It is easy to move from sentimental worship to sentimental national-ism and materialism. We need seriously to reconsider, therefore, the quality of our chapel services and other corporate gatherings, including our com-mencement exercises. How might we better enable our students and faculty to experience the utter mystery and holiness of God?

The Peril of Cultural and Religious Nostalgia

It should be clear that, in seeking to deepen our sense of reverence for the God of the Gospel, I am not advocating any nostalgic restoration of a collapsed Christendom. Nor am I calling for our Christian schools somehow to save Western civilization from its present parlous state, valuable though such a project would be. Such a salvage operation is the program of cultural conservatives such as Patrick Buchanan. Surely he is right, like Oswald Spengler a century before him, to lament the decline of the West—so great has been its 2000-year contribution to the well-being of the world. Hence Buchanan's plea that Americans increase our fertility rate, impose restrictive trade agreements, and put quotas on immigration. The West must batten down the hatches against the barbarians who are threatening to swarm up from beneath the decks of European and American culture. For Buchanan and many others, Christian faith cannot survive apart from the survival of Western civilization. Thomas Fleming and his associates at the Rockford Institute make such fear the very basis of their summons for the re-creation of a European and North American Christendom:

> A people that thinks dinner consists of eating a deli sandwich from Arby's while watching *Friends* is neither Christian nor civilized. A public that pays top dollar for tickets to see Barbara Streisand or Michael Jackson should probably have its collective eardrums punctured, and the business and political leaders who are spotted reading Tom Clancy novels on air-planes should not be allowed to vote in school-board elections or con-tribute money to their alma maters. The official America of TV, public schools, and pop culture is no longer part of Western civilization; it has become something more like a cultural concentration camp designed to produce servile consumers whose highest ambition is early retirement and escape from responsibility.[7]

Fleming, like Buchanan, does not deny that such a restored Christendom would rest on military power and thus on "conversions" won by the sword. On the contrary, they celebrate the bloody military victories of old Christendom, chiefly against the invading Muslims—at Constantinople in 717, at Tours in 732, at Constantinople again in 1453, and especially at Lepanto in 1571. It is noteworthy that Santiago de Compostela, one of the most popular medieval shrines, has St. James as its host saint. He is portrayed not only as a pilgrim himself, but also as the "Matamoros," the decapitating Moor-slayer who appeared thirty-eight times during the Reconquest of Spain from Moorish rule, charging down from the sky on a white horse to spur Christian armies to victory over the Muslims. He also became Spain's patron saint, guiding the Conquistadors to the New World and intervening at least eleven times against the pagan natives. Without preening our own righteousness, we can at least avoid a vaunting celebration of events that, however much we might have approved them if we had been living at their hour, serve to shame and stain Christian conscience.

We can also agree with Fleming and Buchanan in denouncing the spiritually trivializing effects of our materialistic culture without endorsing their political prophylactic against them: the renewal of a militarized Christendom. What they both fail to recognize is that Christianity has already survived the collapse of Roman civilization—precisely because its power derives from the triune God rather than the self-renewing powers of civilization—and thus will it outlive the declining and collapsing West. It should come as no surprise that the most vital forms of Christianity in our time are not found in the West but in Africa, Latin America, and the Philippines. Hence the rightness of the call—made a generation ago by the Catholic archbishop of London, the late Cardinal Basil Hume—for the church to reconvert pagan Europe. We would do well to note that churchgoing America needs this reconversion perhaps most of all. Such a revival might well have the side-effect of renewing our public life, but its chief aim would be the renewal of the church and its institutions through proclamation of the Word and administration of the sacraments.

The Christian Case against Consumerism

Christian colleges and universities can participate in such a renewal by their refusal to employ force rather than persuasion in their common life, especially the soul-numbing force of consumerist greed. As the late missiologist Lesslie Newbigin warned near the end of his life, the church's chief task in our time is to disentangle the interests of Christian faith from an unbridled global capitalism. The evils of late-modern laissez-faire economics are not far to find. Our communities are being replaced by impersonal congeries of consumption; slowly ingrained virtues are being replaced with easy comforts and sensate entertainments; and wisdom itself is being replaced by instrumental knowledge. Our time needs another St. Teresa of Avila to declare without false righteousness but with great simplicity, "I thank God for all the things I don't own." Nearer to us in his witness against a degrading monetary materialism stands G. K. Chesterton puncturing our flabby prosperity with his pungent aphorisms concerning what he calls "the horrible mysticism of money."

> [T]he nuisance of all this notion of Business Education, of a training for certain trades, whether of plumber or plutocrat, is that they will prevent the intelligence from being sufficiently active to criticize trade and business properly. [. . .] [The business student] has never been taught to think, only to count. He lives in a cold temple of abstract calculation, of which the pillars are columns of figures. But he has no basic sense of Comparative Religion [. . .] by which he may discover whether he is in the right temple, or distinguish one temple from another.[8]

> To be clever enough to get all that money, one must be stupid enough to want it.[9]

> There is but an inch of difference between the cushioned chamber and the padded cell.[10]

> The whole case for Christianity is that a man who is dependent upon the luxuries of this life is a corrupt man, spiritually corrupt, politically corrupt, financially corrupt. There is one thing that Christ and all the Christian saints have said with a sort of savage monotony. They have said simply that to be rich is to be in peculiar danger of moral wreck.[11]

> The poor can forget that social problem of which we (the moderately rich) ought never to forget. Blessed are the poor for they alone have not the poor always with them. The honest poor can sometimes forget poverty. The honest rich can never forget it.[12]

It goes without saying that wealth, like poverty, has always been with us. Dante complained almost a millennium ago that the single besetting evil of his age was *cupidità*: a consuming worldliness, a disordered love for things, a grasping greed that obliterates all other concerns. It seems, alas, to be the perennial human proclivity.

To teach students and professors alike how to resist the blandishments of comfort and consumption is not to pose a voguish spirituality over against it. As I will argue in the final chapter, a traditionless and non-communal spirituality constitutes but another consumer item at the emporium of our religious culture. Materialism and spirituality are but the perfect reflexes of the other: they indulge a similar kind of subjective self-seeking. The one makes us beasts and the other makes us angels. As Walker Percy reveals, especially in his hilarious novel entitled *Love in the Ruins*, the bestial and the angelic are very close kin. Percy's narrator, a dissolute doctor named Thomas More, discovers this paradox as he ponders his own disordered life. After attempting suicide and while recovering in a psychiatric hospital, Dr. More finds himself lusting after his attendant nurse. Then, like the Prodigal Son, he comes to himself. He recognizes that to soar in pure seraphic possibility is not essentially different than to be sunk in swinish appetites, and that he will remain suicidally dissatisfied until he finds true satisfaction. To be human is to be neither pig nor angel, but enfleshed souls and inspirited bodies, men and women on our journey both from and toward the God who has both made and remade us. Hence More's poignant confession:

> Later, lust gave way to sorrow and I prayed, arms stretched out like a Mexican, tears streaming down my face. Dear God, I can see it now, why can't I see it at other times, that it is you I love in the beauty of the world and in all the lovely girls and dear good friends, and it is pilgrims we are, wayfarers on a journey, and not pigs, nor angels.[13]

Texts That Can Transform Lives

I am not suggesting that we make our Christian schools into enclaves of moral righteousness. But we can indeed make changes which shape our students' lives and form their characters in ways that will glorify God and make human life ever so much more enjoyable. These changes should begin with our core curricula. I believe that they should be much more astringent and demanding than they now are, and that they should be much less present-minded than tradition-minded. Such a radically revised curriculum would not aim to produce a religious version of the literacy that E. D. Hirsch recommends[14]—namely, a mere familiarizing of our students and faculty with key terms that enable us to become mere Christian sophisticates. Sophisticates have been famously defined as those who are educated beyond their intellectual abilities. Nor is there a universal panacea to be found in a Great Texts program. Mark Twain was all too perceptive when he said that such lists should be called the Great *Unread* Books. Even at schools whose curriculum is built entirely on a common core of classical works, students will still use Cliff Notes, smoke pot, plagiarize their term papers, and swinishly swill beer as they do nearly everywhere else. Yet the great texts can be made to come alive when we have our students grapple with them as books and ideas that form a continuous and unified tradition of argument about the essential, life-altering questions and answers. Such great books and ideas will have drastic moral and religious implications for our world only as we teach them slowly and well. A mere week on the *Divine Comedy* simply will not suffice. Slow reading and teaching require careful thinking and writing within the humanities, as something similar is required within the sciences via experiments in problem-solving. Great texts and works demand sustained and concentrated analysis, especially if we interrogate them with the great questions.

A recent Baylor alumna has confessed to me that her own college curriculum did not require her to be formed by serious modes of either thinking or living. While she assimilated great reams of *information* during her four years in the university, she admits that she did almost no *thinking*: no tough-minded engagement with life-shaping books and ideas. Her honors degree had never required her to encounter the overarching moral and religious questions, nor to undertake any serious revaluation or reliving of her life. She admitted the truthfulness of Walker Percy's tart aphorism that "You can make all A's and still flunk life." Thus did she candidly confess that a certain *violence* had been done to her—not the physical violence of date-rape, but the *intellectual* violence that had robbed her of Christian intellectual excellence. She may also have been the victim (rather than the beneficiary) of the OTG system: Only Two Grades, A and B. Students at Harvard have complained, for example, when Professor Harvey C. Mansfield regularly assigns them C's and D's and perhaps even F's. Thus have they wittily renamed him: Harvey C-Minus Mansfield. To placate them, the honest professor now assigns his students not one but two grades: the official A that is necessary for their professional prospects, and the grade that they actually deserve.

In calling for the installation of classic texts and works in our core curricula, I do not want to make a fetish out of tradition. There are evil traditions undergirded by moral and artistic practices that are unworthy of retrieval. Nazi and Communist cultures, for example, are an abomination in the literal sense: they are *ab hominem* (anti-human). Their art and politics and religion are to be studied chiefly to expose their deceits. Nor is there any surrogate salvation to be found in the great books of the Western world, as they are often called. Even the most excellent works of culture can anesthetize their devotees to ethical outrages. Thus did high-ranking Nazi officials, for instance, preside over the crematoria by day and then return home at night to relish recordings of Mozart and to celebrate Christmas with their families.[15]

Yet while splendid literary and artistic works can be used to blunt moral passion and to pervert religious conviction, they can also give them lasting imaginative life. My own awakening had mainly to do with race. I had grown up in an East Texas town which, like all the others, was built on rigid segregation. Blacks could not attend my schools and churches, it goes without saying; but neither could they use the public restrooms, drink from the public water fountains, eat in the public restaurants, nor sleep in the public hotels and motels. Though black-white relations were often cordial and compassionate, there were certain lines that could never be crossed. Segregation and discrimination thus combined to constitute a Southern victory that virtually overcame the loss of the Civil War. Racial superiority was the background noise of our lives, the racket which we could not hear because we heard nothing else. To question the inherited racial order was akin to a fish questioning water or a bird doubting the air.

Mark Twain questioned it, and through his *Adventures of Huckleberry Finn* he made me question my own received assumptions about race. Yet Twain seared my conscience not by overt preaching, but rather by the subtlety and irony that only an accomplished literary text can accomplish. I was struck with special moral force by the scene in which Huck is returning from one of his escapades on the Mississippi. He pretends that there was an explosion on his boat. "Anybody hurt?" his Aunt Sally asks. "No'm," Huck replies. "Killed a nigger." "Well, it's lucky," Aunt Sally responds; "because sometimes people do get hurt."[16] This small exchange, with Huck's aunt blithely assuming that black people are not human beings, served as a veritable bombshell within my small soul. Though I had been taught to sing that "Red and yellow, black and white, they are precious in his sight, Jesus loves the little children of the world," there was little in my own world to reinforce this profound biblical claim. On the contrary, nearly all of our social habits and practices counted against it. Then as now, the church's message hardly registered in a society whose alien values served virtually to overwhelm it. Yet a literary text broke through this hard social crust and awakened me to evils that I had hardly noticed, as Twain reveals how a black man allegedly killed in a river disaster mattered to whites little more than a dog or a cat that had been run over by a wagon.

I was morally jolted yet again by the more celebrated scene wherein Huck ponders whether he should report the whereabouts of the fugitive slave Nigger Jim.[17] In a long moral meditation, Huck grapples with his own conscience. He counts the many ways wherein Jim has become to him the very embodiment of fidelity and unselfishness, of gratitude and guilelessness. To violate him, Huck senses, would be a crime against the very nature of things, a horror of metaphysical proportions. Once again, Twain refuses to lecture or hector. Instead, he depicts Huck's moral moment of truth entirely in ironic terms. Huck's church and society have taught him that to violate the slave system is to contravene the law of God. If Huck does *not* turn Jim in, it follows, he will surely be damned. In a splendidly naïve scene, where Huck thinks he is doing evil rather than good, he rips up the revealing letter he had written to Miss Watson, declaring "All right, then, I'll go to hell." Twain knew well that the courageous Huck was nearer to the precincts of paradise than the gates of hell.

Yet the scene that struck my own racial consciousness with even greater force occurs in William Faulkner's story called "The Bear." There the sixteen-year old Ike McCaslin finds himself examining early nineteenth-century ledgers kept by two of his great-uncles, Buck and Buddy. The two brothers had made half-literate record book entries as they bantered back and forth about the McCaslin family's various dealings with their slaves. The crucial entry involves a black slave named Eunice: "*Bought by Father in New Orleans 1807 $650. dolars. Marid to Thucydus 1809 Drownd in Crick Cristmas Day 1832.*" A second entry reads: "*June 21th 1833 Drownd herself.*" Writing two days later, the second brother adds: "*Who in hell ever heard of a niger drownding him self.*"[18] What young Ike McCaslin has discovered—to his staggering horror, though it had been caused only vague puzzlement in his uncles—is the reason why Eunice had killed herself at Christmas.

The day of the world's divine rebirth, we learn, had been the day of Eunice's deliberate death. For on the feast of the Incarnation, Eunice had first found out the truth that was beyond her bearing. She had discovered that her daughter Tomasina was three months pregnant. This daughter, we also learn from the ledgers, had been fathered not by Eunice's slave husband Thucydus but by Carothers McCaslin, the plantation owner himself. Now, twenty-two years later, this same "Tomy" had been impregnated by this same Carothers McCaslin—that is, by her own father. The next generation of McCaslin brothers finds it incomprehensible that a slave such as Eunice could be reflective enough to have cause for suicide. Blacks to them were mere chattel—objects to be sold in markets and traded in card games—having little more moral capacity than other animals. Yet the brothers' mention of Eunice's self-murder, six months later when Tomy herself died in childbirth, reveals that they were not totally opaque to the truth. Only young Ike had moral powers sufficient to discern why Eunice had taken her own life—in metaphysical renunciation of a system so evil that the father of a slave child could summon this very girl to his bed of carnal lust and father yet another child on her.

Like Twain, Faulkner does not wag his finger with a hectoring didacticism. Instead, he uses subtle artistic indirection to reveal the horror that prompted Eunice's despairing act. In thus recounting Ike's moral reveille as it is gradually but powerfully sounded, he also enables his readers to experience their own shock of recognition. It will be noticed, no doubt, that neither Faulkner nor Twain was an orthodox believer; in fact, Faulkner's fiction quite explicitly repudiates Christianity,[19] despite his use of Christian images and symbols in his allegorical novel called *The Fable*. Far from undermining my call for a distinctively Christian educational culture, this reveals why we must be willing to seize "the spoils of the Egyptians," as St. Augustine called the Christian appropriation of pagan wisdom, even while retaining our right to be critical of it.

Christian Truth-Telling and the Tournament of Narratives

It should be evident that, even as Christians, we cannot stand outside all cultures and judge them from some supposedly neutral point of view, privileging one over the other or selectively retrieving whatever values we deem to be "best." There is no such vantage point, except in utopia—a word which literally means "no place." We are historical creatures through and through. We are formed by the particular stories that constitute particular traditions. Christians claim no other transcendent perspective, therefore, than the one provided in the self-identification of God through the Jews and Jesus Christ, through the synagogue and the church. This perspective is not a timeless and placeless stance above all world-views; it is no Eiffel Tower from which we can assess the passing parade of cultures. Such impartial objectivity was, as we have noticed, the terrible delusion of the Enlightenment. The eighteenth-century *philosophes* meant to seek international peace by overcoming sectional and religious divisions through personal autonomy and universal knowledge.[20] But their allegedly unifying moral abstractions helped produce alas, new and worse wars.[21]

The post-modernists are right to warn against the Enlightenment chimera of a grand neutral metanarrative. They justly remind us that all seeing is a lensed seeing, that we all wear the spectacles of a particular perspective, that we inevitably privilege our own tradition. All study of the past is in fact a revisioning of the past in the light of present concerns. Again, C. S.

Lewis gets the matter right, both in what he denies and what he affirms: "Not, of course, that there is any magic about the past. People were no cleverer then than they are now; they made as many mistakes as we. But they are not the *same* mistakes. They will not flatter us in the errors we are already committing [. . . .]"[22]

Yet to say that there is no such thing as pure and unadulterated knowing or teaching or learning is not to counsel a despairing resignation to anarchy and chaos. It is not to concede that all truth must by privy and self-interested and coercive. Least of all should we be willing to grant that our Christian viewpoint is but another power-move that seeks hegemony at the expense of others. On the contrary, the pluralistic moment in which we live offers Christians a distinctive and enabling opportunity to demonstrate the real character of our faith. It enables us to enter what the late James Wm. McClendon, Jr. called "a tournament of narratives." Our task is to articulate the Christian story as it confronts and engages other accounts of the true and the good and the beautiful. We are called to nothing less than the discernment of how the Gospel impinges upon all humanistic and scientific questions.

In an age that valorizes difference, we should celebrate the countercultural difference that Christian faith makes for educational life. For surely the incarnate Truth—to know whom and to belong to whose Body is to be set free—provides not only alternative answers but also unique and definitive answers to the primordial questions: What constitutes the human person, the quality of the good life, the purpose of social existence, the nature of the physical universe, the structure of political and moral order, etc. I recall my own startlement when an undergraduate professor of modern drama summed up the perennial questions ever so simply: "Who are we? Where are we? And what time is it?"

Charles Scriven, a Mennonite theologian and educator, reveals both the stringencies that are required and the calamities that might be avoided if we were willing to discern everything through the aperture of the Gospel. Rather than leading us down narrow paths and blind allies, avowedly partisan education in the name of Christ opens up the largest of all possibilities—a full engagement with every version of truth:

> The endurance of distinctively Christian vision must be a matter of deliberate design. In its decisions about personnel, curriculum, and student life, the Christian college must renounce congenial neutrality, what is in any case artifice and self-deception, and embrace without apology its own heritage and discipline. In the tournament of narratives, anything less is a recipe for defeat. Anything less marks capitulation to [what McClendon

called] "the unstoried blandness (and the mortal terrors) of late twentieth century liberal individualism."[23]

Critics such as Stanley Fish would find something alarmingly recidivist in Scriven's summons. As we have seen, Fish claims that all cultures are finally incompatible because every culture will sooner or later reveal itself to be ungenerous and intolerant and finally violent. Fish has abundant evidence for his claim. Much of it lies, alas, at our own feet as Christians. There is indeed a terrible danger inherent in the claim that Jesus Christ is not merely one lord and savior among others, but rather the one and only "name under heaven given among men [and women] by which we must be saved" (Acts 4:12). Christians have, alas, committed egregious evils in the name of this glorious Gospel, undertaking pogroms and crusades and holocausts. What Fish fails to comprehend, however, is that Christians have committed such evils in horrible violation, not as a necessary consequence, of the Gospel. We do not enter the tournament of narratives in order to win so much as to engage others in life-giving conversation. Christians are not bent on vain victory in our own name. Rather do we seek to honor the God into whose Story we have been summoned to play our own small role by telling and living it truly. Because the Gospel is no ordinary human story, we do not declare that it is better than other stories. Rather do we insist that it is a stark and scandalous Story like no other—precisely because it is not about victory but loss. It is about the human loss that has become divine victory, and thus about the strength which is to be found in weakness. The Christian narrative tells of the God who has made humanity in his own image, who despite the rebellion and alienation of his people has called out Abraham, Isaac, and Jacob in order to make of them a nation that would be a blessing to *all* the nations, and who has become flesh in the Nazarene Messiah in order to die for the entirety of humanity and thus finally to fulfill the universal Hebraic blessing. It is this Story alone that enables the church—and by extension its colleges—to have the unique capacity to overcome all racial and ethnic, all gender and ideological antagonisms by joining us in the one truly multicultural community.

Membership in this single reconciling community must be marked by neither race nor ethnicity nor gender, neither by nationality nor class nor even intelligence. One belongs to this company solely by faithfulness to the God who has demonstrated his faithfulness in making us his people. "You did not choose me," declares the Christ of the Fourth Gospel, "but I chose you" (John 15:16). Lives formed according to this Story are not shaped by a smorgasbord of selections autonomously exercised. To be "in Christ" (2 Cor. 5:17) is, as St. Paul says, not to have a merely private and individual relationship with Jesus, but rather to belong first and last to his Body. The church, in turn, requires a life of worship and service and devotion. It also requires a Christian educational culture that will shape both bodies and minds by the disciplines and habits necessary for Christian existence.

The Christian college cannot be equated with the Christian church. On the contrary, we welcome the Muslim and the Buddhist, the atheist and the New Ager, to our table of academic learning. Christian schools should have no desire to fence this table with padded protections. We must be willing to subject the Christian narrative to its most drastic critics—including Nietzsche and Emerson and Whitman. We must also be willing to make common cause with humanists and pagans whose values and virtues we often share. I refer not only to "the noble Greeks and Romans," but also to aboriginal and non-Western cultures. We must even run the risk of de-conversion, should either our students or our faculty become *un*persuaded of the Gospel. Yet the convinced unbelievers in our midst have their own requirements to meet: they must always remain our generous interlocutors rather than our contemptuous despisers.

One final and truthful word must be spoken, albeit with fear and trembling. Our welcome to Hindu and Sikh and secular students alike must be so generous that we do not merely tolerate them and thus trivialize their differences with us. Our commonality does not lie in some storyless and deracinated humanity that we supposedly share. Christians believe that we have something far deeper and more concrete in common with them—namely, our shared creation and redemption in the God of the Gospel. Faith in this Lord requires that we extend non-Christians the hospitality that takes them seriously. Such seriousness requires us not only to honor their own narratives by studying the texts and traditions that undergird them, but also to contest these narratives with our own. This contestation must never be harsh or coercive but always generous and persuasive. Even so, our non-Christian students and faculty must be made aware that their own conversion remains a very real possibility. When this happens it is a matter of neither conquest nor defeat, for our one true and only common ground is Golgotha. For there lies, we believe, the one victory in which no human being is defeated. Here is the sole triumph that has the power to establish a Christian educational culture amidst our multicultural and anticultural age, and thus to enable our own mutual and perpetual conversion. Not the least effect of such repeated conversions will be the replacement of a sappy religious sentimentality with a rigorous Christian skepticism, as I next propose to argue.

Chapter 7

Christian Skepticism vs. Religious Sentimentality

A healthy dose of Christian skepticism and disbelief would serve as a much needed antidote to the suborning of the Gospel to things both worthy and unworthy. Such salutary disbelief is especially needed as a prophylactic against the soft-core spirituality that saps much of contemporary Christianity. An anti-doctrinal sentimentality often rules the worship and the art of our churches, where self-serving emotions are exalted over true mystery. The church of our time needs a theology that repudiates all saccharine substitutes for the hard thinking that Christian faith requires.

Dogmas and Creeds and Religious Pornography

As in so many other matters, Flannery O'Connor foresaw our reduction of transcendent faith to sentimental subjectivity. She likened it to the scientific process whereby the wings can be bred off chickens to produce more succulent white meat. O'Connor said that it is possible to breed the moral and theological sense out of people in a similar way. She described our current generation as a brood of wingless chickens. This is what Nietzsche meant, she explained, when he declared God dead. It also means that nihilism is the atmosphere of our age, the gas that we all breathe, whether inside or outside the church.[1] The church has often made Christianity nearly indistinguishable from the coziness of a warm blanket and the kindliness of a golden heart. With typical tartness, O'Connor added that a golden heart is a positive interference for the writing of fiction. This may have also been what O'Connor had in mind when she declared that Christians are often forced to suffer *by* the church more than they suffer *for* it.

What sustains both faith and fiction against such incipient nihilism is Christian disbelief. We have already heard O'Connor explain the need for such faithful skepticism in a letter to an Emory University freshman named Alfred Corn. Faith is indeed a gift, she counseled Corn, but it is a gift that must be constantly cultivated and enlarged. Faith grows and deepens through concrete acts of charity, she explained. These deeds are prompted, in turn, by a discernment of the divine image in other persons. Only sacred sight can perceive their true worth. Such holy seeing is invigorated by imaginative more than abstract thinking, especially as in practicing the art of Christian skepticism:

> Even in the life of a Christian, faith rises and falls like the tides of an invisible sea. [Faith is still] there, even when [you] can't see it or feel it, if [you want] it to be there. You realize, I think, that [faith] is more valuable, more mysterious, altogether more immense than anything you can learn or decide upon in college. Learn what you can, but cultivate Christian skepticism. It will keep you free—not free to do anything you please, but free to be formed by something larger than your own intellect or the intellects of those around you.[2]

O'Connor believed that Christian dogma is what forms the Christian imagination into something larger than our own intelligence or the intelligence of those around us. Knowing that the word dogma is a pejorative term for most Americans, O'Connor boldly capitalized it, confessing in the upper case that "My stories have been watered and fed by Dogma."[3] She rejected the popular view that dogma divides while ethics unite and that, since the practical and the useful are what truly matter, we can dispense with dogma. So long as everyone loves Jesus, according to the prevailing sentimentalism, doctrinal claims can be shelved. O'Connor believed, on the contrary, that dogma must become central rather than remaining peripheral. It is the distilled essence of God's self-identification in Israel and Christ, and thus the true means for understanding both ourselves and our world. "Dogma is an instrument for penetrating reality," she declared. "It is about the only thing left in the world that surely guards and respects mystery."[4]

For Flannery O'Connor, mystery is not synonymous with puzzle and riddle, for they are the conundrums that balk the mind and stifle understanding. Nor is mystery another name for a spirituality so vague that it cannot distinguish between John of the Cross and Max Lucado. "To St. Paul and the early Christian thinkers," wrote Claude Tresmontant, one of O'Connor's favorite biblical scholars, mystery was "the particular object of intelligence, its fullest nourishment. The *musterion* [a Greek word that can also be translated *sacrament*] is something so rich in intelligible content, so inexhaustibly full of delectation for the mind that no contemplation [of it] can ever reach its end."[5]

Such delectations of mind and imagination also require Christians to make unmistakable declarations about what we do not believe. We cannot avoid the fact that Christian faith is inherently polemical. Every doctrinal claim implies its counterclaim, every affirmation its negation. Karl Barth learned this lesson in his encounter with the Nazis, who pronounced his writings illegal and who banned him from teaching in German universities. In response to the Nazi attempt to establish a national church that would be an organ of the German state, Barth led the Confessing Church to develop the Barmen Declaration, a document wherein every *credimus* ("we believe") is followed by its corollary *damnamus* ("we repudiate"). The first article, for example, declares that "Jesus Christ, as he is attested for us in Holy Scripture, is the one Word of God which we have to hear and which we have to trust and obey in life and in death." Lest the *Deutsche Christen* of the Nazi church—or anyone else—mistake what this means, a clear reference to *der Führer* follows: "We reject the false doctrine that the church could and should recognize as a source of its proclamation, beyond and besides this one Word of God, still other events, powers, historic figures, and truths as God's revelation."[6]

Perhaps we need a new Barmen Declaration for Christian faith and practice in our time, a theological manifesto setting forth the things we do not and will not believe, precisely because we believe in Jesus Christ. Christopher Morse has developed such a theology for a church that, despite its seeming prosperity, nonetheless dwells in a *status confessionis*—a time of such great peril that the church must declare itself against the evils of the age. In *Not Every Spirit: A Dogmatics of Christian Disbelief*, Morse argues that faithful skepticism is an ecclesial imperative rooted in Scripture. Already in the New Testament the summons is unmistakable. "Beloved, do not believe every spirit," we read in I John 4:1, "but test the spirits to see whether they are of God; for many false prophets have gone out into the world." The Gospel of Mark shares this same disdain for untrue claimants to the Truth: "And then if anyone says, 'Look, here is the Christ!' or 'Look, there he is' do not believe it. False Christs and false prophets will arise and show signs and wonders, to lead astray, if possible, the elect" (13:21–22). "If even an angel from heaven should preach a false gospel," says St. Paul, "let him be accursed" (Gal. 1:9).

These deceiving spirits and false prophets and fake Christs are to be broadly understood, Morse claims, as anyone or anything making wrongful claims to our attention and allegiance. Christians are called to name these Antichrists and to refuse them our fealty—even as we are also required to

disbelieve once revered beliefs that have ossified into lifeless propositions. Yet
Christian skepticism does not mean a principled doubting of everything.
Such easy cynicism would be altogether as sentimental and self-serving as the
easy optimism it rejects. Christian disbelief is a positive testing of what
is true and false by a single criterion: "By this you know the Spirit of
God: every spirit which confesses that Jesus Christ has come in the flesh is
of God, and every spirit which does not confess Jesus is not of God"(I John
4:2–3).

There are many so-called Christian "spirits" now at work in our churches, denying that "Jesus Christ has come in the flesh." These gnostic and dis-
carnate substitutes are especially evident in the sappiness of much
contemporary Christian culture. This is not to say that sentimental piety
always produces flaccid faith. There are many staunch witnesses to the gospel
who are sustained by art more saccharine than sacred, and by worship more
superficial than substantial. Such devout souls live out their Christianity in
ways that transcend the limits of their piety, even as many theologians must
be saved in spite of their better taste and more orthodox theology. Yet the
spiritual outrages being committed in the name of Christ cannot be dismissed as mere passing fads. They have come virtually to dominate the evangelical Protestant world.

Consider the following examples from a so-called Christian Book Fair.
A T-shirt company called Living Epistles advertised a sweatshirt labeled "The
Lord's Gym." It featured not Arnold Schwarzenegger but Jesus Christ as the
pumped-up, steroid-laden body builder. He is pressing himself up on a pile
of rocks, blood gushing from his crown of thorns, with an enormous cross
on his back that reads "The Sins of the World." The caption beneath dares
anyone to "Bench Press This!" On the other side of the shirt, Jesus's palm is
pierced with a railroad spike and covered in blood. Inscribed beneath are the
words "His Pain, Your Gain." Other T-shirts shouted such slogans as
"Salvation Is Not for Wimps," "Jesus Loved You So Much It *Hurt*," "His
Blood's for You," and "God Made Grandmas So Kids Could Feel His Hugs."
Bumper stickers declared that "Real Men Love Jesus" and "My Boss Is a
Jewish Carpenter." A keychain featuring a soccer ball contained the slogan
"Jesus Is My Goal."

Such spiritual pap can be made to fill even book-sized containers.
Consider, for example, one of the fair's prize-winning titles: *Lord, I Haven't
Talked to You Since the Last Crisis*. Another much-touted work, *Jesus Christ,
CEO*, describes our Lord as an executive who turned twelve ordinary men
into managers of the most successful company the world has ever known. A
fresh infusion of Christian skepticism would disdain such books, even as it

would help deliver publishers from the temptation to get rich by manufacturing toilet tissue with the words "Get Thee Behind Me, Satan" printed on every sheet.

There are countless other examples of Christian kitsch. At an Easter service held at a Baptist church in South Carolina, puppets popped up from behind a screen and wagged their muppety heads while singing "I Found My Thrill on Calvary Hill" to the old Fats Domino tune. Twenty miles south of Nashville, Tennessee, a Christian entrepreneur named Charles Budell has set up a miniature golf course in which windmills and water-hazards have been replaced by "biblical" obstacles. Christian golfers can tee off at the Garden of Eden, get past the Devil, and end up in Heaven. Along the way, one putts into Noah's Ark, drops onto Mt. Sinai, and visits the tomb of Christ. On the seventeenth hole, the ball disappears into a shaft with Satan's picture on it, only to emerge beneath a red cross. "See," says Budell, "you beat the Devil." Angels are seated near the eighteenth hole, where the ball sinks into an opening with the word RAPTURE emblazoned above it.

It may be protested that such gross parodies of the gospel are too silly to be dignified with criticism. These sacrileges would be laughable were their effects not so deadly. T. S. Eliot once observed that our unconscious habits, especially our leisure lives, serve to shape our souls and form our imaginations far more decisively than all our deliberate efforts to acquire high culture. Neil Postman's argument about American culture at large is even more alarmingly true of evangelical churches in particular: we are amusing ourselves to death.[7] We are promoting a worldly gospel of happiness and success that offers no serious engagement with the deepest needs and desires of the world.

The Triumph of Triviality

A sub-Christian religion devoted not to the Fatherhood but the Daddyhood of God—it might also be called Kiddyanity—can be seen most vigorously at work in much of contemporary worship. It has arisen, no doubt, in protest against the Laodicean lifelessness of much traditional worship. Seeker services aim at introducing the unchurched masses of our post-Christian culture to the rudiments of the faith, teaching them the elementary truths of the gospel in ways that liturgical worship and doctrinal preaching may not. Yet I wonder whether childlike beginners in a dumbed-down, user-friendly Christianity will ever grow up—whether such seekers will ever become finders and keepers of what the book of Jude calls "the faith which was once for all delivered to the saints." It is more likely, I fear, that they will subject themselves to apostolic wrath. St. Paul warns against a permanent infancy in faith. He pronounces fierce judgment on the Corinthians who remain milk-drinking believers, never learning to hunger for the hearty bread and to quaff the good wine of the Gospel.

Asked whether early Christian worship sought to be "user-friendly," Robert Wilken answers, "Not at all—in fact, just the opposite." In fact, the early church's liturgy was quite "different from anything pagans had experienced." Without bloody sacrifices, but with extensive use of the Bible and with sermons stressing its peculiar doctrines, not least its "historically grounded talk of a dying and rising God," the church invited pagans to enter "a wholly different world than they were used to." Far from being "seeker sensitive," the ancient church made it difficult to join, requiring converts to complete a training process that took two years. Even church architecture communicated this "insensitivity" to pagan needs. "The altar at a Greek temple was in front of the temple and represented that worship was a public event open to all. In Christian churches, the altar was inside. Worship was something the church gave one the right to enter into."[8]

Wilken recommends a similar approach in our own time. "I think seeker-sensitive churches use a completely wrong strategy. A person who comes into a Christian church for the first time *should* feel out of place. He should feel this community engages in practices so important they take time to learn. The best thing we can do for 'seekers' is to create an environment where newcomers feel they are missing something vital, that one has to be inculcated into this, and that it's a discipline." The practice of the primal Christians that "would most impress our secular culture today," Wilken declares, was the "devotion to a celibate life of prayer" that arose in the third century. It "deeply impressed pagans. It was radical. They saw that Christians were willing to spend themselves for their beliefs." "For people to give themselves wholly to a life of prayer and chaste living," Wilken notes, was for these primitive believers to provide "the most powerful argument for the truth of Christianity." Wilken observes that, in startling contrast, many seeker-churches have become quite lax about divorce and re-marriage, and thus that their overflowing services may indicate how thoroughly they have accommodated themselves to the disordered sexuality of contemporary American life.[9]

Our new ease in Zion, our friendly familiarity with the Lord God of the cosmos, can be discerned in old-fashioned liberal no less than in new-fangled evangelical churches. Edward Farley laments that the relevance-driven worship practiced in many old-line Protestant congregations prompts one not to exclaim "holy, holy, holy" but "nice, nice, nice." In *A Far Glory*, Peter

Berger argues that we are witnessing "the triumph of triviality" even in many liberal churches. With the anger of an Amos, Berger laments the frontal hugs that might bring sexual harassment charges in other settings, the vigorous applause that follows the choir's or the soloist's performance (as if the true audience were not God but the congregation), and the raucous laughter that the preacher's well-rehearsed one-liners evoke. "Sermons [in such churches] are political harangues," Berger complains, "and 'prayers' the recital of political platforms." Berger offers a bitter litany of other liturgical offenses:

> One could go on: To the embarrassed handshakes mislabeled "the kiss of peace." To the preacher mounting the pulpit in full sacerdotal regalia, only to begin his sermon with a hearty "good morning." To the dedicated removal of every vestige of poetic beauty from the language of the liturgy [. . .] into prose resembling that of a mail-order catalogue. I think that what all these changes add up to is the statement that nothing extraordinary is going on, that what is happening is a gathering of ordinary people enjoying the experience of community.[10]

Such loss of awe and mystery, such commodification of God into the gratifier of our own needs, flattens the imagination of wonder and otherness. If God is only a kinder and gentler version of ourselves, there is nothing ultimate to inspire our worship or command our service. No wonder that Flannery O'Connor likened sentimentality in religion to pornography in art: they both cultivate immediate sensate experience for its own sake. Oscar Wilde was correct to observe that all bad art is sincere, just as Thomas Merton rightly complained that a bad book about the love of God is still a bad book. So does the poet and mystical writer Kathleen Norris protest the removal of the fierce psalms of lament and imprecation from contemporary lectionaries. These cursing psalms remind us, says Norris, that wickedness cannot be conquered by mere niceness. Without anger, she adds, even the praise of God dissolves into a "dreadful cheer,"[11] a smiling blindness to the world's woe, a gleaming-gummed oblivion to what Luther called the bruised human conscience.

Leander Keck complains in a similar vein that our churches have replaced "the theocentric praise of God" with an "anthropocentric utilitarianism." This inversion serves to tame and domesticate the living Lord of Scripture and tradition by ridding him of his jealousy and wrath. God is "reduced to the Great Enabler [who] has little do except warrant our causes and help us fulfill our aspirations." Hence Keck's baleful assessment of contemporary Christian worship: "The opening line of the Westminster Confession [which declares that the chief end of man is 'to glorify God and to enjoy him forever'] is now reversed, for now the chief end of God is to glorify us and to be useful to us indefinitely."[12]

How can we avert this rampant desire to reduce knotty Christian particularities to gassy religious generalities? William Temple, the archbishop of Canterbury during the 1950s, offered considerable aid when he declared Christianity to be the world's most *materialistic* religion. Redemption is an outward and visible and public thing wrought by the flesh-assuming and world-inhabiting God through his space-and-time occupying people. The objective work of Jesus Christ is the center of the Christian life, and all subjective conversions are based upon it. In fact, these conversions are themselves enabled by the gift-giving grace of God. Our "decisions for Christ" announce that our faith is indeed intentional; it is uniquely ours, not merely the reflexive product of our parents' influence or the communities that formed us. Yet such decisions are always the product of the church's witness, not of a lonely and merely private encounter with God. Even the deepest personal experience of saving grace can never be commensurate with the gift of salvation itself. This was Karl Barth's point in response to an evangelical reporter who is said to have asked him, when he was visiting the United States in 1962, whether he had ever been saved. "Yes," Barth is rumored to have replied. "Then tell us about your salvation experience," the report eagerly requested. "It happened one afternoon in A.D. 34, when Jesus died on the cross."

Those who have reduced the Gospel to an acronym—WWJD: What Would Jesus Do?—ignore this fundamental distinction between Christ's objective work and our subjective appropriation of it. As the Son of God slain for our sins and raised for our redemption, Jesus has a life qualitatively different than ours, even as he is also totally identified with us. To ask what Jesus would do assumes that Christians share equality with Christ as the second person of the Trinity. Diogenes Allen puts the matter exactly the other way around. He starkly observes that, in a certain sense, Christ does not need us: "Jesus is Lord because of who he is, not because he has followers. [. . .] He is Lord because he is the Son of God. It isn't because of us that he is the Son of God."[13] A more faithful question thus needs to be asked, even if cannot be turned into four convenient capitals: "What does Jesus Christ, because of his unique life and death and resurrection, uniquely enable his disciples to do through their participation in the life of his people called the church?" The difficult answer is that he is the only Savior who, having accomplished their redemption, empowers his followers to do works even greater than his own (John 14:12). Like John the Baptizer in Grünewald's Isenheim Altarpiece—the long-fingered prophet anachronistically present at

Golgotha, pointing away from himself to the crucified God—we can make witness, in both word and deed, to the salvation that we ourselves could not possibly have accomplished.

The recrudescent nineteenth-century theology of Christian subjectivism finds its literary equivalent in the Christian chic of salvation through autobiography alone. Hence the rage for telling one's own story as if it were God's story—when, by contrast, we are called to *conform* our fallen and false stories to God's one true Story. An important Christian writer recently declared, when asked about the sources of her art, that she writes entirely out of her own experience—her family, her friends, her church. Surely this is to forget that the gospel liberates us from a subjective concentration upon our own little snail-shell world. It gives us new lenses for perceiving both ourselves and our world, delivering us into the great unexplored realm of the Not Merely Me. Luther in his 1535 lectures on Galatians declared life in Christ "carries us out of ourselves, that we should not lean upon our own strength, our own feeling, our own person, and our own works, but upon God, and upon his precious promise and truth, which cannot deceive us."[14] Christian art consists not in the transmission of often-deceptive autobiographical experience into fictional guise, but rather its radical transfiguration into the one undeceiving form: the form of the Cross and the Resurrection.

The Counter-Witness of Peter De Vries

Christopher Morse cites Matthew's inclusion of the Old Testament figure of Rachel—right in the midst of the Christmas story—as an example of such cruciform narrative art. "Along with the sound of wise men and shepherds, of the angels and all the heavenly host praising God and singing," writes Morse, "there is this other sound—the sound of 'a voice heard in Ramah, wailing and loud lamentation, Rachel weeping for her children; she refused to be consoled, because they were no more.'"[15] In the Genesis narratives, Rachel is depicted as the mother of Jacob's final and most beloved sons, Joseph and Benjamin. Her life had begun brightly when Jacob kissed her and wept for gladness at finding a Hebrew woman to marry amidst the unwanted Canaanite women. Yet Rachel's lot in life soon proved unhappy. Not only did her father Laban inveigle Jacob into marrying her sister Leah, but even after her long-deferred marriage to Jacob, Rachel remained childless for many years. The fertile Leah was a reproach to her, having borne Jacob six sons and a daughter. At last God took away Rachel's shame by giving her Joseph, the future rescuer of his family. But in bringing Benjamin into the world, Rachel "travailed, and she had hard labor," as Genesis 35:17

bluntly states. She died in childbirth and was buried by the roadside. Jeremiah remembers Rachel's grave alongside the path that the Israelites took into exile, and he hears her still refusing all consolation. Like these exiled children of Abraham who have no prospect of returning, her children are no more.

Yet Jeremiah also hears the voice of comfort addressed to Rachel and to all who suffer with her. "Thus says the Lord: 'Keep your voice from weeping, and your eyes from tears. [. . .] There is hope for your future'" (31:16–17). It is this thread of hope that Matthew picks up from Jeremiah. Herod has slaughtered all the young sons of Israel, but there is still hope for all the world's Rachels in this singular Child who has been spared. Yet it is a dark kind of hope, a hope that points to this same Son who shall be forsaken on the cross. This is no easy consolation, no sweet and sentimental assurance that everything will work out well. It is the faith that does not spurn disbelief, but that deliberately rejects all false comfort. "By not believing in any consolation short of God's own descent into hell in Christ," Morse declares, "the refusal of Rachel becomes a faithful witness pointing to the Resurrection."[16] God alone, the God of Golgotha, can provide solace that is not saccharine. All surrogate hopes must be doubted and rejected.

Peter De Vries's novels give fictional life to the disbelief that eschews oleaginous substitutes. I am not claiming De Vries to be a Christian in what he affirmed, only in what he negated—namely, in his refusal to be cozily consoled when the children were no more. Many of De Vries's readers know that his most celebrated novel, *The Blood of the Lamb*, has autobiographical origins. Both De Vries's sister and daughter died in childhood. After his sister's death, De Vries once told me, his mother refused ever again to sing in church. Yet her minister, in making a pastoral call, had the gall to inquire about her silence, failing to see that this Dutch-immigrant mother was a latter-day Rachel, refusing to be comforted by anyone but God—and not readily even by him. De Vries offers poignant protest against the cancerous death of his own daughter, even as he lets his mother's mute voice be heard, through his narrator, Don Wanderhope. Wanderhope has lost his brother to leukemia. In the novel as in life, a minister has come to proffer the hope that Wanderhope knows to be bogus. He will not take solace in a God whose sovereignty makes him the direct cause of every occurrence, both human and natural. Hence Wanderhope's wail of disbelief: "My sensation, rather than fear or piety, was a baffled and uncomprehending rage. That flesh with which I had lain in comradely embrace [was] destroyable on such short notice, by a whim known as divine? [. . .] Who wantonly scattered such charm, who broke such flesh like bread for his purposes?"[17]

When Wanderhope's own daughter Carol dies of leukemia at age eleven, his disbelief is no longer partial but total. He refuses to find any relief in the notion that her death is the work of God's beneficent will. Instead, he engages in his own willful inversion of the central Christian claims. It is not Christ who is slain from the foundation of the world for the sins of the world, but little Carol herself who is the innocent creature needlessly destroyed. This fountain filled with blood has not been drawn, as in William Cowper's hymn, from the veins of Emmanuel but from his own helpless child. Wanderhope thus addresses the dying Carol as his "lamb," and he strokes her hair as "precious fleece." He describes her needle marks and incisions as "stigmata." Carol dies at the hour when other children are frolicking their way home from school, even as it is also the hour of Christ's death: three o'clock in the afternoon. The abandonment that occurred at Calvary may not have been the act of substitutionary atonement wrought by God in Christ, De Vries suggests, but a fearful sign of God's perpetual truancy amidst human anguish.

One wonders whether De Vries the ex-Calvinist might have been rescued from such horrible fears if he had been taught a doctrine of divine sovereignty that did not insist on God's omnicausality. Calvin chose his final adjective carefully when he declared that "all events are governed by God's secret plan."[18] That God's providential will for the world is not transparent but hidden from human sight requires that we walk by faith, that we struggle through the valley of doubt as well as the shadow of death. Yet if God's work were completely concealed, human history and individual life would be random and rudderless, the chaotic product of an accidental universe. Both Catholic Scholasticism and Protestant Orthodoxy sought to steer a middle course between such false notions of divine transparency and divine opacity by insisting on the distinction between first and second causes. God's primary will does indeed superintend the working of all things together for good (Rom. 8:28). Yet there are secondary causes—both natural and human, at once free and contingent and necessary—that may temporarily deflect, even if they do not finally defeat, God's providence. Sentimental Christianity spurns this distinction, trying instead to make evident the God who remains hidden even in his incarnation. It encourages either cozy feelings of assurance that the Lord works everything to our benefit, or else cozy communities assured that they are God's only hand and feet in the work of peace and justice. Christian disbelief disavows such sentimentalities.

Even with sentimentalism set aside, we are still left to deal with the terrible death of Carol Wanderhope. In the scene that follows, De Vries hints at the one true way to avoid the twin evils of divine omnicausality and godless accidentality. Don Wanderhope had bought a cake for Carol's birthday, but he had inadvertently left it in the Catholic church where, on the way to the hospital, he had stopped to say one last desperate prayer for her recovery. Staggering both from grief and from the liquor he has drunk to numb it, Don suddenly remembers the cake and returns to the church to get it. In a gesture of pure metaphysical fury, Wanderhope flings the confection in the face of the crucifix hanging over the church door. Yet just as Jeremiah hears God answering the inconsolable Rachel, so does De Vries disclose a strange solace in this act of defiance. A bleary-eyed Wanderhope envisions Christ wiping the icing from his eyes "very slowly, very deliberately, with infinite patience. [. . .] Then the cheeks were wiped down with the same sense of grave and gentle ritual, with all the kind sobriety of one whose voice could be heard saying, 'Suffer the little children to come unto me . . . for such is the kingdom of heaven.'"[19]

Even as Jacob wrestles with the angel all night until he has been blessed, even if his battle with God leaves him permanently lamed; as Isaiah protests that God absconds behind the blank wall of Israel's exile; as the Psalmist laments that the wicked prosper while the faithful and the righteous languish; as Ecclesiastes complains that life is a great weariness under a sun that rises and also goes down without producing anything new; as Job angrily contends with the God who has subjected him so unspeakable suffering without due cause; and as Rachel mourns in Ramah that her children are no more—so does Peter De Vries have his characters decline all comfort that is not real comfort. Don Wanderhope refuses to believe that his daughter's death is either the mechanical execution of a divine plan or the random result of godless chance. His encounter with the cake-spattered Christ suggests, instead, that God has strangely subjected himself to the sin and rage of his people. This is indeed a dark revelation. Perhaps it explains why De Vries claimed, ever so wittily, to be nothing more than a backslidden unbeliever. Yet his fiction makes powerful witness against the soggy spirituality of our age, confronting us with a cross which demands our disbelieving rejection of all false faith. De Vries's insistence on the difficulty of authentic faith can also assist us in recovering a true sense of holiness in Christian worship, as I shall argue in the ensuing chapter.

Chapter 8

The Ugly, the Beautiful, and the Holy in Christian Worship

The way to avoid triviality and sentimentality in worship, and thus truly to honor the God of the Gospel, has been shown to us by Evelyn Underhill in her classic work of 1936, entitled simply *Worship*. There she draws a decisive distinction between private prayer and corporate worship. Prayer is an asking, Underhill argues, worship an offering. In prayer, we petition God's mercy for our own sin and misery and need, even as we also beseech his interceding grace for the sins and miseries and needs of others. In worship, by contrast, we offer praise and thanksgiving to the Lord God for his unsurpassable worth.[1] Though over-simple and needing qualification, Underhill's distinction is essentially right. Our English word *worship* derives from the Anglo-Saxon *weorthscipe*: "worth-ship," the giving of honor and blessing to the One who possesses true worth. The word was once used to address monarchs and other dignitaries, "your worship" being an alternate expression for "your lordship." This old meaning is still evident in the marriage vows of the unrevised Book of Common Prayer—now, alas, sanitized from the service: "With my body I thee worship." Worship is the church's public testimony to God's incomparable worth. To do it rightly is to offer reverence for God not only in his goodness and truth but also in the beauty of his holiness. To do it badly is to dishonor God in our own falsity, evil, and ugliness.

The Uneasy Christian Regard for Beauty

"From a Judaic-Christian point of view the very association of God and beauty, let alone the idea that they are co-essential, is [. . .] trivial." So writes James Kirwan in a book called simply *Beauty*.[2] Kirwan has cause for his drastic claim that there is no essential Christian link between God and beauty. We find, for example, that the God of Holy Writ is described by only two of the three medieval transcendentals—*bonum* and *verum* but not *pulchrum*. Scripture often declares God to be good and true, but rarely if ever does it speak of his beauty. *To kalon*—the Greek word ordinarily translated as "beauty" or "the beautiful" in the aesthetic rather than the moral sense— appears in only two New Testament contexts: once in Matthew 5:16 to describe the "beautiful" works which Christians are called to let shine in the presence of others; and again in John 10:11 and 14 to describe the "beautiful" shepherd who is Jesus Christ. Proverbs 31:30, by contrast, is a typical text from the Hebrew Bible: "Charm is deceitful, and beauty is vain." Nowhere in either Testament is there any exaltation of beauty in the aesthetic sense; on the contrary, there is a direct prohibition against the making of images for God, lest perhaps they be beautiful.

The commandment against images sets Israel apart from pagan religions. The ignoble Amorites and Jebusites and Hittites, like the noble Greeks and the Romans, sought to placate and manipulate the forces and powers of nature by making personified statues of them, whether in animal or human form. Yahweh is no such power or force: He is the maker and redeemer of heaven and earth, the self-identifying Spirit who must be worshipped without the aid of such idols. Jaroslav Pelikan argues that the Mosaic command is directed against what is potentially idolatrous in all three of the medieval transcendentals. Worship of the True can produce rationalism, just as worship of the Good can lead to moralism. Yet something profounder even than the fear of idolatry is at work in the Second Commandment. It is also a warning, says Pelikan, against the subtle and seductive powers of beauty.[3]

It is important to distinguish a biblical conception of beauty from its classical counterpart. The Greeks understood beauty in relation to the harmony and proportion, the symmetry and balance of nature. Just as the natural world has its own splendid pairings and hierarchies, the parts being subordinated to the whole, so should human creations of beauty imitate the great replicating and subordinating patterns of nature. Even systems of thought should be built on correspondences and proportionalities that reveal their rootage in the order of the natural world. This classical understanding of beauty was no less spiritual rather than natural. The transient forms of both natural and human beauty—as Plato first taught and as Augustine taught after him—are to be honored for their participation in the transcendent Forms.[4] George Macdonald saw the matter clearly a century and a half ago: "If the flowers were not perishable," Macdonald wrote, "we should cease to contemplate their beauty, either blinded by the passion for hoarding the bodies of them, or dulled by the [. . .] commonplaceness that the constant presence of them would occasion. [. . .] The flower is not its loveliness, and its loveliness we must love."[5]

The Platonic Christianity espoused by Augustine and Macdonald is a necessary but insufficient warning against the dangers of beauty when it is understood as harmony and hierarchy. Human fallenness has also set the original order of things terribly askew. After the Edenic calamity there is a dread disproportion and cacophony built into human existence. Once this primordial human disorder has spread into the natural world—by contagion, as it were—we can no longer look upon the creation as an affair wholly of symmetry and order: it is also the realm of terror and blood. "Red in tooth and claw" is Tennyson's terrifying description of the natural order in his celebrated poem on metaphysical doubt, *In Memoriam*. After a century characterized chiefly by mass killings—Pope John Paul II calls ours "the culture of death"—it is even more difficult to speak of human history as having any intrinsic beauty and glory.

Both Jews and Christians refuse to surrender history to the realm of the ugly. They both see God's beauty at work principally in his people called Israel and the Church. In Jesus Christ, moreover, the God who is beyond all images has made the unique image of himself. Christians believe, therefore, that God himself has lifted the ancient prohibition against depictions of divinity. Yet the alien kind of beauty embodied in Christ and his community militates against any straightforward or untroubled exaltation of the beautiful. The new Christian sanction given to images of the Holy One did not go unopposed even within the church, especially during the iconoclastic controversies of the ninth and tenth centuries. Even when Christ and the saints and the events of their lives were artistically represented, Byzantine artists took considerable care not to depict them in realistic or naturalistic terms. Instead, they suffused these holy figures with the presence and spirit of divinity. In the iconography of Eastern Orthodoxy, for example, one never beholds a wretchedly abandoned and abjectly human Jesus such as one finds in the Isenheim Altarpiece of Matthias Grünewald. Even from the cross, the Christ of Byzantine art remains Pantocrator, the maker and ruler of all things. Yet gradually in the West, the realistic and naturalistic impetus won out, as the figure of Jesus became ever more human, until at last he became merely human and sometimes even subhuman.

This sorry trajectory reached its nadir, perhaps, in Victorian renderings of Jesus. They reveal an odd correlation between the loss of Christ's transcendent otherness on the one hand, and the advent of religious sentimentality and sweetness on the other. One can witness this transmutation not only in Warner Sallman's immensely popular *Head of Christ* but also in Heinz Hoffman's similarly celebrated portrait of Jesus in Gethsemane. There he is depicted as a noble and stately figure who prays, not with anguished face and blood bursting from his brow, but with serenely calm face and devoutly folded hands. Thus has Jesus become the meek and mild Exemplar, the pale Galilean who, as Walter Pater protested, has conquered the world with his grayness. Such a savior could never have raised his voice or stared sharply or appeared in any way forbidding.

The proclivity for religious sentimentality, as we have seen throughout this book, is still very much with us. It still associates the Holy with things lovely and sweet, soothing and comfortable. Christian faith is thus made—rather it is remade and distorted—into something pretty and pleasant. Even the cross, a crude instrument of cruelty and death, is turned into a matter of décor and fashion. Against this prettification of Christ there arose another and truer tradition that links the Holy with the ugly and the grotesque. G. K. Chesterton explained this strange connection in an essay written in 1907. There he argued that Dickens always envisioned Christmas in grotesque terms, celebrating the happiest of events by means of goblins and ghosts, the bulb-nosed and the miserly. Dickens' figures are forbidding because their transformation is meant to be at once remarkable and real. "We have a feeling somehow," writes Chesterton, "that Scrooge looked even uglier when he was kind than he had looked when he was cruel. The turkey that Scrooge bought was so fat, says Dickens, that it could never have stood upright. That top-heavy and monstrous bird is a good symbol of the top-heavy happiness of [Dickens's Christmas] stories."[6]

Beauty, says Chesterton, is often allied with sadness. The reason, perhaps, is that beauty is often an outward and fleeting thing. The lovely face, like the gorgeous autumn scene, cannot last. Ugliness, by contrast, is always with us, and its lastingness makes it open to joy in ways that beauty is not. Those who are natively ugly can end, of course, in rancor and resentment, especially if their unsightliness is not their own doing. But at least they are not likely to be stuffed with self-importance. In his essay "On Gargoyles," Chesterton remarks that "[t]he ugly animals praise God as much as the beautiful. The frog's eyes stand out because he is staring at heaven. The giraffe's neck is long because he is stretching toward heaven. The donkey has ears to hear—let him hear."[7] A friend once wisely remarked that she has never met a stutterer who wasn't a kind person. Though they fumble grotesquely at our most distinctively human act, stammerers suffer a disability that is not wholly evil. Pretentious claims do not often issue from stumbling tongues. Insofar as deformity frees us from a top-heavy seriousness about ourselves, it offers an avenue to the Holy. Satan, Chesterton wittily remarked, fell by force of his gravity. Utopias, he added, are grim and joyless places precisely for being so dignified. They have no room for the frolicsome, the foolish, the grotesque. These latter folk, like the unfallen angels, can still fly because they can still take themselves lightly.[8]

In a world obsessed with utopian notions of beauty and health, it is not surprising that we have sought to remove ugliness from public view. A former student confesses that, if his mother continues to undergo her periodic face-lifts, her cheeks will eventually meet at the back of her neck. It is not only the marks of age and suffering that scandalize us. Our increased aversion to deformity has also brought an end to freak shows. This much-touted gain in sensitivity marks a certain loss in charity. The late Christopher Lasch argued that, for all our alleged "sensitivity," we do not truly care about the lame and the halt, the blind and the deaf, the fat and the mad—candid English monosyllables and biblical words all. If we really cared about them, said Lasch, the grotesque would become the object, if not our laughter, then certainly our tears.[9] Instead, we seek to define them out of existence with our lumbering euphemisms: the hearing impaired, the temporarily disabled, the mentally challenged. Refusing thus to rename—and thus to deny—the hard reality of his own wheel-chair existence, the writer Reynolds Price insists on calling himself a *gimp*.[10]

Yet it is important not to glorify the grotesque, as if grotesquerie and malformity were always markers of truth. Hispanic religious art which discerns Jesus almost entirely as the *crucificado*—depicting him in the gruesomeness of his bloody scourging and death——no doubt seeks God's beauty in the ugliness of his Son's mortality. But in failing to discern Christ's victory over the deadly forces of sin and death and the devil, it threatens unconsciously to revel in the macabre. Much of the decadence that produced Fascism was characterized by such *Liebestot*, such love of death. The aberrancies of our own time often mark a certain perversity rather than revealing the real. Backward caps, opaque glasses, spiked hair, blackened lips, tattooed skins, and pierced penises are more likely—during these latter decadent days—to signify falsity than truth. Such willful ugliness is meant, of course, to mock the cult of prettification and niceness. I suspect that it also reveals something quite unintended. The youthful obsession with body-piercing, for example, may disclose a secret desire to suffer. The young know, at some hidden depth of their being, that our culture practices a great deceit in teaching them to live on the dry crusts of pleasure alone. They become voluntary stigmatists in protest against such deceit: they submit to the brief pain of needles while truly hungering for the slow joy of sacrifice. Their nose and navel rings may thus point, albeit ever so dimly, to another piercing—to a nailing that was meant for the transgressions and iniquities of the world.

The Strange Gaiety of the Grotesque

Gaiety and the grotesque are rightly linked whenever physical ugliness points to our spiritual incompleteness, and thus to our need for radical alteration. Rarely are the grotesque satisfied with their condition. Their cracked appearance often reveals a certain rent in their souls. They are able to acknowledge this inner fissure as the seamlessly well-formed are not. Haunted by dreams of his own failures in charity, Scrooge is gradually made capable of conversion. His late-won happiness is all the more notable for following so dramatically upon his life-long misery. Thus does he find salvation in the most fundamental sense: something lasting is saved from the wreck that once was his life. From having been grotesquely sad and evil, Scrooge becomes grotesquely gay and good.

Such misshapen characters have a bewildering effect on readers. They unsettle our certainties about the way things are constituted. We know that something is wrong with these torqued creatures, that they are departures from the norm, but we are not sure that their crookedness of form is their real problem, nor that they could be cured by being made normal. Geoffrey Galt Harpam illuminates this troubling paradox:

> When we use the word "grotesque" we record, among other things, the sense that though our attention has been arrested, our understanding is unsatisfied. Grotesqueries both require and defeat definition: they are neither so regular and rhythmical that they settle easily into our categories, nor so unprecedented that we do not recognize them at all. They stand at a margin of consciousness between the known and the unknown, the perceived and the unperceived, calling into question the adequacy of our ways of organizing the world, of dividing the continuum of experience into knowable particles.[11]

Flannery O'Connor is the writer whose fiction reveals most clearly how the grotesque throws our complacent assumptions off balance, and thus how it can help us recover a true vision of both wholeness and holiness. Her work is filled with freaks and misfits, with imbeciles and lunatics, with the club-footed and the wooden-legged, with young women who—lacking all utopian comeliness that would make men desire them—have acned faces and clump about in Girl Scout shoes. Yet O'Connor's grotesques are not odd for the sake of oddity. They are skewed souls whom the Holy straightens and rectifies, albeit at great cost.

"A Temple of the Holy Ghost" is an O'Connor story that makes startling use of the grotesque to disclose the nature of the Holy. It concerns an unnamed twelve-year old girl whose two chief personal traits—her intellectual brilliance and her religious insight—are also the two chief sources of her sin. This unnamed brainy child likes to make fun of the dim-witted. Two country boys who have come to court the girl's two visiting cousins are the special targets of her contempt. In their love of sentimental gospel songs, the Wilkins brothers know nothing of the mystical faith and exultant hymnody of the child's own Catholicism. And so the girl scorns their membership in the Church of God, even as she mocks the Baptist preacher who offers pious prayers at her school. The story's precocious young protagonist thus makes the two gifts that one cannot possibly earn or deserve—native intelligence and religious faith—into a cause for spiritual pride. She has become, in fact, a little monster of presumption.

Yet such grotesquerie is always complicated, never one-dimensional, in O'Connor's work. The story's anonymous smartalice also possesses an acute religious sensibility. At night the child makes a dogged effort at her prayers. She searches her conscience and recalls at least some of her sins. She thinks of Christ on the road to Calvary, falling under the weight of his crushing cross. Knowing that she lacks all saintly powers of longsuffering, she hopes instead to become a martyr—"if they killed her quick."[12] Despite her uglifying pride, therefore, this twelve-year old has a potential for spiritual beauty that her pubescent cousins lack. She is outraged, for example, at their mockery of the nun who had given them a formula from I Corinthians 6 to fend off fresh young men in the back seats of cars. Sister Perpetua had told the girls to say, "Stop sir! I am a Temple of the Holy Ghost," in the assurance that the groping boys would then desist. Such unworldly advice strikes the two cousins as hilariously wrongheaded. The sexually innocent child, by contrast, is touched by it. The news that she is nothing less than the dwelling place of God "made her feel as if somebody had given her a present."[13]

The nameless little girl learns what it means to be a temple of the Holy Ghost only after her cousins return from a freak show at the local fair. They tell the curious child about the hermaphrodite whom they had seen there. He earns his living by exhibiting his sexually mixed features to voyeurs wanting to confirm that they are not as he is.[14] Yet he makes the spectators' perverse *frisson* the occasion for his own confession: "God made me thisaway and if you laugh He may strike you the same way. This is the way He want-

ed me to be and I ain't disputing His way. I'm showing you because I got to
make the best of it. I'm expecting you to act like ladies and gentlemen. I
never done it to myself but I'm making the best of it. I don't dispute hit."[15]

Unlike the town's Protestant preachers who—as religious harbingers of
our secular purists—finally shut the freak show down, the Catholic child is
not scandalized by the story of this hybrid creature with his strange creed.
Perhaps because she has seen crucifixes that are beautiful in their ugliness,
she responds to her cousins' report with neither pity nor horror, but with a
reverie that ends in real reverence. She dreams that the freak is the liturgist
in a church service, leading the people in a litany of radical affirmation:

> "God done this to me and I praise Him."
> "Amen. Amen."
> "He could strike you thisaway."
> "Amen. Amen."
> "But he has not."
> "Amen."
> "Raise yourself up. A temple of the Holy Ghost. You! You
> are God's temple, don't you know? Don't you know? God's Spirit has
> a dwelling in you, don't you know?"[16]

By the story's end, the proud little protagonist has been transformed.
Her humbling began with her perception of the Holy within the
hermaphrodite. In her childlike way, she came to see that the freak's deformity defeats our standard definitions of formliness, even as his faith exposes
the terrible inadequacy of our conventional belief. Thus does he enable her
to discern the mysterious frontier that lies between the known and the
unknown, the perceived and the unperceived. He represents, in fact, an
"answer to a riddle that was more puzzling than the riddle itself."[17] The narrator's confessed conundrum concerns the relation of the ugly and the Holy.
The riddling answer is that the freak, in his faithful embrace of his own ugliness, inhabits the realm of the Holy. He dwells there not only because of his
disfigurement but also because of his attitude toward it. Though deprived of
the sexuality that most moderns regard as the defining center of their being,
the hermaphrodite does not complain. He avoids the twin sins of anger and
self-pity because he has access to a non-naturalist view of the world. His
faithfulness enables him to see that he is no mere genetic accident. For while
he may indeed be a freak of nature, his life is first and last the will of God.
He is a creature in whom God's Spirit dwells mightily, and he is beautiful in
his ugliness.[18]

Flannery O'Connor reveals that even the highest Platonic conceptions of beauty cannot be made neatly to fit Christian faith. As her nihilist character called The Misfit declares, in a celebrated confession made in her most famous story, "Jesus thown everything off balance."[19] Christ has unhinged all conventional moral harmony, The Misfit complains, so that there is a radical asymmetry between divine grace and human deserving. More than any other modern theologian, Hans Urs von Balthasar answers O'Connor's challenge to envision a new and distinctively Christian understanding of beauty, making it the focus of his entire theology. He rightly locates it nowhere other than in the grotesqueness of the cross. Balthasar sees Jesus Christ himself as the truly transcendent form of beauty, the source and aim of all immanent loveliness. Yet the Incarnate Son is neither the static mirror of an unchanging God nor the reflected glory of a changing world. Balthasar argues, on the contrary, that Jesus dramatizes and expresses the fullness of God's own living beauty, and that he does this in his archetypal passage through the whole of reality, most especially in the ugliness and deformation of his suffering.

Balthasar also insists that Gethsemane and Golgotha constitute a radiant darkness, blinding even as they enlighten. As the one form-breaking form (to use the paradoxical language of Paul Tillich), the cross does not disclose God in a schematism of unambiguous logic and clarity. On the contrary, Christ embodies both the extinction of all meaning in his death as well as the restoration of all meaning in his resurrection. For von Balthasar, therefore, to worship God in the beauty of his holiness is to maintain the radical apophatic insistence that we know God chiefly by knowing what he is not—uncreated, invisible, immutable, etc. Truly divine beauty also preserves the distinction emphasized by pseudo-Dionysus: the ever greater wonder at our unlikeness and dissimilarity to the Father, even in our ever increasing praise for his drawing near to us in the work of the Son and the Spirit.[20]

This mind-staggering truth that we know the God of Jesus Christ both ever less and ever more—yet also at one and the same time—has profound aesthetic consequences. It teaches us to see the strange beauty that we could not otherwise see. The peacock was the bird that enabled Flannery O'Connor to discern what is wondrously disproportionate in divine beauty. O'Connor was drawn to this odd bird, she confesses, by no ornithological desire to fill out her collection of assorted fowl with another exotic addition. Having seen only a picture of a peacock, she nonetheless felt an instinctive attraction to it. His disproportion, she discovered, is his essence. His lumbering large feet, his blue-black waist coat, his vainglorious strutting, his unearthly scream, his skinny ugly legs, his long dragging tail which, when unfurled, looks from the rear like a pathetic set of underwear—all of these peacock parts, O'Connor notes, are quite "incommensurate with the whole." No work of traditional beauty is *this* anomalous creature—not so long as we are bound by the ordinary criteria of the commensurate: symmetry and balance, wholeness and proportion.[21]

The peacock's actions are even stranger than his appearance. When he screams, he seems to be trumpeting what O'Connor calls "the message the earth most needs to hear," as if he were giving "a cheer for an invisible parade." The peacock cannot be commanded to utter his eschatological cry, and even less can he be coaxed into spreading his tail. He makes his audience wait. This shuddering display of the cock's glorious tail is, of course, a mating gesture meant to attract the peahens. Yet it is not entirely a sexual summons. The peacock also struts when no hens are present. He seems determined to display the splendor of his arched green-bronze tail even when there is no purpose for doing so. The peacock's exhibition of his "galaxy of gazing, haloed suns," as O'Connor calls it, needs no reason for its magnificent array; it exists for its own splendid sake. Men have been known to remove their hats when the cock unfolds this "map of the universe," O'Connor reports, and once an "old Negro" woman cried out "Amen! Amen!"[22] The nameless priest in "The Displaced Person" offers deliberate theological analogies when he witnesses the peacock's unaccountable act of glory. "The Transfiguration," he declares, adding that "Christ will come like that!"[23] So it is that divine beauty, when discerned through the aperture opened at Calvary, proves to be a strange and jarring kind of beauty. It entails what St. Paul called the "much more" of God's unexpected and undeserved grace (Rom. 5: 9–10, 17, 20), and thus is it linked to the disproportionate and the incommensurate.

The Beauty of True Worship

Faith in the disproportionately and incommensurably beautiful Savior enables Christians to discern yet a second and even stranger kind of beauty: the beauty that the world regards as ugliness. Plotinus called ugliness the "Principle contrary to Existence." James Kirwan explains: "The ugly is what is not in accordance with the soul, is that which has not been entirely mastered by pattern, by Ideal-Form, and which the soul, as divine, resents and shrinks from. (An ugly soul is one abandoned to bodily sensations, one which abandons its true nature: 'in self-ignorance we are ugly')."[24] It is not difficult to see how Christians such as St. Augustine appropriated the work of Plotinus. The ugly, in this Christian reading of things, are the sinful, those who have abandoned their true nature, not only for a sensate animal existence (as Plotinus thought), but also for a self-sufficient angelic existence (as Augustine rightly described the ugliness of pride). Since ugliness is fundamentally a matter of the soul rather than the body, it follows that beautiful bodies can disguise ugly souls, even as ugly bodies may be animated by beautiful souls.

It follows that true worship must disclose the strange beauty of Christ's own brokenness and ugliness. A Christological beauty requires indeed that worship never be aestheticized. We are not permitted to make worship into a high-brow performance designed for God's tasteful elite—a lovely concert followed by an eloquent lecture. The early Christians knew nothing of the later splendors in music and architecture and liturgy that would become the hallmarks of high-church worship. Neither did my own Baptist forebears despise dignity and restraint and exaltation in worship; quite to the contrary, these original Baptist Southerners in the Charleston tradition knew them to be the very means both for acknowledging and experiencing God's mysterious otherness-in-nearness. Yet never did they make decorum in worship an end in itself; they sought it for the sake of simplicity and sobriety and the avoidance of all aesthetic pretense. Baptists of the South who belonged to the Sandy Creek tradition had cause—then even as now—to complain that an elaborate formality can convert worship into a cold and passionless thing. They knew, and not only from the church at Laodicea, that lukewarm Christianity, like lukewarm love-making, is an obscenity.

To celebrate the all-consuming glory of God in worship is to admit its impracticality, its unnecessity, even its wastefulness. It does the world no obvious good. The supreme importance of worship derives, on the contrary, from the desire to grant God all glory and blessing without regard to its human usefulness. Karl Barth illustrated such sacred irrelevance by telling of a French priest who continued to celebrate the Mass, together with a handful of worshippers, even though their church had suffered a direct hit from a German bomb. As the walls gave way and the roof began to collapse, this priest and his little flock of faithful souls continued with the service, offering God their praise and adoration amidst great calamity and ruin. Such worship accorded indestructible witness, says Barth, to the truth set forth in Romans 3:4: "Let God be true though every man be false." I recall the similar testimony of the English Christians who, when I worked in their midst during a sabbatical year, explained what it was like to worship at their central London church during the Blitz. The Congregationalists at Paddington Chapel worshipped every Sunday during those dreadful months, even though their church was once struck by a Nazi rocket. They recall, with considerable regret, their mistaken decision to cancel public worship on the Sunday following the war declaration of September 1, 1939. More than all the British and American bombers combined, these Christians came to understand that such undaunted exaltation of the triune God constituted their ultimate opposition to Hitlerism, especially when they sang such hymns as "How Firm a Foundation."

Most worship occurs in ordinary time, not amidst the overt crisis of war. Hence the need, I believe, for worship to celebrate the strange beauty of divine holiness by following the pattern of the Christian Year. Massey Shepherd, the distinguished Episcopal liturgist, argues that true worship constitutes a total reordering of space and time. The history of Israel's many divine deliverances, culminating in Jesus Christ's deliverance of our whole species at Golgotha, reveals that God himself has entered the two chief dimensions of finite life in order to make them divinely beautiful. Spatially, the Christian Year attests that the cosmos is not collapsing helplessly upon itself in final entropy and annihilation. By working our way from Advent to Lent and back again, we learn that Jerusalem remains the center of this hurtling cinder flung off from the sun—not because it is the seat of something called Israel or Christendom, but because it is the Place of the Skull: the site of the cross. And this old Jerusalem, true worship teaches us, is the city that shall also be made the center of the New Heaven and the New Earth. Thus do geographical and eschatological metaphors intersect to form worshipful ways of radically reordering ordinary space.

Shepherd argues that the liturgical year also radically reshapes our conventional notions of temporality. God's time does not circle about in a repetitive cycle of sameness, locking us into the glad-but-sad round of the seasons. For all of its transient beauty, nature's circle forms a great zero of annulment, canceling with wintry destruction all that has been wrought with vernal semination. The church's year, by contrast, is not circular and negating but linear and creating. Its first half moves from Advent through Christmas and Epiphany to Ash Wednesday and Lent, thence to Maundy Thursday and Good Friday and Holy Saturday. Here we remember the great and terrible signs of our alienation from God, even as we rehearse his mighty acts to redeem them. Pentecost is the middle period of fifty days—from Resurrection and Ascension to the Outpouring of the Spirit—that prepares us for the second half of the liturgical year. There the church's worship moves steadily forward toward the Final Advent by appropriating the great fruits of Pentecost. We return every November to ordinary Advent, says Shepherd, not in dreary repetition but in the confident conviction that God has moved us further along the road toward Kingdom Come.[25] Unlike the fleeting joys of spring soon to be annihilated by the coming winter, the Christian calendar reverses the relentless inevitability of pagan and scientific time. Third chances and new beginnings are intrinsic to the rhythms of this unearthly beauty.

Much work needs to be done on the various liturgical acts that give clarity and profundity to the seasons of the Christian Year: hymns and songs that are at once musically rich and poetically memorable, anthems and other forms of "special music" that enhance rather than replace congregational singing, litanies and responsive readings that focus our attention not on ourselves but on God, testimonies that deepen rather than cheapen the power of the Gospel, prayers that confess both our faith and our sin in ways neither trite nor hackneyed, celebrations of baptism and the Lord's Supper that serve to re-forge our identity with the vast communion of other Christians, both living and dead, both distant and near. In all of these acts of worship, we need to discover how better to honor the grotesque and cruciform beauty of God's holiness.

I am steadfastly convinced that faithful preaching remains at the heart of Protestant worship. When it fails, it is likely that everything else will be empty of substance. Barth was right to call preaching the Protestant sacrament, having a status tantamount to the Mass. St. Paul makes clear that the Gospel is not something to *be* proclaimed so much as it is proclamation *itself*. "Faith comes from what is heard, and what is heard comes by the preaching of Christ" (Rom. 10:18). To proclaim Christ's beauty is, as we have seen, not to give way to any sort of comforting pleasantness but to be schooled in the angular realism of the cross. Any sermon that can be preached without the illumination of its shadow-casting Light is sure to be ugly in the ultimate sense, however lovely its immediate appeal. The lectionary, provided that it is not determined by the requirements of religious correctness, is an aid to meeting this enormously difficult challenge. It prevents ministers from having a narrow canon of their own choosing and thus from riding their favorite hobby-horse texts. It calls them to follow the steady but arduous progress of the Christian Year across the whole trajectory of the Bible.

Yet there is nothing canonical about the lectionary. Barth rightly complained that it privileges the four gospels over everything else, as if they were uniquely revelatory in ways that the Pastoral Epistles and the Acts and the Apocalypse are not. The lectionary also threatens to quench the Spirit-prompted freedom of the preacher to address the clamant issues of the hour, speaking the pertinent Word to crises that cry out for prophetic address. Nowhere do contemporary lectionaries prove more fallible than in their tendency to elide the most difficult and often the most important sayings of Scripture. One of the approved readings for Ascension Day, for example, is taken from Revelation 22. It conveniently omits the text's unsavory warning that outside the gates of Paradise "are the dogs and sorcerers and fornicators and murderers and idolaters, and everyone who loves and practices falsehood." In a sub-biblical desire not to offend tender sensibilities—yet with utter tone-deafness to ordinary ironies—the editors also excised the following warning: "if any one takes away from the words of the book of this prophecy, God will take away his share in the tree of life and the holy city."

Finally, however, the gravamen of worship lies not in what is said and read, nor what is prayed and sung, but whether these things serve their only end, which is the praise and honor of the one worshipful God. I have argued, in agreement with the protagonist in Dostoevsky's novel called *The Idiot*, that "The world will be saved by beauty." Prince Myshkin is Dostoevsky's Christ-figure precisely because of his strangeness and oddity. He does not embody the gorgeousness of human beauty but the plain Beauty that was born in a cow stall, the skewed Beauty that has assumed our sin-twisted condition, the cruciform Beauty that, as the Byzantine liturgy puts it, "does down death by death." True worship of the true God—worship which alone can enable evangelical intimacy with the One who is high and lifted up— lies in nothing other than such ugly but holy beauty. This stark paradox of opposites in strange union can also enable Christians to have a right regard for one of the most vexed questions of our time: the place of romance in an hyper-eroticized world.

Chapter 9

A Christian Regard for Romance in an Eroticized World

Among the many places where the church can make its witness to a culture in enormous disarray, surely there are few more important than the life of romance and marriage. Though Christians have built up a venerable tradition of teaching about these matters, there is no evidence that Jesus ever fell in love, much less that he married. There have been scurrilous stories, of course, about his relation with prostitutes such as Mary Magdalene and with such multiply married women as the Samaritan woman at the well, even as it has been suggested that Christ had a homosexual liaison with the so-called "beloved disciple" who lies "close to the breast of Jesus" (John 13:23, 21:20). We can dismiss such speculations as the futile bewitchments that they are. But we cannot get past the fact that romance and marriage were not central to the life of Jesus and that they were not regarded as early Christian virtues. Quite to the contrary, confirmed bachelors and perpetual maidens would seem to have more in common with Christ, romantically speaking, than do those of us who have been either married or given in marriage.[1]

The chief of the apostles also seems to have had an extraordinarily low view of romance, attributing erotic longings to mere animal lust. The only cause for marriage, according to Corinthians 7, is to bank the fires of sexual desire. Paul thus enjoins his fellow Christians to remain in his own unmarried state. If they cannot so restrain themselves, as he famously says, "It is better to marry than to burn" (1 Cor. 7:9 KJV); i.e., to be "aflame with passion," as the RSV has it. As we shall have occasion to notice, our chief bachelor saint is perhaps confusing love with lust. Frederick Buechner has succinctly described the difference. Lust, says Buechner, is "a craving for salt in a man dying of thirst."[2] However that may be, the stark fact remains that there is not a single case of romantic love reported anywhere in the New Testament.

149

Given this obvious New Testament disregard for romance, what are lat-ter-day Christians to make of it, especially when the secular world pays non-stop homage to Eros? When chocolates and cards, when cakes and candies, when dinners and love-notes are being exchanged on Valentine's Day, what are Christians to do? Are we to turn up our collective noses and smugly declare: "St. Valentine was an early Christian martyr whose feast day fell on February 14, a day which therefore became confused with a pagan celebra-tion of romantic love that occurred on that same day, the day when birds were believed to begin mating again as winter wound down"? Are we thus to say that Valentine's Day is the sign of the world's commercialized unbelief, and that we will have none of it? I believe that there is a better way of retain-ing what is right about the biblical suspicions of romance. We may also look for the Christian counter-evidence that there is something not only won-drous about romantic love, but also something sacred and even potentially saving about it. To do so, we must first acknowledge the good causes for rejecting romance and marriage, only then arguing that they may and must be redeemed.

Romance Rejected

Our ancient Jewish forbears were a good deal less spiritual and far more earthy about matters of sex and romance than the early Christians were. The Baptist preacher and prophet Warren Carr puts the matter pungently. The Old Testament, says Carr, has its own four-letter word for sex: *know*. For our Hebrew ancestors, sexual intercourse between man and woman was the ulti-mate expression of physical knowledge and personal communion. "And Adam *knew* Eve." The Jews believed, as we do not, that there is no such thing as safe sex. For them, as for all wise people, the act of becoming one flesh is an extraordinarily dangerous thing. Precisely because it is laden with such great capacity for glory and goodness, it is also freighted with a terrible potential for evil. C. S. Lewis makes the astonishing claim in *The Screwtape Letters* that sexual cohabitation creates a permanent and unbreakable rela-tion, either for good or for ill, between a man and a woman. As the devil's minion named Screwtape asserts: "The truth is that wherever a man lies with a woman, there, whether they like it or not, a transcendental relation is set up between them which must be eternally enjoyed or eternally endured."[3] While Lewis may offer an overheated reading of 1 Cor. 6:16 ("Do you not know that he who joins himself with a prostitute becomes one body with her?"), he is certainly right to insist that sexual congress is no mere recre-ational activity without lasting consequences. He is making the same point as G. K. Chesterton, who declares that "[t]he man and the woman are one flesh—yes, even when they are not one spirit. [Humanity] is a quadruped."[4] The church has thus made drastic provision for this oddly quadrupedic life by creating the only true and "safe" environment for sex—namely, the sworn fidelity and lifelong companionship of monogamous marriage.[5]

Exactly because of the great peril inherent in all sexual relations, many Christians have been called to follow the path of Jesus and Paul by abjuring marriage altogether. The *negative* reasons for rejecting romance are not far to find. We need go no further than the story of David and Bathsheba in 2 Samuel 11 and 12. Perhaps because he was the king of all Israel, David may have thought himself immune from ordinary restraints. He felt no need to douse the flames of passion when he beheld the naked beauty of Bathsheba as she washed herself in a neighboring courtyard. Demanding the pleasures of her body as his own and exploiting his virtually untrammeled powers as king, he arranged for the killing of Uriah, Bathsheba's husband. He would have indeed gone unpunished but for the courage and insight of a truth-telling prophet named Nathan, whose parable of the rich man who stole the poor man's land made David discern the evil he had done. "You are the man" is the prophet's simple but searing indictment, and "I have sinned against the Lord" is the king's penitent reply (2 Sam. 12:7, 13).

This confession may seem altogether too pious, as if the violations done against the dead Uriah and the pregnant Bathsheba were of little matter—given David's quick restoration to his regal state. Yet Scripture always goes beyond the obvious. When we commit sexual sin—as when we commit all other sins—we rip apart the world's moral and spiritual order. Garrison Keillor brings home this point by telling of a friend—Keillor calls him Jim Nordberg—who confessed his own temptation to adultery. A woman at Nordberg's office was finding him more interesting and attractive than his wife did. He had lied, therefore, about his real reason for attending a professional conference in Chicago with this woman. Though their adulterous affair was likely to go undetected, he could not silence his conscience. Waiting for the woman to pick him up, Nordberg considered the implication of his act:

> As I sat on the lawn looking down the street, I saw that we all depend on each other. I saw that although I thought my sins could be secret, that they are no more secret than an earthquake. All these houses and all these families—my infidelity would somehow shake them. It will pollute the drinking water. It will make noxious gases come out of the ventilators in the elementary school. When we scream in senseless anger, blocks away a little girl we do not know spills a bowl of gravy all over a white tablecloth.

> If I go to Chicago with this woman who is not my wife, somehow the
> school patrol will forget to guard the intersection and someone's child will
> be injured. A sixth grade teacher will think, "What the hell," and elimi-
> nate South America from geography. Our minister will decide, "What the
> hell—I'm not going to give that sermon on the poor." Somehow my adul-
> tery will cause the man in the grocery store to say, "To hell with the
> Health Department. This sausage was good yesterday—it certainly can't
> be any worse today."

In refusing to commit an act that our age makes almost obligatory, Nordberg
had discerned, as Keillor says, that "[f]ar from being hidden, each sin is
another crack in the world."[6]

Sexual sin creates a fissure in the heart of human existence because, in
violating others, we first of all damage God. The triune Lord has graciously
sought, from the very foundation of the cosmos, to enter into a deep mutuality with his creation, becoming incarnate so that we in turn might participate in God's own triune life. He thus demands that we display our true
intimacy with him by way of true mutuality with each other. He will tolerate nothing less than faithful love. To break faith and trust with another person is thus to dishonor God. Monogamy and monotheism are related in
more than an etymological way. Worship of the one true God and holding
true only to one spouse are often synonymous activities.

The immense difficulty in achieving trusting and lasting fidelity in love,
even among God's covenanted people, was made evident to early Christians
not only in the story of David and Bathsheba but also in the sex-sodden society of the first-century Mediterranean world. Theirs was a highly eroticized
culture, as a reading of Robert Graves's *I, Claudius* or a glance at the ruins of
Pompeii will reveal. One of the most notorious Pompeiian drawings depicts
a priapic man whose penis is so large that a crane is required to lift it. The
late Roman Empire was hyper-sexualized in ways very much akin to ours.
Madonna and MTV might well have aired on late-night Roman television.
Yet the early Christians began to reject romance for *positive* no less than negative reasons. There were better things to do with one's life than to make sex
its be-all and end-all. When Paul declares "It is well for a man not to touch
a woman" (1 Cor. 7:1) he is not revealing himself to be sexually repressed, as
former Episcopal bishop John Shelby Spong believes. He is declaring that
some eras are so sexually decadent that Christians need to make radical
counter-cultural gestures, to commit subversive acts against the dominant
cultural paradigm, even while remembering patiently with G. K. Chesterton
that "decadence also decays."

Many early Christians sought to wage guerrilla warfare against the sex-drenched culture of their day. During the third and fourth centuries, the wilderness monastics of Egypt, for example, heeded the call of Paul to put their bodies under subjection. They took seriously the Apostle's declaration that Christians should be athletes practicing a radical *ascesis* for the sake of the Gospel. Paul thus likened his own self-denial to a boxer who did not beat the air with his fists: "I pommel my body and subdue it" (1 Cor. 9:27). The Desert Saints make declarations that, in being even odder, are all the more aptly astringent. Abbot Cyrus of Alexandria, for instance, declares that the sin of lust is committed primarily in the imagination, the adulterous act being but ancillary to it:

> If thou hast not these imaginings, thou art without hope: for if thou hast not the imagination thereof, thou hast the deed itself. For he who fights not in his mind against sin, nor gainsays it, sins in the flesh. And he who sins in the flesh, hath no trouble from the imagination thereof.[7]

Such injunctions against erotic fantasies are an affront to contemporary hedonism, even as Paul threatened the idol-making silversmiths at Ephesus. He and the early Christian monastics did not repress their sexuality so much as they sought to master and redirect it toward trans-corporeal ends.

The Call to Celibacy and the Recovery of Virginity

It is important to remember that Christians do not need to be monks and nuns in order to reject romance for a celibate life. There are Christian singles who have been called by God to redirect their sexuality into other forms of Christian life than marriage. We who are wedded believers owe them great honor and gratitude. It is important not to suspect that such Christian celibates have merely repressed their sexuality or that they are closet homosexuals. Very often these believing singles feel themselves summoned to correct the sexual idolatry of our culture. There are also widows and widowers who elect not to remarry, even though they had been happily married and though they seem obvious candidates for second weddings. Having had an initial vocation for marriage, they feel themselves called to a second life of singleness.

Kathleen Norris is a Presbyterian laywoman who has also become a Benedictine oblate—a tertiary member of the most ancient order of Christian monastics. She spends a good deal of her time in monasteries precisely to remind herself, both as poet and wife, that celibacy and singleness are meant to be a blessing rather than a curse. In her fine book called *The*

Cloister Walk, Norris says that the real mark of our cultural perversity is that we have come to regard virginity not as an honor but as a burden, believing that the sooner we lose it the better. Our culture has turned sex into entertainment, she says, converting orgasm into yet another goal—akin, say, to scoring a touchdown. "To channel one's sexuality into anything besides being sexually active," writes Kathleen Norris, "is seen as highly suspect; it leaves celibacy vulnerable to being automatically labeled as infantile or repressed."[8] Morris reverses a commonplace aphorism to offer her own disturbing apothegm: we *undress* for success. Sexual unrestraint at work in collegiate men often causes them to ignore and even to spurn collegiate women whose passions are not equally disordered. These virginal women often become convinced, in turn, of their unattractiveness. They often resign themselves to a solitary life, only to discover—upon leaving college and entering the world of mature men who can recognize their true loveliness—that they are indeed fit for connubial life.

The British writer William Rees-Mogg has proposed a new set of vows for contemporary couples who marry chiefly because of their sexual compatibility:

> "I take thee for my wedded wife because I have found it enjoyable to have sex with you; so long as you continue to be attractive to me and I do not find sex preferable with someone else I expect to continue to be married to you; if you become old or ugly or peevish or poor or ill I shall leave you if you have not already left me; in the meantime I shall cherish you financially and will take you to parties where we can shine before our set."[9]

Walker Percy is even more vitriolic in his denunciation of our cathouse culture. He says that many American couples first have sex and then introduce themselves. The time will come, Percy prophesies, when our men and women will approach each other like dogs—nose to tail, and tail to nose, sniffing. It is also noteworthy that many contemporary couples have reversed the ordinary progression that once led to wedlock: first they move in together, then they buy a house, then they have a child, and finally they get married.

With one-third of American girls having had sex by the time they are fifteen—and with boys becoming sexually experienced even earlier—we have cause to fear the long-term consequences for an entire generation that has lost the possibility of virginal love being consummated in marriage. The Victorian celibate poet Gerard Manley Hopkins declares, in his poem called "Spring," what is vital in virginity. In fact, he petitions Christ himself—the son of a teenaged girl, Hopkins helps us remember—to transform the rising sap of youthful love into a guileless freshness that will remain permanently virginal, even if it is in the experience of married love rather than celibacy:

> What is all this juice and all this joy?
> A strain of earth's sweet being in the beginning
> In Eden garden. — Have, get, before it cloy,
> Before it cloud, Christ, lord, and sour with sinning,
> Innocent mind and Mayday in girl and boy,
> Most, O maid's child, thy choice and worthy the winning.

Given the rampant devirginizing of young people in our time, perhaps the summons of the church to them is not only that they *preserve* their virginity but that they seek to *recover* a chastity that would otherwise seem lost. Kathleen Norris, developing an idea from Thomas Merton, understands this strange possibility of restored virginity when she speaks of a certain immaculacy of judgment and purity of perception that young people can retain, by God's grace, even when they are no longer sexually virginal:

> It is in adolescence that the fully formed adult self begins to emerge, and if a person has been fortunate, allowed to develop at his or her own pace, this self is a liberating force, and it is virgin. That is, it is one-in-itself, better able to cope with peer pressure, as it can more readily measure what is true to one's self, and what would violate it. Even adolescent self-absorption recedes as one's capacity for the mystery of hospitality grows: it is only as one is at home with oneself that one may be truly hospitable to others—welcoming, but not overbearing, affably pliant but not subject to crass manipulation. The difficult balance is maintained only as one remains virgin, cognizant of oneself as valuable, unique, and undiminishable at the core.[10]

It not surprising that, amidst the fetid swamps of contemporary sexuality, many people are choosing to nourish their "undiminishable" core through a life of singleness. Such solitude is Christian only if it is not an avoidance but a calling, a clear summons to an alternate way of redemptive life. Norris argues, in fact, that the chief aim of Christian celibacy is not so much non-genital love but the cultivation of non-exclusive friendships for the sake of God and the world. Husbands and wives can love only one spouse truly, whereas celibates can have many spiritual spouses of both genders and many ages. These Christian celibates thus offer a radical sign of the Kingdom by attending to the needs of others without making them the objects of bodily scrutiny and desire. Norris quotes an anonymous Benedictine sister on virginity:

"This is something I carry very deeply within [. . .] that I carry very secretly . . . virginity is centered in the heart and could be named 'singleness of
heart.' [. . .] Virginity is a state that returns to God in wholeness. This
wholeness is not that of having experienced all experiences, but of something reserved, preserved, or reclaimed for what it was made for. Virginity
is the ability to stay centered, with oneness of purpose."[11]

I understood this truth for the first time when one of my Roman
Catholic students came seeking my counsel about becoming a nun. It was an
exceedingly odd experience for a Baptist teacher of theology, especially when
the student told me she had not yet talked with her priest or her parents. I
quickly discerned that this young woman does not despise men nor hate the
prospect of sexual intercourse. She confessed, on the contrary, that she wants
to marry and to have children. But she was wondering whether, like St. Paul
and a great host of other Christian virgins, she may be called to live a celibate life. She knows that when Paul urged men not to touch women (1 Cor.
7:1), he was not speaking out of fear and contempt. He was confessing, even
if a bit harshly for our tastes, his deep respect for a life to which he had not
himself been called. So do contemporary Christians owe honor to those who
have been called to reject romance and marriage. They are our brothers and
sisters in the household of God.

Romance Redeemed

We adverted to the lustful love-story of David and Bathsheba as a
reminder that there are good biblical reasons for rejecting romance as it is
conventionally conceived. Yet there are other Old Testament texts that hail
romance for its power to produce life-shaping, life-binding love. The most
famous, of course, is the long erotic love-poem called the Song of Solomon.
Less obviously romantic, but deeper in its implications, is the love story of
Jacob and Rachel. It is a happy story, though it begins with an almost
macabre comic twist. It will be remembered that the trickster Jacob has had
to wait fourteen laborious years after he was tricked into marrying the wrong
woman, the unlovely Leah, before at last he gets his beloved Rachel. In one
of the Bible's most poignant scenes, Genesis 29 records that Jacob had first
met Rachel at the well where she had come to water her father's sheep. There
Jacob had felt an almost magnetic allurement to Rachel. It led him to perform an act of exquisite courtesy and aid: he removed the heavy stone from
the well's mouth, and he drew the water that her sheep needed to drink.
Jacob used his masculine strength to relieve Rachel's feminine burden. It is
only after Jacob had *earlier* shown Rachel kindness and deference that he

later displayed his romantic love. "Then," we read, "Jacob kissed Rachel, and wept aloud." He was shedding tears not of grief, of course, but of joy—the joy for having met the mystery of love in this woman who approached him not as a seductress but as a woman in need.

The Scots poet Edwin Muir (1887–1959) has caught the quality of married love in a poem called "The Annunciation." He gives it an evocatively religious title in order to liken nuptial union to the Word received by the Virgin Mary:

> Now in this iron reign
> I sing the liberty
> Where each asks from each
> What each most wants to give
> And each awakes in each
> What else would never be,
> Summoning so the rare
> Spirit to breathe and live.
>
> Then let us empty out
> Our hearts until we find
> The last least trifling toy,
> Since now all turns to gold,
> And everything we have
> Is wealth of heart and mind,
> That squandered thus in turn
> Grows with us manifold.
>
> Giving, I'd give you next
> Some more than mortal grace,
> But that you deifying
> Myself I might deify,
> Forgetting love was born
> Here in a time and place,
> And robbing by such praise
> This life we magnify.
>
> Whether the soul at first
> This pilgrimage began,
> Or the shy body leading
> Conducted soul to soul
> Who knows? This is the most
> That soul and body can,
> To make us each for each
> And in our spirit whole.[12]

Marriage is a kingdom made of steel because, far from entrapping spouses, the bars of its covenant serve to liberate them. Like the Virgin Mary at the Annunciation, they are freed as they surrender themselves to each other, not offering what one would only reluctantly grant, but both giving and receiving nothing less than everything. In the economy of love, the smallest of gifts are golden treasures, and to waste them is to multiply them. Yet there are dangers inherent in the glories of marital love. To make it divine, making mere spouses into gods and goddesses, is to deny the wondrous earthiness of connubial bliss, located as it always is in the temporal and fallible particulars of ordinary human life. Nuptial love thus remains a paradoxical and indissoluble mixture of the physical and the spiritual when it is truly whole.

Muir is confessing I suspect, that lasting love begins in the kindness and friendship that deepen gradually and mysteriously into life-companionship. I admit that this is how I met and married my own love. Suzanne Coppedge was first of all my friend in Christian faith. We were both members of the Baptist Student Union on our college campus. I can recall the day and the time and the place where it first occurred to me that this young lady was not only my friend. It came about on an August afternoon in 1961 as I drove through a small East Texas town called Hughes Springs. There I happened to see her walking along the streets, after we had both returned from doing summer mission work. I saw suddenly that she was the woman whom I cared about as I did not care about other women. Gradually I came also to see to that she was the woman I wanted to marry and to spend my life with. This gift came to me very much as God's grace comes to all of us. It was not something that I had sought, much less deserved. It was a strange and unbidden gift. It was the soul-staggering wonder that this lovely person could love one so unlovely. This may have been what Martin Luther meant when he declared marriage to be our largest human metaphor of God's own grace. When a student once asked me to explain why salvation is not a matter of our own free choice, but wholly God's gracious gift, an offering that we gladly receive rather than bravely choose, I could do no better than to make this stammering reply: "If you had ever fallen in love, you might understand."

It was the troubadour poets of medieval Provençal who first began to make the connection between romantic love and divine grace. Dante Aligheri is the pre-eminent poet of this great tradition. Dante found himself morally and spiritually transformed by his vision of divine glory at work in a young maiden named Beatrice Portinari whom he encountered on the streets of thirteenth-century Florence. His love for her drew him out of himself into a larger, indeed into a transcendent world of goodness and truth and excellence. The God who had become incarnate in Jesus Christ had now displayed his glory in the innocent beauty of this young girl. His vision of her did not issue in marital love for Dante because the marital conventions of his day did not permit it: she was to remain his extraordinary ideal, not to become his ordinary spouse. But such Christian romance did flower into marriage when, two centuries later, Martin Luther fell in love with a nun named Katarina von Bora. It was given to Luther, the Augustinian monk and radical ascetic, to discover not only the holy calling of celibacy and singleness, but also to rediscover the divine vocation of married love. So great was his love for dear Katie that he confessed he wouldn't trade her "for France and Venice together."

The link between divine and romantic love involves more than the initial wonder of being loved undeservedly. For this love to be sustained in marriage, it also requires radical acts of forgiveness. Just as God repeatedly pardons our sinful waywardness, so do married partners sustain their love through repeated reconciliations. Nuptial love is such a difficult endeavor that it prompted one of Luther's jauntiest sayings: "It takes courage," said Luther, "to enter both marriage and tournaments." Luther was speaking not of our modern athletic engagements, of course, but of those fearful medieval jousts where knights carrying lances hurtled full tilt at each other on horseback. Such headlong conflict, Luther suggests, often characterizes marriage. "Think of all the squabbles," Luther joked, that "Adam and Eve must have had in the course of their nine hundred years. Eve would say, 'You ate the apple,' and Adam would retort, 'You gave it to me.'"[13]

In a more pensive mood, Luther called marriage "a school for character." What he meant, I think, is that character is the product of habituated practices which we perform without regard to our personal feelings. We seek the good of our spouse, not because we are "in the mood," as the old Glenn Miller tune has it, but because, as the Book of Common Prayer declares, it is "meet and right and our bounden duty." Many modern marriages fail because, as my colleague Scott Moore says, we have come to regard marriages as an extended form of dating. They work only as long as the couple continues to "like" each other, to have fun together, and thus to find each other "interesting" and even "entertaining." True marriage, by contrast, means loving one's spouse precisely when he or she is unlikable, often even unlovable. For only then can marital love be likened to the love of God. Thus do some elderly couples who have long since "fallen out of love" find themselves caring for each other, with an unaccountable dearness, in the midst of the infirmities that the late years bring.

Without the binding ties of sworn fidelity, romantic love is soon broken. Ironically, it is the happy imprisonment of wedlock that sets romance free to flourish. C. S. Lewis has the satanic Screwtape take delight in our confusion about romance: "'being in love' does very often, in western Europe [and the United States] precede marriages which are made in obedience to the Enemy's [God's] designs, that is, with the intention of fidelity, fertility, and goodwill. In other words, the humans are to be encouraged to regard [romance] as the *basis* for marriage a highly coloured and distorted version of something the Enemy really promises as its *result*."[14] The German martyr Dietrich Bonhoeffer also understood the reversed relation of love and marriage. In a sermon written from his prison cell at Tegel for the wedding of his niece Renate Schleicher and his former student Eberhard Bethge, Bonhoeffer declared:

> Marriage is more than your love for each other. It has a higher dignity and power, for it is God's holy ordinance, through which he wills to perpetual the human race till the end of time. [. . .] In your love you see only the heaven of your own happiness, but in marriage you are placed at a post of responsibility towards the world and mankind. Your love is your own private possession, but marriage is more than something personal—it is a status, an office. [. . .] As you first gave the ring to one another and have now received it a second time from the hand of the pastor, so love comes from you, but marriage from above, from God. As high as God is above man, so high are the sanctity, the rights, and the promise of marriage above the sanctity, the rights, and the promise of love. *It is not your love that sustains your marriage, but from now on, the marriage that sustains your love.*[15]

Incompatible Marriages and Serial Divorces

Lewis and Bonhoeffer are both reminding us that, for more than a thousand years, Christians were not married because that they had first fallen in love. Usually by way of familial arrangements, virtual strangers were united in the sacrament of marriage. With the church's support as well as its sanction, they were able to bring children into the world, to nurture them in the Gospel, and to remain faithful to each other until death. Insofar as romance blossomed amidst such sworn fidelity, it did so because of the marital ties that blessedly bound them. It's a lesson the contemporary church could well learn. Romance is the most dubious of marital foundations. The deep commonalities of friendship, of mutual concerns, but chiefly of a shared life in the Body of Christ—these are the things that enable and sustain marriage.

Hence Stanley Hauerwas's celebrated dictum: "We always marry the wrong person." He means, I assume, what both Lewis and Bonhoeffer mean: that if we marry in order to be happy, and if we define happiness in standard trouble-free terms, then we are bound to wish we had married someone else. If forgiveness and reconciliation are the positive basis for the vocation and discipline of marriage, there are negative requirements as well. We are often called to hold our peace when our spouse has offended us, rather than ventilating our wrath. So are we also summoned to accept each other's foibles rather than trying to reshape them to our own liking. The alternative is hellish recrimination. A former student who had recently married confessed that she and her husband had decided to have "a completely open and honest marriage." Rather than tolerating offenses, they vowed to call each other immediately to account. The result of such graceless "honesty" was altogether predictable: they engaged in perpetual warfare. The likelihood of their enjoying sexual communion, even on their honeymoon, was destroyed until they learned to accept and to forgive each other's weaknesses and offenses. Again, Bonhoeffer speaks deep wisdom in this matter:

> *God gives you Christ as the foundation of your marriage.* "Welcome one another, therefore, as Christ has welcomed you, for the glory of God" (Rom. 15:7). In a word, live together in the forgiveness of your sins, for without it no human fellowship, least of all a marriage, can survive. Don't insist on your rights, don't blame each other, don't judge or condemn each other, don't find fault with each other, but accept each other as you are, and forgive each other every day from the bottom of your hearts.[16]

At the heart of marriage lies the integrity that only faith in the incarnate God can prompt. We can fool almost everybody but our earthly spouse and our heavenly Spouse. They know when we are authentic and when we are fraudulent. We can fake marital love no more than we can pretend to trust God. Because marriage often reveals our deceptions, both of ourselves and of others, we often resort to divorce rather than face the unpleasant truth. The huge incidence of divorce—more than half of all American marriages end there—may derive from this desire for a truthless and character-free bliss. Samuel Johnson observed in the eighteenth century what is inherently contradictory about divorce when he described second marriages as "the triumph of hope over experience." G. K. Chesterton was similarly appalled upon discovering, already in the 1930s, the all-too-easy grounds for legitimate divorce in America: "If Americans can be divorced for 'incompatibility of temper,' I cannot conceive why they are not all divorced. I have known many happy marriages, but never a compatible one. The whole aim of marriage is to fight through and survive the instant when incompatibility becomes unquestionable. For a man and a woman, as such, are incompatible."[17] We are not wed because we are sexually or temperamentally or even religiously compatible, but because we are called to the difficult and rewarding vocation of life together.

The dread of matrimonial difficulty may partially account for the late marriages that many couples are now making. Young people are today abstaining from marriage—though certainly not from sex—until they are well into their thirties, even their forties. Some of these singles reject married life for selfish reasons—in order to remain unattached, uncommitted, permanently "free" to arrange their lives in whatever fashion they choose. Such a self-centered program is the precise recipe for damnation—perhaps not only in the life to come, but also in the present hell of selfishness. The Cornish poet Jack Clemo altered St. Paul's saying to fit those who would seclude themselves in such icy solitude: "It is better to marry than to *freeze*."

When I have lamented the paucity of collegiate romances, the conspicuous absence of couples holding hands on campus, I am told that these young men and women are too busy preparing for their careers to deal with the vexations of romance in their twenties. Yet ours is a sadder world, I believe, for having so few couples who are glistening with the excitement and wonder of youthful and virginal love, and fewer still who are starry-eyed at the prospect of marriage. I believe that there is no calendar either for romantic love or divine grace. Just as the Spirit blows when and where it wills, so is romance not a thing to be scheduled. The risk of romance is very much akin to the risk of faith, and it requires the same growth and cultivation as faith. For if romance is not redeemed, it can indeed become a fatal attraction.[18] It sometimes issues in broken hearts and, alas, in broken lives. Yet we will never know the glories of the romantic love that issues in lifelong married companionship unless we are also willing to risk its disappointments and to undertake its sometimes painful developments.

The vogue for delayed maturation in marriage over against immediate gratification in unattached singleness derives, I believe, from the strange late-modern conviction that the world owes us bliss. Sigmund Freud, for all the limits of his outlook, spoke deep truth when he declared that the purpose of psychotherapy is to reduce screaming rage to ordinary unhappiness. The detective novelist P. D. James shares Freud's astonishment about the modern notion that we deserve unbroken enjoyment for the whole of our lives. For James, by contrast, a quiet and often stoical endurance is the chief requisite for both religious faith and nuptial love. Thus does she salute our forebears for enduring often unblissful marriages, assured that these too had their reward:

> Those [unhappy couples] who were able to survive the more turbulent years of youth and middle age often found in each other a reassuring and comforting companionship in old age. They had a far smaller expectation of happiness, admittedly, and a far lesser tendency to regard happiness as a right. All our brightly minted social reforms, the sexual liberation since [World War II], the guilt-free divorce, the ending of the stigma of illegitimacy, have had their shadow side. Today we have a generation of children more disturbed, more unhappy, more criminal, indeed more suicidal than in any previous era. The sexual liberation of adults has been bought at a high price and it is not the adults who have paid it.[19]

Marriage is the place where boys are meant to become men, just as it enables girls to grow into women. As Genesis says, we are called to leave our fathers and mothers, to cleave to each other, and thus to become adults. The essence of married adulthood is mutuality and complementarity. The novelist John Updike once observed, ever so unfashionably, that the very existence of women is an appeal to the kindness of men. Men with their masculine might and brute strength can dominate women, even as women with their feminine charm and neediness can maneuver men. These fundamental perversities are the sorry legacy of the Fall. But in true marriage men can cease to lord it over women, even as women can cease to stage-manage men, as we both join in confessing our common dependence on the triune and self-giving God.

The Augustinian injunction "to put our loves in order" is nowhere truer than in marriage. By loving all things in God, the great African saint does not intend anything gauzy or mushy but something ever so concrete: to make the love of God the orienting point for everything—for all our thoughts and words and deeds. This doesn't mean that we need to do nothing other than ponder God in every moment of earthly bliss. Dietrich Bonhoeffer observed, for example, that the man who thinks about God while lying in his wife's arms is even holier than God. Roman Catholics are agreed, insisting that sex in marriage has a triple purpose: communion, procreation, and pleasure. The most recent Roman Catholic Catechism quotes none other than Pope Pius XII from a discourse he gave in 1951:

> The Creator himself [. . .] established that in the (generative) function, spouses should experience pleasure and enjoyment of body and spirit. Therefore the spouses do nothing evil in seeking this pleasure and enjoy-

ment. They accept what the Creator has intended for them. At the same
time, spouses should know how to keep themselves within the limits of
just moderation.[20]

Protestants and Catholics and Orthodox are of one accord in their insistence
that, whenever we love our spouses in true carnal love—just as when we love
our neighbors as ourselves—we are also loving God.

Even for many who rightly order their loves in God, the chief biblical
treatise on marriage has given them grief. For the Paul who speaks in
Ephesians is alleged to be an unreconstructed misogynist. There is little
doubt that the Apostle uses unegalitarian language in defending the mystery
of marriage. He declares that the wife finds her freedom in subjecting herself to her husband, even as the husband finds his humility in exercising
headship over the wife. As always, it seems, both liberals and conservatives
manage to mangle the apostolic message. Liberals are horrified at any appeal
to authority, since for them it implies not only the inferiority but perhaps
even the Talibanic enslavement of women. Conservatives, all too eager to put
women in their secondary place, insist that Paul forbids women either to
preach or even to teach anyone but children. What left and right both miss
is that these strange sayings are not about illegitimate power and domination
but about legitimate authority and relation. Surely Paul is calling for a mutual acquiescence, a glad marital commonality that is indecipherable and
impossible apart from life of glad subjection to God that is possible only in
Christ's Body: "This is a great mystery, and I take it to mean Christ and the
church" (Eph. 5:32).

Just as the church is a community of radical self-surrendering interde-
pendence, so does Christian marriage entail something far deeper than legal
rights and pre-nuptial contracts that lay out duties and responsibilities in
graceless egalitarian terms. Christian marriage requires, on the contrary, the
radical equality found only in *total* relinquishment. The husband is called to
be the head of wife only as Christ is the head of the church. Far from being
a swaggering savior or domineering lord, he is the Suffering Servant who lays
down his life for the church, even as the husband is called to sacrifice himself for his wife—and just as she, in turn, sacrifices herself for him. Married
Christians are summoned happily to submit themselves to each other as the
only way of turning youthful romance into lasting love and lifelong regard.
For then are we made not only one flesh but also one life, a communion of
minds and bodies and souls in the romance that can be redeemed because
our love has been ordered to the love of the God. Such a life, whether in marriage or celibacy, also requires a spirituality that is first outward in order that
it might become inward.

Chapter 10

The Outward Faithfulness
of Inward Christian Piety

The final chapter returns to the point at which we began—with a contention that has enormous consequences for church and culture alike. The contemporary obsession with spirituality, among Christians as well as those who call themselves religious but not Christian, surely betokens something worthy of the church's attention. I am not convinced, however, that the current vogue for spirituality should be embraced without making important historical and theological distinctions. I contend, moreover, that these distinctions will lead us to prefer the term "piety" rather than "spirituality." Such inward piety, I will argue, springs from the outward life of faith as it is lived in the church, especially through doctrinal preaching and sacramental worship. Only when it is thus focused and grounded and transformed, I will conclude, can the church benefit from the resurgent spirituality of our time.

The Dangerous Vagueness of Spirituality

The term "spirituality" is perilously vague. It is an abstract noun that has become so devoid of theological content that it can be attached to almost any modifying phrase. An electronic web-search for the word "spirituality" received 10,000 responses. Even when the genitive "of" was added, there were still several hundred sites. Here are but a few of the many "spiritualities" advertised on the Internet: the spirituality of unity, the spirituality of work, the spirituality of simplicity, the spirituality of intimacy, the spirituality of non-violence, the spirituality of the body, the spirituality of imperfection, the spirituality of perfection, the spirituality of indigenous cultures, the spirituality of food, the spirituality of letting go, the spirituality of the feminine, the spirituality of the good herb, the spirituality of aging, the spirituality of the religious educator, and—perhaps most revealing of all—the spirituality of wildness.

This last sort of "spirituality" is described rather ungrammatically as follows: "religion that is lived, felt, and experienced—rather than simply believed—real and ecstatic and visceral. Wicca, neo-paganism, ecospirituality, shamanism, totemism, shapeshifting, therianthropy, nature magic, animal and plant lore, and earth-based spirituality of all kinds." Surely the one thing missing from this sorry litany is the spirituality of abortion. Once spirituality is made but another shopping item in the spiritual bazaar of self-interest, it can be put to purposes that are truly demonic. Hence the confession of a wise and skeptical friend: "Whenever I hear the word 'spirituality,' I grab first for my wife and then for my wallet."

With uncanny prescience, C. S. Lewis anticipated what is potentially perilous in the current vogue of spirituality. In his space novel of 1944 entitled *Perelandra*, Lewis depicts a demonic scientist named Weston as an advocate of an immanentist life-worship that has remarkable parallels to contemporary spirituality. Weston has contempt for the transcendent God who creates and judges and redeems the world. He will have nothing to do with the incarnate Lord who requires that we worship him rather than his creation, who commands that we live not for this world alone but also for the Life beyond life. Weston's anti-Christian philosophy proves predictably anti-humanistic, as the denial of the God who has become human issues finally in a hatred of humanity itself. Weston worships the dynamic and impersonal life-process instead. He scorns "mere humanity" in the name of a vitalism as vacuous in its rhetoric as it is vicious in its ethics:

> The majestic spectacle of this blind, inarticulate purposiveness thrusting its way upward and ever upward in an endless unity of differentiated achievements towards an ever-increasing complexity of organisation, towards spontaneity and *spirituality*, swept away all my old conception of a duty to Man as such. Man in himself is nothing. The forward movement of Life—the growing *spirituality*—is everything. [. . .] To spread *spirituality*, not to spread the human race, is henceforth my mission.[1]

No such monstrous imprecision attends Paul's use of the word "spiritual" in the New Testament. He sets up a clear contrast between the life of the flesh (*sarx*) and the life of the spirit (*pneuma*). The conflict lies not between the body (*soma*) and the soul (*psyche*), but rather between a way of life confined to the earthly horizon of human self-seeking, on the one hand, and the heavenly life dedicated utterly to the Spirit of God, on the other. Hence Paul's straightforward declaration: "To set the mind on the flesh is death, but to set the mind on the Spirit is life and peace" (Rom. 8:6). Far from exalting the incorporeal world at the expense of the corporeal, Paul makes clear that the deadliest "works of the flesh" are not only outward and bodily but also—and chiefly—inward and spiritual: "idolatry, sorcery, enmity, strife, jealousy, anger, selfishness, dissension, party spirit, envy [. . .] and the like" (Gal. 5:20–21).

Nor does Paul ever regard the gifts of the Spirit as something that can be acquired by human yearning or native capacity. The natural human desire for God given in the created order of things has been perverted and forfeited in the Fall. The Prayer Book puts our condition pungently: "There is no health in us." Our *salus* can be restored only through the salvation offered by the gift of God in the life, death and resurrection of Jesus Christ. Union with God and participation in the divine life, by way of the ascending and reigning Christ, occurs only through the gift of the Spirit called faith. And this total entrustment of one's life *to* God it is itself enabled *by* him. It is a faith *in* Christ that is worked through the faith *of* Christ:

> Some biblical scholars point out that the Greek preposition connected to the word "faith" [e.g., in Rom. 3:21 and Phil. 3:9] can be translated "of" as well as "in." [. . .] The two possible translations are complementary. [. . .] The gospel leads to faith in God that comes, not through the law of Moses, but through the faith of Jesus. Jesus trusted God. Jesus obeyed God. Though Jesus was crucified because of his trust in God, God raised Jesus from the dead, thereby vindicating Jesus' trust in God and vindicating God. God's power to restore life and to restore fellowship with those from whom Jesus had been alienated is now revealed.[2]

The objective and totally finished character of Christ's already accomplished act makes possible our own subjective and partial appropriation of it. Thus do the New Testament words "spirit" and "spiritual" refer primarily to the life of Christian faithfulness—a faithfulness that is inseparably outward and inward. It is noteworthy that these words do not produce a biblical term akin to our "spirituality."

Spirituality and Piety

Declan Marmion points out that Jerome, in the fifth century, was the first Christian theologian to use the word *spiritualitas*. "So act as to advance in spirituality," Jerome advised recently baptized believers. He used the word to mean very much what Paul meant—to advance in a life of total devotion to the Spirit received in baptism, and thus in opposition to the life of sinfulness. Between the sixth and eleventh centuries, the word took on a decidedly supernatural sense. Spirituality referred to a life lived not according to nature but according to the counsels of perfection contained in the Beatitudes and omitted from the Commandments. *Spiritualitas* was thus put in contrast with *corporalitas* or *materialitas*. By the twelfth and thirteenth centuries, a further shift had occurred. The opposition between "spirituality" and the ordinary meanings of the word "flesh" had become virtually complete. *Spiritualitas* was now a monastic word set over against *carnalitas* and *mortalitas*, even *brutalitas* and *animalitas*. It referred to the incorporeality and eternality of the soul, while the latter words described the consequences of original sin.[3]

These changes in the various meanings of spirituality were accompanied by another and even more consequential shift. Jacques Leclercq observes that two kinds of theological schools had developed in the high middle ages, with two kinds of theology as the result. Schools for clerics were situated in cities and near cathedrals. With a curriculum based on the seven liberal arts, they sought to train future clerics for the "active" pastoral life. Such "school" theology was centered on an oral style of education based principally on the question-and-answer method. A problem was propounded, various authorities were adduced, and a solution was thus found. The intention was to inculcate clear, impersonal, unambiguous knowledge—even if it meant recourse to jargon. Magnificent though its accomplishments were in such theologians as Aquinas and Abelard, "scholastic" theology became gradually equated with rote learning and specialist argot.[4]

Over against it there arose a monastic theology that was tied to a rigorously ascetic life of prayer and worship and work. Because the monasteries were located in rural retreats that revered silence, it became a written as much as an oral style of theology. It was not taught by schoolmasters, but by abbots or abbesses who sought to tutor their monks and nuns in the "contemplative" life. This intensely personal kind of theology was based more on spiritual desire than intellectual inquiry. It thus had recourse to poetry and metaphor rather than to precise technical terms. Monastic theology did not seek to cultivate the *knowledge* of God through abstract reasoning, so much as the *experience* of God through concrete imagination. As with the ancient desert saints, so with these medieval monastics: they were concerned less with routing heresy than with overcoming temptation. They wanted to honor and praise God by means of an ever-enlarged participation in God's own life. Mystical union with God rather than propositional understanding of God was their goal. It is noteworthy that the most famous of these monastic theologians, Bernard of Clairvaux, made his motto *Credo ut experiar* rather than *Credo ut intelligam*.[5]

It is also noteworthy that, in his *Institutes of the Christian Religion*, John Calvin cites Bernard of Clairvaux more than any other theologian except Augustine of Hippo. Not at all the desiccated logician of divinity that he is often made out to be, Calvin called prayer "the central practice of the Christian life," and the longest chapter in the *Institutes* is devoted to prayer. Yet Calvin did not share the monastic conviction that the heart's desire is a sure guide to life in God. "The heart," Calvin starchily declared, "is a factory for the perpetual making of idols." Perhaps this explains why Calvin chose the word *pietas* rather than *spiritualitas* to describe the Christian life of total devotion to God. The old Roman word, redolent with rich social and political connotations, helped guard against a potentially delusory inwardness. It connoted, instead, a sense of duty and responsibility, even patriotism; a deep devotion and loyalty to one's family and homeland; but also a kindness and tenderness towards others in need. In every case, *pietas* pointed the Romans to a reality beyond themselves— namely, to a huge sense of indebtedness to their country, to their parents, and of course to their gods. Calvin insisted, therefore, that a truly inward piety has its grounding in such outward acts of faith.

Both English and American Puritans followed Calvin's practice by employing the word "piety" for their own devotional practices. They too knew the perennial human temptation to confuse our fallen longings with the motions of the Holy Spirit. They thus insisted that life in Christ takes us *out* of ourselves—out of our pathetically small subjectivities—into the grand objective realm of the *not merely me*: into the eternal world of God's own justifying grace and sanctifying holiness. In the Puritan tradition, prayer itself was not understood as an entirely inward act of private and personal devotion. As the Westminster Shorter Catechism makes clear, prayer is one of the three "outward and ordinary means whereby Christ communicateth to us the benefits of redemption." The other two "outward means" are the Word truly preached and the Sacraments rightly celebrated. In all three activities, Christians are recipients of theological gifts that make the life of piety inseparable from the life of worship and doctrine.

Their deadly separation occurred only during the Enlightenment. I believe that it is a mistake, therefore, to regard the current fashion for spirituality as a reaction against the cerebral kind of deistic theology that arose with the Enlightenment. Certainly the seventeenth and eighteenth centuries did mark a new turn to the outward and observable world that can be known rationally and scientifically. It is also true that a deistic theology followed from it. Yet even this empiricist turn was not purely outward and objective; it was also deeply inward and subjective. The notion that nature can be viewed neutrally was an intellectual deceit. It was but another lensed way of seeing, a new kind of subjectivism now disguised as pure objectivity. Even Descartes's famous formula—*Cogito, ergo sum*—is marked by its emphasis on the thinking subject: *I* think. Surely this highly individualized, subjective, autonomous and reflexive self is the chief creation of the Enlightenment.[6]

It is no accident that a new and often non-doctrinal kind of pietism arose alongside the new secular rationalism as its close cousin. The Age of Reason was also the Age of Piety. It was the epoch not only of Leibniz and Bayle, Toland and Paley, but also of Wesley and Zinzendorf, the Freemasons and the Rosicrucians. They were all marked, albeit in different ways and degrees, by the modern turn to the sovereign subject whom Karl Barth calls the Absolute Man:

> [Enlightenment] man knows that he is linked with, and ultimately of the same substance as, the God significant for him in this double function. God is spirit, man is spirit too. God is mighty and so is man. God is wise and benevolent, and so is man. But he is all these things, of course, infinitely less perfect than God. Man's way of being these things is confused and fragmentary, but it *is* the same way. [. . .] Has not [this Enlightenment] man in fact asked himself and himself given the answer he apparently wished to hear from some other source? This is the question of which, thus expressed, man in the eighteenth century was not aware. This was the absolutism also inherent in his inner attitude to life; he assumed it to be self-evident that in taking himself into account, and himself answering the account, and then acting in obedience to it he was also showing the existence of God. [. . .] He believed—even in this inmost place we find him prey to a strange vicious circle—that by virtue of the reality of his own existence he could vouch for God and in so doing for the possible existence of God.[7]

Spirituality as Sanctification

I believe that much of contemporary spirituality is an extension of the delusory sovereignty that characterized Enlightenment mentality. Such pernicious self-referentiality can be overcome, I believe, only if we learn to cultivate a theologically grounded piety. At its best, the new concern with the spiritual life reflects a laudable desire to make Christian faith a matter of the heart no less than the head, a discipline of devotional practices rather than a repetition of doctrinal propositions. J. I. Packer, citing Henry Rack, offers a helpful definition of a distinctively Christian spirituality: it is an "enquiry into the whole Christian enterprise of pursuing, achieving, and cultivating communion with God, which includes both public worship and private devotion, and the results of these in actual Christian life."[8] Diogenes Allen makes a similar reading of spirituality as an attempt to deal seriously with the church's primary concern for holiness of life: "Christian spirituality concerns sanctification [. . . .] the work of God the Holy Spirit, bringing to fullness the work of Christ, in the church, the body of Christ. Sanctification runs through the entire work of all the great theologians of the past and colors virtually *everything else* that they wrote [. . . .][9]

Anything less than a rigorous spirituality will make for a subjectivism that turns us into caricatures of ourselves rather than the Christian persons we are meant to be. The Greek *persona* means "mask." We cannot be persons at all without wearing masks, for masks enable us to assume our rightful roles. The poet W. H. Auden once observed that there is no real distinction between the sincere and the insincere, but only between the sane who know they are wearing masks and the insane who do not. This is especially true of Christians. We perform our various earthly callings and tasks only as we wear one mask above all others: the mask of Christ. To wear any other is to ignore Luther's warning: "The moment I consider Christ and myself as two, I am gone." John Fletcher of Madeley, an eighteenth-century Anglican who quotes this saying of Luther, makes clear what is at stake in "putting on Christ." It requires, says Fletcher, a renunciation of

> [. . .] all separate existence in Adam and from Adam. You will take Christ to be your life, you will become his members by eating his flesh and drinking his blood, you will consider his flesh as your flesh, his bone as your bone, his righteousness as your righteousness, his cross as your cross, and his crown (whether of thorns or glory) as your crown. You will reckon yourself to be dead indeed unto sin, but alive unto God, through his dear Redeemer. You will renounce propriety, you will heartily and gladly say, "Not I, but Christ liveth, and only because He lives I do, and shall live also."[10]

The Pauline insistence that we "put on Christ" accounts, I believe, for the Apostle's strange admonition that we not be caught naked at the Second Coming (2 Cor. 5:3). To wear the *persona* of Christ, Paul indicates, is to be clad with the garments of righteousness. The metaphor of clothing as a covering for sin runs throughout the Bible, from the moment the Lord God replaces the first couple's pathetic fig leaves with leather skins, to the proper dress that Jesus requires for those who are driven in from the streets to feast at the king's banquet (Matt. 22:11–14). If nakedness is a metaphor of our fallenness, then dress becomes something other than mere protection from the elements. We make theological no less than sartorial statements with our attire.

It is noteworthy that many highly spiritual folks in our time do not find anything extraordinary about their outward personification of Christ. Convinced that only the inward and spiritual truly matter, they enter the presence of the Lord wearing backward baseball caps, thigh-high skirts, muscle-preening polo shirts, and knockabout shoes. Thus do they make unconscious declarations that, for them, the act of worship is nothing extraordinary. It requires no drastic reclothing. Black Christians deny this false distinction. They worship God in the beauty of their best apparel. They want their clothes to reflect God's own glory. They have no dress-down days at their churches. They approach God, instead, in the splendor of their dress, outwardly embodying the claim that we are meant to be God's own well-clothed royalty, enjoying the marriage feast of the Lamb in *style*.

It has now become almost a commonplace to observe that, unlike these faithful black Christians, many people now identify themselves as "spiritual" but not "religious." Robert C. Fuller is one of their chief defenders. In a book entitled *Spiritual, But Not Religious: Understanding Unchurched America*,[11] Fuller praises the spirituality that rejects the special authority of the Bible, the unique divinity of Jesus, the fallenness of humanity, and especially the church as a corporate community wherein sin is overcome and lives are re-conformed to the image of God. Doctrines and institutions are moribund and stifling for such spiritual people.[12] Robert Wuthnow is keenly disagreed. He shows what is almost inevitably self-centered about the contemporary turn to the inner self as the ultimate locus for an encounter with God. He quotes Thomas Moore's immensely popular *Care of the Soul* as evidence of the literal *self*ishness that underlies Moore's call for people to cultivate the sacred in everyday life and thus learn to be content with themselves. "Dropping the salvational fantasy," says Moore, "frees us up to the possibility of self-knowledge and self-acceptance."[13] No longer is the soul regarded the transcendent, unitary seat of selfhood implanted by God; it has become what Wuthnow calls the "dispersed self." Rather than defining itself in relation to received teachings and doctrines and social institutions, this new sort of soul creates its own ever-fluid identity through "a wide variety of encounters and experiences, including moments of interaction with sacred objects, such as trees and automobiles. Broadly speaking, it is a dispersion of experiences, themselves widely separated in space and time, with different people, and of varying significance."[14]

Formality and Spiritual Formation

Ours is hardly the first age to have contested the relation of the subjective and the objective, the inward and the outward. It was a much agitated issue between Puritans and Anglicans in the seventeenth century. Bishop Lancelot Andrewes declared, in resistance to Puritan plainness, that we worship God not only with our heads but also with our hats. Preaching at St. Paul's Cross in London during 1625, John Donne also responded to Puritan critics of the Church of England: "[I]f I come to extemporal prayer, and extemporal preaching, I shall come to an extemporal faith, and extemporal religion; and then I must look for an extemporal Heaven, a Heaven to be made for me." "Let us not *pray*," Donne concluded, "not *preach*, not *hear*, slackly, suddenly, unadvisedly, extemporally, occasionally, indiligently. Let all our speech to him, be weighed, and measured in the weights of the *Sanctuary* [. . . .]"[15] An ad hoc kind of Christianity leads, so Donne contends, to a faith that is so self-absorbed that even Paradise must exist primarily for him alone.

Donne and his fellow establishmentarians were accused of stifling the Nonconformist freedom to cultivate an inward and personal piety, replacing it with a stiff and unfeeling adherence to the Book of Common Prayer. Ramie Targoff demonstrates that the Book of Common Prayer, a work that has influenced worship in the Anglophone world perhaps more than any other, was much more than Thomas Cranmer's clever theological compromise between Romanists on the right and Calvinists on the left. It was the product, instead, of the Church of England's deliberate insistence that carefully scripted public worship shapes and transforms Christian worshippers in indispensable ways. Without such formal rigor and beauty, the spiritual life can dissipate into chaos and inconsequence.

Sixteenth-century Anglicans hardly came upon their conviction afresh. Aristotle had insisted two millennia earlier that there is a causal link between ethics and habits. Moral virtue depends, according to Aristotle, on practices that we carefully learn and often repeat. As important as doctrinal orthodoxy always remained, the early church agreed with Aristotle, insisting that its public liturgy formed the character and lives of Christian worshippers. Gradually, especially in the late Middle Ages, this link between the public and the personal was obscured. As the Latin mass came to be celebrated behind the rood screen, so that parishioners could neither see it nor even hear it in their own language, the Catholic church supplied them with *Lay folks' Mass Books*. These worship guides, Targoff shows, encouraged individual worshippers to undertake their own meditations and examinations of conscience as the monks said and sang the service beyond the wall. Catholics rejected a common liturgical text, even in the vernacular, on the grounds that it would distract laypeople from their private devotions.

The Anglicans regarded the Puritan exaltation of original prayers and extemporaneous sermons as an odd return to Catholic practice—insofar as it made worshippers into virtual non-participants at a service which itself lay at the mercy of the minister. Like Luther, these Anglicans exalted the aural over the visual. When we worship, Luther insisted, we should stick our eyes in our ears. Richard Hooker, the chief defender of the Book of Common Prayer, also agreed with Calvin that human nature is far too weak and fallible ever to rely on a spontaneous spiritual life: we always need external props and aids. Yet Hooker was not concerned only about religious order and control. The bookless and unreading masses convinced him of their need for standardized liturgical practices that would deepen devotion to God in ways that private promptings of the Spirit do not.

Like the Puritans, the Anglicans sought the transformation of the human heart. Yet the heart remains a notoriously invisible and unreliable thing, whereas outward postures and gestures and enunciations can be both seen and measured, as can communicants kneeling at an altar or serving each other bread and wine. The Puritans charged that such public repetition of Prayer Book confessions and litanies encourages hypocrisy. Andrewes and Donne and a host of other Anglicans rejected this easy divide between the authentic and the theatrical. We become the things that we perform, they argued, for it is the outward life that shapes the inward. The Lutheran theologian Joseph Sittler offered similar wisdom when he was asked, not long before his death, what single piece of advice he would offer the late twentieth-century church. "Watch your language," said Sittler. Sloppy worship produces sloppy existence before both God and our neighbors. Stanley Hauerwas and William Willimon make the link between liturgy and ethics far more drastic: "You begin by singing some sappy sentimental hymn, then you pray some pointless prayer, and the next thing you know you have murdered your best friend."[16]

The Outward Shaping of the Inward Life

I confess that my own heroes in the Faith are men and women whose outward and public faith exhibited their inward and private piety. C. S.

Lewis is altogether typical. Once when two of Lewis's friends came to collect him for a day's trip away from Oxford, they noticed that Lewis was walking up and down in his garden while they sat impatiently in the car. When Lewis finally joined them, his friends demanded an explanation: "What were you doing out there while we sat here waiting for you?" "Oh," replied Lewis, "I wouldn't dare leave home without first saying my prayers." Prayer, for C. S. Lewis, was an outward, even visible, habit that shaped his inward and spiritual life. His prayer life was also rooted in hard study. When Lewis was asked what kind of devotional reading he most favored, his interlocutor perhaps assumed that he would answer by naming something like Oswald Chambers's *My Utmost for His Highest*. Instead, Lewis replied that his spiritual life was enriched by such theological treatises as Athanasius's *On the Incarnation*. Lewis was not boasting. He was making the salient point that a piety which is not based upon—and which does not lead to—a profounder *knowledge* of God is a bogus and bankrupt piety. It comes as no surprise that Lewis opposed innovations in worship. The moment our attention is drawn to the service itself, rather than the God whom we are meant to serve, worship is broken:

> Every service is a structure of acts and words through which we receive a sacrament, or repent, or supplicate, or adore. And it enables us to do these things best—if you like, it "works" best—when through long familiarity, we don't have to think about it. As long as you notice, and have to count, the steps, you are not yet dancing but learning to dance. [. . .] The perfect church service would be one we were almost unaware of; our attention would have been on God.[17]

Piety is rooted in action as well as prayer and worship. Gerard Manley Hopkins, the great Jesuit poet of nineteenth-century England, was once asked by his friend Robert Bridges for advice about overcoming his inveterate unbelief. Bridges expected Hopkins to reply with a lengthy theological treatise. He received, instead, a two-word reply: "Give alms." Hopkins's point was simple: the Christian faith requires our habituation to self-giving outward practice in order for it to issue in a life of God-loving inward belief. This is hardly to suggest that Hopkins found his ethical and spiritual life easy. On the contrary, it was often agonizing. His "dark" or "terrible" sonnets, as they are often called, declare the awful otherness and hiddenness of God, no less than the wondrous nearness and dearness of God. The heavenly Father and Lord of Jesus Christ, as Hopkins understood profoundly, is not our heavenly chum. He is the sovereign, free and living Lord who comforts only as he also frightens. Hence Hopkins's fearful question in his sonnet that begins "Thou art indeed just, Lord": Could God's love do him any greater harm than the depredations of his worst foe?

> Wert thou my enemy, o thou my friend,
> How wouldst thou worse, I wonder, than thou dost
> Defeat, thwart me?

Hopkins insists that the Gospel is never something that we can comfortably *assume* to know in advance, something that we need only *apply* either here or there. On the contrary, the Gospel always awaits our astonished rediscovery; indeed, our constant and trembling re-conversion. The reason is not far to find. Christ's cross is at once the place of God's supreme light as well as his complete darkness. To bear it faithfully is to be vexed no less than cheered. Bishop Kallistos Ware thus sums up the fearful wisdom of Abba Agathon, one of the desert saints of ancient Egypt: "Prayer is the hardest of all tasks. If we do not find it difficult, perhaps it is because we have not really started to pray."[18]

Hopkins was so convinced of the link between the outward and inward life that he joined his friends at Oxford in practicing what they called "the discipline of the eyes." They believed that what we *see* shapes our souls. To behold ugliness and vulgarity and crudity—whether on television or billboards—is to risk the twisting and perversion of our very lives. Karl Barth also believed that what he *heard* shaped his soul. He began every day by listening to Mozart for an hour and then praying for another hour.[19] Barth was not seeking to put himself into something as silly as "the mood for prayer." He wanted, instead, to hear earthly echoes and musical parables of the heavenly Kingdom, so that when he prayed he might participate in the very life of God. In order that his prayers not become mere subjective meanderings among his own small-minded concerns, Barth always prayed aloud, even though he prayed alone. Only in prayer, Barth observed, do we not wear masks. There we stand naked before God. Because such nakedness cannot be publicly displayed, Barth was loath to exhibit his own piety:

> The witness of the disciple consists in the fact that he refrains from attesting his piety as such. If he is to display the Kingdom of God, and proclaim it from the housetops (Mt. 10:27), he will not make a show of his own devoutness but keep it to himself, allowing God alone to be the One who judges and rewards him. This restraint will be a witness to the pious world with its continual need to publicise itself, and perhaps even to the secular world. It will speak for itself—or rather, it will speak for that which does seriously and truly cry out for publicity.[20]

The Wesleys as Exemplars of True Piety

What, then, are we to conclude from these distinctions and examples about the outward and visible faith in Christ that forms the basis for an inward and invisible piety? I believe that the resurgent interest in the life of prayer will prove itself lasting rather than faddish only if it issues in a renewed emphasis on doctrinal preaching and liturgical worship. These are the places *par excellence* where we become public Christians of the kind whose devotional life is not subjectively self-serving. Hence my disagreement with Alister McGrath's commendation of Archbishop Donald Coggan's claim that "The journey from the head to the heart is one of the longest and most difficult that we know." This may have once been true of those who espoused a certain kind of Catholic or Protestant scholasticism, but I do not believe it to be true today. "Theological correctness" is a problem only to a miniscule minority. There may be few remaining dispensationalists who open their Scofield Bible every morning to trace the divine ordering of the successive ages, even as I suppose there is a tiny tribe of Calvinists who ponder the Canons of Dort every night before bed. But surely the chief difficulty of our time is that our piety is too little rooted in theology, not that it is dominated by doctrinal considerations.

The journey from the heart to the head is not only the most difficult but also the most necessary in our subjectivist and emotionalist age. We need to balance Bernard's *Credo ut experiar* with Augustine's *Fides quaerens intellectum*. Experience of God will be something other than terrible self-delusion only if it is grounded in *intellectum*—in an ever-greater knowledge and understanding of God. The terrible Christian scandal of our time, as I have sought repeatedly to emphasize, is that a sappy sort of spirituality over-emphasizes the heart at the huge expense of the head. I concede that there is legitimate worry about a false emphasis on knowledge. Yet learning becomes a temptation to arrogance and a distraction from true piety only when it is disordered—i.e., when it is loved more than God and thus when it becomes a substitute for the love of God.

From the medieval monastics to Wesley in the eighteenth century, this has not been the case. The great devotional writers of the West have all stressed the interstitial relation of knowledge and piety: *the love of learning and the desire for God*, as Leclercq entitles his splendid book. "From his arrival at Clairvaux to his entry into Heaven," Leclercq writes, "the real, the only Bernard was, indissolubly and simultaneously, a learned man and a man of God, a thinker and a saint, a humanist and a mystic."[22]

Our best Protestant pietists are agreed. "It is a fundamental principle with us," John Wesley declared, "that to renounce reason is to renounce religion, that religion and reason go hand in hand, and that all irrational religion is false religion."[23] Thus did he write and publish digests of several major Enlightenment thinkers, including David Hume and John Locke. Wesley wanted his followers to engage their piety with the most rigorous philosophical thought of their era. He sought also to master the best science of his time, convinced that "the book of nature is written in an universal character, which every man may read in his own language."[24] Nor did Wesley ever stop stressing the importance of what George Whitefield called the "externals"—the ordinary (and often uninspiring) daily practice of self-denial, the routine doing of good for people in trouble, the sometime dutiful observance of prayer and fasting.

For both of the Wesleys, private piety is rooted in the life of public faith. "There is no holiness," John insisted, "that is not a social holiness." He and his brother were profoundly concerned with the amelioration of human suffering—poverty and illiteracy, sickness and criminality, hunger and homelessness. Yet they were not romantic about God's "preferential option for the poor." Sin infects the penniless no less than the rich, even though it does greater harm in the wealthy than the poor. Poverty can be the occasion for a terrible envy, just as prosperity can induce an even more damning complacency. Both rich *and* poor need saving. Charles Wesley's hymn gets the matter exactly right: it is not the poor who are God's "preferential option" as such, but the "humble poor" whose neediness has opened them to the grace of God as cushioned and comfortable are not. Two of my former students who serve as co-pastors of an inner city Baptist church in Trenton, New Jersey, happily confess that they are never laden with the unhappy suburbanite task of persuading their parishioners that they need God.

The Wesleys learned, to their pain, that the path of radical Christian practice is strewn with hazards and threats. It's a lesson easily forgotten among suburban Christians. Charles and John did not speak of their Christian "walk," therefore, but employed far more militant metaphors: "struggle," "contest," "battle," "warfare." "Soldiers of Christ, arise," Charles Wesley cries out in one of his best hymns, "and put your armor on." "Wrestle and fight and pray," he adds, "tread all the powers of darkness down and win the well-fought day." This call to Christian arms was no idle analogy. The Wesleys repeatedly stirred up riots in places where they were preaching. In a town called Devizes, for example, the local Anglican ministers were so riled by their influence on the masses that they aroused a mob against them. These ruffians first stoned and then flooded with firehoses the house where the Wesleys were staying. The hooligans ripped off the shutters and drove the preachers' horses into a pond. Local Methodist leaders were ducked in this same pond; others had bulldogs set upon them, their homes looted, their businesses ruined.

Charles Wesley is not to be compared with the composers of contemporary praise songs, whose poetic worth is negligible if even detectible. That Charles stole his hymn tunes from the drinking ditties sung in taverns is a canard. He was a poet of the first rank who was ever so careful to fit his text to appropriate music. That the two Wesleys often made their witness in public houses—outraging their owners—has contributed to this popular misconception, as has a certain confusion over the musical term "bar tune" or "bar form," which has nothing to do with inebriating liquor! One of Charles Wesley's most remarkable hymns, "Jesus, Lover of My Soul," may have been written, in fact, in response to the frightening incident at Devizes. It is a deeply mystical, even a spiritually erotic hymn; for it speaks openly of Jesus as the spouse and lover of Christians. Yet there is nothing smarmy about the intimacy with Christ that Wesley enjoins. Set to a minor key by Joseph Parry, it has a haunting quality that makes one tremble at the thought of fleeing to Christ's breast as our only security in the midst of life's floods and storms, whether human or natural. We are naked to evil, Charles Wesley confesses, unless Christ shields us:

> Other refuge have I none, hangs my helpless soul on thee;
> leave, ah! leave me not alone, still support and comfort me.
> All my trust on thee is stayed; all my help from thee I bring;
> cover my defenseless head with the shadow of thy wing.

The revival led by the Wesleys did so much to relieve human misery that they may well have prevented the political violence that devastated France in 1789 from occurring in England. Yet while they were opposed to the American Revolution, the Wesleys were far from political conservatives. John especially abominated the institution of slavery. One of his last acts before dying was to call the abolitionist William Wilberforce to his bedside, encouraging him in his battle against the slave trade. Earlier he had written Wilberforce a letter declaring slavery to be "that execrable villainy which is the scandal of religion, of England, of human nature."[25] Two days before his death, Wesley penned his final letter, again to Wilberforce: "Reading this morning a tract wrote by a poor African, I was particularly struck by that circumstance, that a man who has a black skin, being wronged or outraged by a white man, can have no redress; it being a *law* in our Colonies that the *oath* of a black man against a white goes for nothing. What villainy is this!"[26]

It would be a sign of true Christian seriousness if our contemporary advocates of spirituality were to condemn elective abortion and capital punishment with equal vehemence.

The Centrality of Preaching and Hymns for Worship

The Wesleys, like their medieval counterparts, understood that preaching helps guarantee the reciprocal relation of heart and head. Instead of constantly asking what can God do *for* us?—how we might come to feel more pious or to be more holy or to act more spiritually—doctrinal preaching enables us to ask the far profounder question: What does God want to do *through* us? The Good News is that God is determined to create a radically redemptive community, a new people whose benefits are not meant primarily for themselves but for God and the world. This transformed Body is sustained by wisdom that the world regards as folly—the preaching of Christ crucified (1 Cor. 23). Hence Paul's insistence that the Gospel is not something to be preached so much as it is preaching itself. "Faith comes from what is heard," he declares in Romans 10:17: *fides ex auditu.*

The *Shema* calls Israel not to *see* God but to *hear* him, for hearing is the organ for receiving and obeying commands. The eyes have lids that can gaze or blink back or shut out; they are the organs of vision and surfaces. The ears have no such flaps; they are pierced with truths that require heeding or spurning. This is not to discount vision, even though Scripture constantly stresses the priority of faith over sight: Jesus congratulates those who have not seen but nonetheless believe, even as Paul declares that "we walk by faith, not by sight" (2 Cor. 5:7). The eyes provide vision that leads to understanding, and thus are they ever so important. But understanding follows from faithful obedience rather than being a prior condition for it. *Credo ut intelligam*, declared St. Anselm; he believed in order that he might understand. Saving faith cannot do without understanding, but it is often enabled and perennially sustained by faithful proclamation, by preaching that issues in transformed personal and communal life.

The preaching that engenders authentic piety must be founded on the bedrock claims contained in the great confessions of the Church. They are not only reflective distillations *of* Christian experience but also a powerful spur *to* Christian experience. The larger our theological claims, the larger our encounter with God, both communally and personally. Charles Spurgeon once declared, for example, that anyone having a small creed also had a small church. Heresy is deadly, among other reasons, because it leads to counterfeit religious experience. For a religious person to have a false idea of God,

William Temple once observed, is to be worse off than having God not at all: it would be better to be an atheist. Contemporary Christian spirituality could be rescued from an enormous vapidity by learning even such basic doctrines as justification by grace alone and sanctification through faith alone. Both doctrines teach that what God in Christ has done *for* us he insists also in doing *in* us.[27] So would a renewed emphasis on the doctrine of the Trinity help to overcome our pernicious individualism. Only because we believe that God has a rich and complete life unto himself—as the three persons of the Holy Trinity give themselves utterly without stint to each other—do we also believe that the communal God is free to act in our behalf, delivering us from our present misery. Such deliverance comes only as our communities of faith enable us to participate in God's own triune life of total self-surrendering love.

Good preaching and teaching will sustain Christian piety only as they are inseparably tied to good worship. As I have sought repeatedly to show, such worship must rely more on ceremony than spontaneity. Liturgical worship need not be high falutin' and altogether solemn. It can often be quite simple and uncomplicated and joyful, as the worship of the Taizé community demonstrates. Yet it must be ceremonial if it is to avoid the shallowness of spontaneity that we've heard John Donne complaining about. Ceremony, by reaching deliberately for the artificial, can plumb the depths of genuine significance, as Thomas Howard explains:

> Through the imposed, we meet the natural. Through the prescribed, we meet the sincere. This is always and everywhere true. No tribe, culture, civilization, or society has ever operated on any other assumption.
>
> Birth rites, puberty rites, marriage rites, death rites: no one gives the back of his hand to these things. Huns, Florentines, Saxons, Watutsis, and Athenians all agree here. If you are approaching something significant, or *if you want to discern the significance of an event*, you must submit to ceremony.[28]

Contemporary spirituality can also be given dignity and depth through the quality of church music as well as the character of the preaching and praying. Especially for those of us who stand in the non-creedal traditions, the heart of our theology lies in our hymns. They are our sung creeds: they often set forth what we believe and practice more sharply and freshly than either our prayers or our sermons. Yet in many evangelical churches, our richly theological hymns are being rapidly replaced with religiously vacuous praise songs. So far as I can see, these choruses are useful mainly in helping young Christians memorize scripture. Yet they threaten to arrest believers in

a perpetual milk-drinking adolescence, since these praise songs are very
rapidly becoming standard fare for adult worship. Let it be clear that I am
not making an elitist call for high-toned anthems and complex cantatas, nor
for a return to hymns with archaic words and unsingable tunes. But I do
believe that we must reclaim the theologically and imaginatively rich theology that characterizes the greatest of both our ancient and modern hymns.

Consider, for example, four works that few of my students know—
including, alas, few of the seminarians whom I teach: "A Mighty Fortress Is
Our God," "Love Divine, All Loves Excelling," "When I Survey the
Wondrous Cross" and "Come Ye Sinners, Poor and Needy." Then consider
a praise song that they *all* know: "Majesty." The three hymns and the one
gospel song, both in their lyrics and their melodies, make us shudder with
awe, tremble with thanksgiving, stand aghast at Golgotha, mark the wonder
of Christ's intimacy with us, and ponder the cost of our glad surrender to the
God who has yielded himself up for our sake. The praise song, by contrast,
has rhymes that are banal, a tune that is saccharine, and a meaning that is
sentimental if it is discernible at all. What is the nature of this "Kingdom
authority [that] flows from his throne unto his own"? Surely it is not the
magisterium of the one holy catholic and apostolic church!

A serious case can be made for Isaac Watts's "When I Survey the
Wondrous Cross" as the sublimest hymn in the English tongue.[29] It com-
bines deep theology with deep piety. Yet the original words even of this
unsurpassed poem have been doctored. It originally began with these lines:
"When I survey the wondrous cross, / Where the *young* Prince of glory died."
Watts was willing to confess—at least in his bravest moments—that Jesus
did not die as a tired old codger, full and weary of years, but as a man on the
very threshold of adult achievement. Thus did Watts stress, in single word,
both the horror of Christ's early death as well as the wonder that the Gospel
is meant for *all*—for the exuberant young no less than for the exhausted old.
Yet even worse damage has been done to Watts's great hymn by squeamish
spiritualizers who have excised its most vivid stanza. There Watts links the
outward gruesomeness of Christ's saving act with the drastic inward effects
that it works in us:

> His dying crimson, like a robe,
> Spreads o'er his body on the tree:
> Then I am dead to all the globe,
> And all the globe is dead to me.

The gore that drenched Christ's naked body became his gown of glory. Here
was no noble martyr's death. Here the King of the cosmos bore our sin away

in the stream of his own blood. Nothing other than such Love can demand our bodies and souls, our minds and hearts, our very lives, our all. Nothing else can rescue us from a vague and often heretical spirituality, prompting a strong outward faith that sustains a vital inward piety. Nothing less can constitute the basis of a Christian culture that might invigorate the life of the church and its academies, and thus the life of the world as well.

Conclusion

There is no better way to conclude these essays on the church's engagement with culture than by re-visiting Robert Jenson's seminal essay of 1993, "How the World Lost Its Story." There Jenson makes the case that modernity has ended with the loss of what he calls a "narratable world." From the Greek tragedies through Dante and Shakespeare and Jane Austen finally to James Baldwin, western culture shared the assumption that, in all good stories, "each decisive event is unpredictable until it happens, but immediately upon taking place is seen to be exactly what 'had' to happen." Jenson cites Aristotle's own example: the blinding of Oedipus. We have no way of knowing Oedipus will tear out his eyes in horror at discovering the terrible truth about himself that he had failed to see; but when Oedipus does blind himself, we know immediately that "the whole story must lead to and flow from just this act." It was also assumed—again in the West if not the East—that most of our lasting literary stories are thus fitted to the "real" world—that is, they realistically describe "the world as it is prior to our storytelling." Such narrative confidence once meant that we could truthfully interpret our lives according to these stories about how the world really is, even as we could tell our own life-stories in ways that made them true to this same world.[1]

As Jenson points out, these modern Western assumptions were secularized versions of the Jewish and Christian practice of reading Scripture as the world's true story: as God's own narrative of the world's Fall and Redemption and Glorification. Just as there was a universal Storyteller, so was there a universal story. Advocates of the Enlightenment sought, by contrast, to retain confidence in the reliability of a narratable world while dispensing with faith in the God who had once been embraced as the Author of the world's narrative. Though successful for nearly four centuries, the Enlightenment experiment has finally and miserably failed: "If there is no universal storyteller," declares Jenson, "then the universe can have no story line." The loss of a narratable world entails a drastic moral loss as well: deeds no longer have discernibly moral consequences: we are left with a world where one thing simply follows another without any necessary relation. Someone may pull out his eyes for no reason at all. The moral future is jeopardized no less than the moral past. No longer is there any God to guarantee that one's own

185

actions, like the world's drama itself, will issue in any future good. As Jenson observes, "Promises, in the postmodern world, are inauthentic simply because they are promises, because they commit to a future that is not ours to commit."[2]

Post-modernism has been famously defined by Jean-François Lyotard as "incredulity toward metanarratives"—the impossibility, that is, of capturing the meaning of all things in any single account of them, whether biblical or secular. Jenson is wiser to say simply that the venerable Western confidence in a narratable world has collapsed into shards and fragments. He cites the fiction of Sartre and Joyce, the paintings of René Magritte, the dramas of Samuel Beckett, and the music of Frank Cage and various rock groups as revealing the disintegration of our once venerable faith in a coherent and truthful storyline. The moral collapse of Enlightenment humanism is even more pronounced than the literary, as we are now left with only fragmentary moral truths and patchy ethical systems.[3] The post-modern rejection of the Enlightenment attempt to have God and the world on its own rationalist terms constitutes, as we have noticed, something other than ill tidings. Post-modernists have helped Christians disentangle themselves from a false alignment of the church with the Enlightenment project. Much of my effort in this book has been to carry out this salutary disengagement, even as I have sought to demonstrate that post-modern fragmentation and disintegration also characterize much of the church's contemporary witness, especially its worship. The classical hymns of the church rely, for example, on the full biblical narrative of primal Catastrophe, costly Restoration, and hopeful Consummation. Many praise-choruses, by contrast, ignore the first two, while retaining a syrupy version of the last. As with the moral virtues, so with Christian doctrines: they constitute an indivisible unity. To isolate one Christian claim at the expense of the others, to treat a distorted fragment of Christian faith as if it were the whole, is to betray not only the Gospel story but also the divine Storyteller.

What, then, must be done? Again, Jenson offers an apt answer. Now that our secular-pagan culture can no longer make dramatic and thus moral sense of people's lives, the church can no longer tell the world how to make its story come out right religiously—namely, by showing how the Gospel re-narrates the world's own account of its life. Hence the necessity of a radical counter-witness: "if the church does not *find* her hearers antecedently inhabiting a narratable world, then the church herself must *be* that world." This has been our central theme: the call for the church to create its own culture—morally and academically, aesthetically and religiously shaping the lives of God's people, thus offering a real alternative to the collapsed Enlightenment culture of the post-modern world. As Jenson makes clear, this newly constituted world requires an unabashed return to *liturgy*: to worship whose strange beauty and uncanny power form a world centered upon the story of the triune God,[4] a communal world where deeds have consequences and where promises can be made and kept. Only then can the chief error of modern Protestantism—though once its chief accomplishment—be overcome:

> Protestantism has been modernity's specific form of Christianity. Protestantism supposed that addresses of the gospel already inhabited the narratable world in which stories like the gospel could be believed, and that we could therefore dismantle the gospel's own liturgical world, which earlier times of the church had created. Protestantism has from the beginning supposed that real action is in the world, and that what happens "in church" can only be a preparation to get back out into reality.[5]

Toward this summons to the faithful liturgical witness of the church—so that the really important things are made to happen in the church, precisely in order that the world might know its true story—I propose eight theses. Obvious though they seem, I have found that they challenge the often non-ecclesial faith of my evangelical students:

1) that there is no such thing as a solitary Christian;

2) that we can identify ourselves as Christians only insofar as we belong to Christ's Body called the church, where we are radically dependent on each other;

3) that our private life of prayer and devotion arises out of the foregoing life lived in the Body of Christ, and not the other way around;

4) that we enter this community at the choosing and command of Christ, who thus enables our free decision to follow him;

5) that, because Jesus Christ alone is the Word of God incarnate, we honor him as Lord over all things: the sole Criterion for proclaiming the Word of God in the church and for interpreting the Word of God in Scripture.

6) that the Christian life is marked by its transformative communal living and countercultural practices based on our justification and sanctification in Jesus Christ;

7) that the outward and visible marks of this communal existence in Christ are the Word faithfully preached, the sacraments rightly administered, and church discipline regularly practiced;

8) that baptism and communion are not chiefly our own actions per-
    formed for Christ, but signs of his incorporation of us into his Body
    by dying and rising and reigning for our sake.

To do justice to each of these unremarkable claims would require another book. Suffice it to say, all too briefly, that students often balk at even the
very first thesis. Because their own faith seems solitary, they think of analogies that would validate their aloneness with God. "What about the ship-
wrecked person on a island having no other possessions than a Bible, though
with provisions of food and shelter for the long-term future: wouldn't he or
she, reading the Scriptures and coming to saving faith, constitute a solitary
Christian?" The answer, of course, is No. Whence came this Bible? It did not
fall from the sky. The canonization of Scripture may be said, in fact, to be
the first authoritative act of the church. To read this Book aright, therefore,
is already to dwell in communion with the saints. Who but the great chorus
of past saints now rejoicing in the church triumphant, interceding for all the
living, could enable this lonely soul to hear and heed the Gospel? And who
but the Holy Spirit, moving in the heart and mind and will of the castaway
islander, could reveal the story of the triune God and his people to be the
one absolutely true story?

To the question, again asked by my evangelical students, whether being
Christian means having a personal relation to Jesus Christ, the answer, of
course, is Yes. This phrase means, quite precisely, having relationship with a
Person. Yet how do we encounter this Person? If we answer that we speak to
him in our prayers or that we experience his presence in our lives, as surely
we must, how are we to be assured that these prayers and this presence are
authentic? They could instead be the result of our unconscious auto-sugges-
tions or the product of our visceral well-being. Only as we encounter Christ's
own person in his Body called the church—as we worship and work together with other Christians in the name of the triune God—do we encounter
the living Lord. And only thus can we be rescued from subjectivism and ego-
centrism, from a sentimental familiarity with God that leads to spiritual self-
sufficiency and that often masks itself as authentic faith. Christian existence
is profoundly relational, therefore, for it is profoundly dependent on other
Christians in a common reliance on a common Lord. Our life of private
devotion is thus prompted by our public life in the church, as we seek to
pray and work and think in conformity to the great company of saints and
martyrs that comprise the two-millennium-old Faith.

"Yet do we not come into such faith," I am asked yet again, "by our own
solitary decision to trust Jesus Christ as our personal Lord and Savior?" The

short answer is: No. Certainly the act of faith is ours, and certainly our lives are shaped by choices concerning the Gospel as well as many other things. Yet the lifelong act of faith belongs to us only because it is first God's gracious gift. It is given to us, moreover, only as the Good News has been graciously borne to us by the faithful witness of the church. Never, therefore, is Christian faith a solitary decision. As we have seen, it is the faith *of* Jesus that enables our faith *in* Jesus. The question of saving faith is always a question of Who calls and who answers, of Who gives and who receives, of Who authors and finishes and who is authored and finished. In John's Gospel, Jesus insists on the primacy and finality of his own choosing: "You did not choose me but I chose you" (15:16a). So does Luke call Christ himself God's "Chosen One" (Luke 23:35), just as he calls Christ's disciples God's chosen witnesses (Acts 11:41). Over and again, the New Testament makes it plain that being "with" and "in" and "for" Christ is always his doing before it is ours.

Because certain double-predestinarian, Dort-nostalgic hyper-Calvinists have misused such good biblical terms as *election* and *predestination*, certain evangelicals have become afraid of them. The chief Apostle had no such fear: "For those whom he foreknew he also predestined to the image of his Son [. . . .] And those whom he predestined he also called; and those whom he called he also justified; and those whom he justified he also glorified" (Rom. 8:29–30). This Pauline shorthand retelling of the gospel story offers a con-catenation of glad claims that lie at the heart of the Gospel. That Israel is God's *predestined* people is the most fundamental biblical premise. That Jesus is God's *chosen* messiah for the salvation of the whole world is the very essence of the Good News. That all Christians have been undeservedly *elect-ed* by the God who in Christ Jesus has refused deservedly to reject us, is our one hope and joy. Election and predestination, it follows, do not concern God's arbitrary choosing of the favored few, nor his even more arbitrary rejecting of the unfavored many.

To be numbered among the rejected, to be against Christ, is to seek our own salvation, to believe that God owes us his grace because we are religious, to think that our own goodness and righteousness make us worthy of God's honor. To belong to the elect, by contrast, to be "in Christ," is to live and move and have our very being in total and utter reliance on God's prevenient grace. The good word "prevenience" means simply that God's grace always comes before and enables all of our faithful responses to his will. Salvation is not akin, therefore, to a political decision to vote Libertarian or an econom-ic choice to purchase a Buick, and least of all to selecting a gift at the shop-ping mall. Nor is it akin even to choosing between good and evil, for Satan is not the equal of Christ. Though still powerful, Satan has already been defeated at Golgotha. As the one true Victor over evil, Christ elects us who are evil in order to transform us into images of his goodness. To believe, in sum, is to be given and to receive and to live according to this one true Gift: the sheer unearned mercy of saving faith in Jesus Christ. How wise it was, therefore, for Blaise Pascal—a seventeenth-century Roman Catholic theologian with considerable Calvinist sympathies—to declare that we would not seek God unless he had already found us. P. T. Forsyth, a British Congregationalist theologian who lived and worked a century ago, put the matter of God's sovereign initiative ever so clearly:

> The Gospel descends on man, it does not rise from him. It is not a projection of his innate spirituality. It is revealed, not discovered, not invented. It is of grace, not works. It is conferred, not attained. It is a gift to our poverty, not a triumph of our resource. It is something which holds us, it is not something that we hold. It is something that saves us, and nothing that we have to save. Its Christ is a Christ sent to us and not developed from us, bestowed on our need and not produced from our strength, and He is given for our sin more than for our weakness.[6]

Lest my argument seem not only Calvinist but also Catholic, I should add that my fifth thesis denies the claim of the Roman communion to be an extension of the Incarnation. Catholics are right to point out that the early church flourished without an official Scripture for nearly three centuries, and that the Bible itself was canonized by the church. Yet there can be no conflation of the Gospel and the church, as if they were undifferentiated realities. Jesus Christ, as the Word of God made flesh, remains Lord over both the church and the Bible. While Scripture is our written witness to Christ, the Gospel governs the church's proper interpretation of it. Wherever there is a seeming conflict between books and passages of the Bible, the one that more fully proclaims the Gospel is to be considered more authoritative. The theological oneness of men and women in Christ set forth in Galatians 3:28, for example, trumps any literalist reading of the command that women "learn in silence with all submissiveness" (1 Tim. 2:11).

So do Jesus and his Gospel rule over the church. Its bishops and elders, its deacons and councils—no less than its ordinary believers—are called to utter the central petition of the Model Prayer: "Forgive us our sins." A repentant church cannot be an infallible church. The Roman Catholic and evangelical Protestant consensus statement on the relation of the Scripture and tradition makes clear the Protestant denial "that Christ has endowed the

Church with a permanent apostolic structure and an infallible teaching office that will remain until the Kingdom is finally consummated."

> For Evangelicals, the Church as the one body of Christ extending through space and time includes all the redeemed of all the ages and all on earth in every era who have come to living faith in the body's living Head. Everyone who is personally united to Christ, having been justified by faith alone through his atoning death, belongs to his body and by the Spirit is united with every other true believer in Jesus.[7]

Even when my audiences embrace these first five theses—and there are few who do!—they often ask a further question: "Isn't anyone who professes faith in Jesus Christ and who relies on nothing other than his saving grace to be counted a Christian?" Not, I reply, unless such reliant faith issues in transformed life within the body of Christ, and unless this transformation redound to the benefit of God's Kingdom rather than our own personal satisfaction. Our brothers and sisters in the Eastern Orthodox tradition get to the heart of the matter when they describe the Christian life as theosis: the divinizing of all believers into the likeness of Christ. The Eastern church does not call, therefore, for Christians to imitate Jesus through the exercise of ethical choices—knowing well that this can produce moralistic self-righteousness. It summons them, instead, to participate in God's own triune life through the transformative power of the liturgy and sacraments of the church. To become persons in the true sense is to become what the New Testament calls "partakers of the divine nature" (2 Pet 1:4).

The Christian life is rooted in the twin doctrines of justification and sanctification. They are the inseparable sides of a single coin, so that to have one is necessarily to have the other. They are related not as beginning and end, nor as offer and response, nor as possibility and realization, and least of all as "letting" Christ be our Savior and then later "making" Jesus our Lord. Rather do the two conditions occur simultaneously and indivisibly, and they are the systolic and diastolic movements of the Christian life. Ephesians 2:8–10 became the watchword of the Reformation because these verses balance the twin emphases perfectly: "For by grace you have been saved through faith; and this is not your own doing, it is the gift of God—not because of works, lest any man should boast. For we are his workmanship, created in Christ Jesus for good works, which God prepared beforehand, that we should walk in them." Hence the following outline:

Outline of Justification and Sanctification

A. Justification or Reconciliation by Grace Alone (*sola gratia*)

B. Sanctification or Regeneration through Faith Alone (*sola fide*)

1. Completely without regard to our own merit, but solely by the faith *of* Christ
1. Completely by the gift of faith *in* Christ, freely and gladly received

2. Solely by the atoning work of the crucified Savior
2. Entirely through the empowering work of the risen Lord

3. As Christ's once-and-for-all, already completed act, to which we made *witnesses*
3. As the Holy Spirit's ever-continuing, never-ending regeneration of us as *disciples*

4. Depending not at all on *conditional* (i.e. by) good works
4. Signified by a life of *consequential* (thus for) good works

5. So that God constantly turns himself toward us
5. So that God constantly turns us toward himself

6. In total forgiveness of our sin
6. In total transformation of our lives

7. This is what God does *for* us, as we are completely passive and receptive
7. This is what God does *through* us, as we remain completely active and engaged

8. Hence our utter *equality* in sin and therefore in pardon
8. Hence our utter *inequality* in guilt and therefore in holiness

9. As we are given the heavenly Mercy that prompts confession and repentance
9. As we face the hellish Judgment that fills us with fear and trembling

10. Entering this life sometimes but not always through sudden conversion
10. Continuing in this life through lifelong conversion and slow growth in grace.

11. As we are *made* Christians in the singular, unrepeated act of *baptism*
11. As we *remain* Christians in the ever-repeated acts of the *Lord's Supper*

12. Hence real motive for evangelism and missions
12. Hence true source of ethics and social action

This sketch suggests already the elaboration of my seventh thesis to those who ask whether they are not sufficiently Christian when they gather in small Bible study and prayer groups, engage in joint evangelism projects, and volunteer at relief agencies, especially such a noble one as Habitat for Humanity? No, I answer, not if you do these things without the prompting of preaching and the sacraments and church discipline. This reply would be small-minded if it were a call to mere church certification—as if we could not be Christians without an ecclesiastical stamp of approval. It was not mere institutional validation that the early Baptists practiced when they instituted a vigorous program of church discipline that lasted well into the previous century. All church members were held accountable to exacting moral and spiritual standards that were enforced by ex-communication. Together with preaching and the sacraments, church discipline reminds us that the Word of God stands over against us, makes transcendent demands on us, and enables a counter-cultural way of life not possible by even the staunchest human effort.

Authentic preaching is centered upon the central themes and narratives of the Bible as well as the doctrines of the church, rather than focusing upon personal experience or current moral and political concerns or even verse-by-verse commentary on Scripture. All three synoptic gospels, no less than the book of Acts, make clear that Jesus calls his disciples above all else to *proclaim* the Glad Tidings. "Go into all the world and preach the gospel to the whole creation" (Mark 16:15). The Lord's Supper can never stand alone, for this reason, but must always serve to complete and fulfill the proclaimed Word. For both good and ill, therefore, preaching remains the Protestant equivalent of the Catholic Mass. Protestantism's high regard for the proclaimed Word derives, as we have seen, from Paul's celebrated declaration that "faith comes from what is heard, and what is heard comes from the preaching of Christ" (Rom. 10:17). The Gospel is not only a message to *be* preached, Paul makes clear, but also preaching itself. Authentic proclamation is not, therefore, a word *about* God; it is the Word *of* God. Hence these biblical adjurations stressing the unique and final authority of Christian proclamation: "Hear the word of the Lord." "Repent and believe the gospel." "Come and follow me." "Woe be unto me if I preach not the gospel."

The test of authoritative preaching is whether it acknowledges that God remains concealed even in his revelation, whether it accentuates God's inexorable otherness, and thus whether it stresses the mystery of divine inaccessibility and incomprehensibility in its very proclamation of the Good News. The greater God's self-identification in Jesus and Jews, the greater also the mystery of his unknowability. The God who stands completely revealed in the cross is, in this very same place, also concealed. This means that, whenever preaching becomes a true address from God, it does not offer a *direct* openness or access to God. Preachers can never set the Word before their hearers as a given and assumed truth, as a reality confidently comprehended before the act of proclamation. The openness to God made possible through preaching is what Karl Barth calls "a becoming open." Because God alone miraculously grants this access to his own life, the efficacy of preaching depends on God alone—not on the eloquence or sincerity or learning of the preacher: "God tears away the veil, the husk, the concealment [. . . .] He removes the incomprehensibility. He makes impossible the possibility of taking offense, of not believing."[8]

The same mysteriously granted gift that makes belief possible through proclamation is also at work in the sacraments.[9] Once more, my appeal to evangelical students is that they discern the need to have their character sacramentally formed by a high doctrine of Baptism and the Supper. Their native inclination is to regard these crucial events as additives or decorations to the Christian life, not their meat and milk. Hence the importance of recognizing that we receive our birth into the Faith through the baptismal pool, just as our life in the Faith is sustained at the sacramental table. Both events demonstrate, yet again, that God is the Author and that we are players in the divine drama, as the British Congregationalist theologian Daniel Jenkins makes clear:

> "[T]he Sacraments bear testimony to what is, from our human side, the incalculability of God's action, to the fact that God retains His freedom in His revelation and that the life of the Church, the Communion of Saints, is 'hid with Christ in God.'"[10]

Even in the believers' church tradition, where baptism is consciously chosen rather than agreed upon by parents, the event signifies much more than our own decision to follow Jesus. Such discipleship would require no sacramental act of death and burial. As baptism by total immersion makes ever so vivid, this is God's act: we are drowned with Christ in a watery grave, plunged into the aboriginal chaos out of which God fashioned the cosmos, in order that we may be raised with Christ as new creations, emerging wet-haired from the waters of life like new-born babies. Thus is baptism an irreversible event, not to be repeated (as some evangelicals are prone to do) to signify renewed faith, much less in transfer of membership to a different denomination or church. We keep recurring to it—remembering our baptism especially as we affirm the baptism of others—as the singular event in which our lives truly begin.

Few if any writers have better limned this understanding of baptism as a lifelong call to conversion than George Herbert does in the first of two poems entitled simply "H. Baptisme":

> As he that sees a dark and shadie grove,
> > Stayes not, but looks beyond it on the skie;
> > So when I view my sinnes, mine eyes remove
> More backward still, and to that water flie,
>
> Which is above the heav'ns, whose spring and rent
> > Is in my dear Redeemers pierced side.
> > O blessed streams! Either ye do prevent
> And stop our sinnes from growing thick and wide,

Or else give tears to drown them, as they grow.
    In you Redemption measures all my time,
    And spreads the plaister equall to the crime:
You taught the Book of Life my name, that so

    What ever future sinnes should me miscall,
    Your first acquaintance might discredit all.

Herbert was a seventeenth-century British poet and Anglican parson (1593–1633) who could easily have made his way into the great world of high political and ecclesial office. He felt himself called, instead, to serve as priest of Bemerton, a tiny Wiltshire parish church near Salisbury. In rain-soaked England, a thick clump of trees may not be a place of coolness and rest so much as a potential refuge for thieves or brigands. The speaker thus casts his eyes skyward toward the light which signals freedom and hope. So it is with his sins: rather than concentrating on their shadowy darkness, and thus becoming fascinated with the very thing he abominates, he looks away from himself to the heavenly place where they have already been cleansed. Nor was his baptism a mere earthly washing. Its pool was supplied by the atoning river of blood that rushed from Christ's rent body. The streams of mercy that there poured forth retain their perennial efficacy many years beyond his baptism. They serve either to stop the rivulets of evil from becoming a flooding torrent, or else they become tears that drown his fledging sins in the river of repentance.

Herbert's riparian metaphors suddenly become temporal and medicinal, as he begins to address Christ himself. His baptism is the true gauge of his years, he confesses, for no matter how soon his mortal life may end, he has been reborn to eternal life. And since sin is an otherwise mortal wound, baptism is the only curative to heal it. In baptism, Christ removed Herbert's name from the Book of Death and re-entered it into his own Lamb's list of the undying. Baptism not only erases past evils; it also guards against the future sins that will surely besmirch his name ("me miscall"). Herbert remains confident that his sinful self is not his true person, but that in Christ he has the fast Friend who will shame away his own reprehensible acts. Thus does Herbert summon Christians constantly to remember their baptism. Just as in moments of dire demonic temptation Luther scrawled *Baptizatus sum* on a slate and thus drove Satan out, so are contemporary Christians called to recognize their baptism as the indelible mark that marks them as God's property rather than their own.

So it is with the Holy Meal: it is God's enabling act rather than a sign of our own brave determination to follow him. Even in the believer's church tradition, where Christians do not gather around the Lord's Table but feed each other with the bread and wine, we become priests to each other because Christ has first gathered and nourished us as the company called by his name. Thus are we ourselves fed by the Lord who is mysteriously present here as not elsewhere. Luther rightly asked why, if Christ be not uniquely present in the Supper, we should bother to perform it? Forsyth declared, in a similarly tart way, that memorials are meant for heroes who have perished. The eucharistic remembrance is no such solemn recollection of a dead man: it entails an encounter with the living Lord, in whose body and blood we dare not partake unworthily, lest he be crucified afresh. Hence my hope that evangelicals will begin to celebrate this Holy Meal, not as the church's infrequent obligation, but as its frequent privilege. Even one who so strongly stressed the primacy of preaching as Karl Barth came, toward the end of his life, to insist upon a weekly observance of the Supper. The sermon, he said, should prepare the congregation for the visual enactment of the event that had been aurally proclaimed.

Again, it is George Herbert who, in "Love (III)," has penetrated to the very core of this life-sustaining sacrament:

> Love bade me welcome: yet my soul drew back,
>   Guiltie of dust and sin.
> But quick-ey'd Love, observing me grow slack
>   From my first entrance in,
> Drew nearer to me, sweetly questioning,
>   If I lacked any thing.
>
> A guest, I answer'd, worthy to be here:
>   Love said, You shall be he.
> I the unkinde, ungratefull? Ah my deare,
>   I cannot look on thee.
> Love took my hand, and smiling did reply,
>   Who made the eyes but I?
>
> Truth Lord, but I have marr'd them: let my shame
>   Go where it doth deserve.
> And know you not, sayes Love, who bore the blame?
>   My deare, then I will serve.
> You must sit down, sayes Love, and taste my meat:
>   So I did sit and eat.

Herbert meditates here on the nature of the Lord's Supper in particular and the Christian life in general. He envisions Christ as an innkeeper who

Conclusion 197

welcomes a tired traveler to what may be a tavern no less than a hostelry. The pilgrim, perhaps dusty from walking rural roads, confesses that he has compounded his mortality with his sinfulness. He is a doubly unworthy guest. Christ reminds him that human capacities cannot be completely ruined by even the worst misuse, since the Creator who grants the gifts also redeems them. Still wanting to find some minimal place merit and standing of his own, the traveler insists on placing himself in service to his host. He learns, instead, that this is the one Table at which we are never hosts but always guests. As Luther said, we are utter beggars who have been escorted to the king's banquet.

* * *

The calling of the church is to embody, in our living and our dying, the Gospel of the world's Host. This Story alone gives the true account of how things really stand, because it alone gives every human life the one plot that is neither tragic nor sinister. The word *host* is a multivalent and theologically rich word, revealing the truth of Aristotle's saying that metaphors, by setting one thing in relation to another, name what was theretofore unnamed. The Latin *hostia* means both victim and sacrifice, and it becomes exactly the right word for naming Jesus Christ as the atoning Lord who, as the one perfectly sinless victim, has been sacrificed in our stead. Because the English word *host*, in another of its derivations, refers to those who entertain guests in their house, it is also related to the words *hospice, hospitable, hospital,* and *hospitality.* Hence the extraordinary paradox: Christ is both the welcoming Lord who invites us to the hospitality of his table, but he is also himself the sacrificial meal whose transformed body and blood we eat and drink. At the same time, he remains the world's Great Physician, and the church is his hospital where we receive his medicinal cure for our sin. Our English word *host* has yet a third rootage—in the Latin *hostis.* Originally meaning *stranger* or *enemy*, it came to signify the *army* that defeats them. Because armies are large, the word *host* also came to signify *a great company* or *multitude.* Hence the many biblical references to the Lord God of Hosts whose angelic army is arrayed against the massive forces of evil.

This little excursus into etymology is a pedantic way of declaring the theme and thesis of these essays: the God of Israel and Christ and Spirit and church is the God who contends for us. We contend aright for him only as we live and tell his Story aright. He is the Host who enables his people to sacrifice their lives to his Kingdom, to offer God's hospitality to all creatures great and small, as we ourselves becomes Christian militants wearing the armor not of terror but of truth. The Story we have truthfully to tell to the nations is the narrative of the triune God who refuses to keep the divine plenitude pent within himself. Just as God cannot and will not be God except in trinitarian mutuality, so God will not be God without his cosmos and his people. Though his world is wracked by an unearthly evil, as Luther calls it in "A Mighty Fortress Is Our God," God refuses to let the forces of sin, death, and the devil reduce the cosmos to a final zero. He wills, on the contrary, that evil be defeated by way of a triumph that will occur, paradoxically, through us. How so? Because the one whom God has chosen—one whom we would never have chosen, because he was despised and rejected, a Man of Sorrows—is on our side. Luther calls him *das Wörtchen*, the little word who, though he seems weak and defenseless, has enormous strength in his enormous suffering. Bringing with him the Spirit and all the gifts of the Spirit, he wins the final battle not alone but through his church militant. He enables its Christian soldiers to march onward by letting everything go— goods and kindred, even this mortal life also. They contend for the Faith in the confidence that God's kingdom abides forever.

Notes

Introduction

1. Christopher Clausen, *The Faded Mosaic: The Emergence of Post-Cultural America* (Chicago: Ivan R. Dee, 2000), 7.
2. Flannery O'Connor, *Collected Works* (Library of America, 1988), 1163.
3. All biblical translations are taken from the Revised Standard Version.
4. Quoted in Francesca Aran Murphy, *Christ the Form of Beauty: A Study of Theology and Literature* (Edinburgh: T & T Clark, 1995), 133.
5. In *The Comedy of Redemption: Christian Faith and Comic Vision in Four American Novelists* (Notre Dame, IN: University of Notre Dame Press, 1988), 67–79, I have dealt with Barth's teaching that the church can make careful and partial endorsements of the Word of God as it is heard beyond the Christian community.
6. John Howard Yoder, "How H. Richard Niebuhr Reasoned: A Critique of Christ and Culture," in *Authentic Transformation: A New Vision of Christ and Culture*, by Glen H. Stassen, D. M. Yeager, and John Howard Yoder (Nashville, TN: Abingdon, 1996): 81.
7. Ibid., 69.
8. Quoted in Robert Knile, *As I Was Saying: A G. K. Chesterton Reader* (Grand Rapids, MI: Eerdmans, 1985), 265.
9. Karl Barth, *Church Dogmatics*, vol. IV, *The Doctrine of Reconciliation*, ed. G. W. Bromiley and T. F. Torrance (Edinburgh: T & T Clark, 1934–69), part 3, i: 102.
10. Ibid.
11. Stanley M. Hauerwas and William H. Willimon, *The Truth About God: The Ten Commandments in Christian Life* (Nashville, TN: Abingdon, 1999), 14.

Chapter 1

1. C. S. Lewis, *The Abolition of Man* (New York: Touchstone, 1996), 23.
2. John F. Kennedy, "Speech to the Greater Houston Ministerial Association," September 12, 1960 (www.tamu.edu/scom/pres/speeches/jfkhouston.html).
3. "Civilization rests on mutual self-control that springs from inner checks on conduct and appetite, which flows from a shared moral vision. In turn, it rests on a shared understanding of human nature, which necessarily flows from a shared understanding of existence, and which entails a shared religion. Indeed, the first societies were united by ties of blood and shared faith" (John Attarian,

"The Only Answer to Modernity's Impiety," *Modern Age* 44, 1 [Winter 2002]: 8.) This statement reveals what is problematic about the notion of a Christian civilization, for it implies that there is a necessary symbiosis between church, society, and ethnicity. The church has been a multicultural community from the beginning, and it has repeatedly been required to differentiate itself from both nation and race. Only in so doing was it able to survive the fall of Roman civilization. As Walker Percy and others have argued, the task for our time is to discover, ever so painfully, how the church can create an authentically Christian life in the wake of Western civilization's advancing collapse.

4. Quoted by Tomoko Masuzawa, "Culture," in *Critical Terms for Religious Study*, ed. Mark C. Taylor (Chicago: University of Chicago Press, 1999), 80.

5. Clifford Geertz, *The Interpretation of Cultures* (New York: Basic Books, 1973), 89.

6. Stanley Fish, *The Trouble with Principle* (Cambridge, MA: Harvard University Press, 1999), 60–61.

7. Ibid., 56.

8. Quoted in Clausen, *Faded Mosaic*, 41.

9. "The very name of Rome sounded to [the peoples whom Rome had conquered] like a great, vital undertaking in which they might collaborate. Rome was a plan for universal organization, an administration which could be admired, a treasury of ideas received from Greece which lent brilliance to all living, a repertory of new feasts and better pleasures. The day when Rome ceased to be this project for things to be done tomorrow, the Empire fell apart." (José Ortega y Gasset, *Invertebrate Spain*, tr. Mildred Adams [New York: Howard Fertig, 1974], 26.) Ortega fails to note that Christians were among those who, at least in the early years, found Rome's unifying project to be quite unsatisfactory. For while Paul appealed to the protections provided by his Roman citizenship in Acts 21:39, he also in Romans 1 condemned the Empire's open sanction of homosexual practices.

10. "Truth, politics and post-modernism," The Spinoza Lectures at the University of Amsterdam (Amsterdam: Van Gorcum, 1997), 44.

11. Richard Rorty, *Philosophy and Social Hope* (New York: Penguin, 1999), 173. It's interesting to note that, for Rorty, loyalty to the democratic state trumps all "merely personal" religious convictions: "[T]he Founding Fathers [. . .] asked people to think of themselves not so much as Pennsylvania Quakers or Catholic Marylanders but as citizens of a tolerant, pluralistic, federal republic" (ibid., 88). As we already suggested and will repeatedly discover, both liberals and conservatives—whether they be Christians or secularists—identify themselves as Americans above all else.

12. Ibid., 88.

13. James C. Edwards, *The Plain Sense of Things: The Fate of Religion in an Age of Values*, quoted in Stanley Hauerwas, "Preaching as Though We Had Enemies," *First Things* 53 (May 1995): 47.

14. Charles Taylor, *Sources of the Self: The Making of Modern Identity* (Cambridge

MA: Harvard University Press, 1989), 32.

15. J. Bottum, "Christians and Postmoderns," *First Things* 40 (February 1994): 32.

16. Barry A. Harvey, *Another City: An Ecclesiological Primer for a Post-Christian World* (Harrisburg, PA: Trinity, 1999), 3.

17. Hardly anyone noticed the subtle horror implicit in the murders that occurred at the Wedgewood Baptist Church in the Fort Worth, Texas, on September 15, 1999. When the gunman entered the sanctuary and began firing his pistol, the young people assembled there assumed that this was yet another stunt-depiction of the devil aimed at benignly frightening them into good behavior. Their formation in the Faith had left them unable to recognize a demonic killer when they confronted one.

18. Fish, *Trouble*, 58.

19. Both of these statements are cited by Clausen, *Faded Mosaic*, 129. He also quotes this remarkable Whitmanesque prophecy of an all-inclusive America freed from the shackles of history: "affection shall solve the problems of freedom yet" (188).

20. Mark Chaves, "Are we 'bowling alone'—and does it matter?," *Christian Century* (July 19–26, 2000): 754.

21. Alisdair MacIntyre, *After Virtue*, 2nd ed. (Notre Dame, IN: University of Notre Dame Press, 1984), 33ñ34.

22. Walker Percy, *Love in the Ruins: The Adventures of a Bad Catholic at a Time Near the End of the World* (New York: Farrar, Straus & Giroux, 1971), 15.

23. Clausen, *Faded Mosaic*, 7, 163, 120.

24. Paul Tillich, *Dynamics of Faith* (New York: Harper & Row, 1957), 15.

Chapter 2

1. *The Sword of Imagination: Memoirs of a Half-Century of Literary Conflict* (Grand Rapids, MI: Eerdmans, 1995), 11.

2. *The Portable Conservative Reader*, ed. Russell Kirk (New York: Penguin, 1982), xi.

3. Lionel Trilling, *The Liberal Imagination* (Garden City, NY: Doubleday Anchor, 1950), vii, xii.

4. Kirk, *Sword of Imagination*, 68–69.

5. Ibid., 209.

6. Ibid., 393.

7. Ibid., 2.

8. Ibid., 180.

9. Ibid., 126.

10. Ibid., 197.

11. Ibid., 13.

12. Ibid., 199.

13. Ibid., 121.

14. Ibid., 368.

15. Ibid., 48.

16. Ibid., 301.

17. Ibid., 331.

18. All the professor's horses and all the professor's men could not trace this statement to Russell Kirk's pen, but the professor vouches for it nonetheless.

19. Kirk, *Sword of Imagination*, 141.

20. I owe this anecdote to Brian Frizell.

21. Ibid., 223.

22. Ibid., 200.

23. Ibid., 388.

24. Ibid., 348.

25. Harry Jaffa, together with Bruce Ledewitz, Robert L. Stone, and George Anastaplo, *Original Intent and the Framers of the Constitution* (Washington, DC: Regnery Gateway, 1994), 38. I owe this point to David Green.

26. Kirk, *Sword of Imagination*, 335.

27. Ibid., 414.

28. Edward E. Ericson, Jr., "Christian, Therefore Conservative," *Modern Age* 44, 1 (Winter 2002): 22.

29. Harold R. Hutcheson, ed., *Lord Herbert of Cherbury's "De Religione Laici"* (New Haven, CT: Yale University Press, 1944), 30.

30. Lewis, "Illustrations of the Tao," *Abolition of Man*, 91–109. It has been noted that Lewis draws no examples from the Koran.

31. *Portable Conservative Reader*, xv.

32. *Sword of Imagination*, 13.

33. *Portable Conservative Reader*, xvi.

34. Since it was built largely by prisoners of war, Spanish Republicans refer to it sardonically, not as the valley of the fallen, but the valley of the pushed.

35. "Thoughts after Lambeth," *Selected Essays of T. S. Eliot* (New York: Harcourt, Brace & World, 1960), 342.

36. Russell Kirk, *Redeeming the Time*, ed. Jeffrey O. Nelson (Wilmington, DE: Intercollegiate Studies Institute, 1996), 15.

37. Kirk, *Sword of Imagination*, 341

38. Ibid., 279.

Chapter 3

1.   Peter Berger, *The Sacred Canopy* (New York: Doubleday Anchor, 1969), 5.

2.   Ibid., 28.

3.   Ibid., 34.

4.   Peter Berger, *A Far Glory: The Quest for Faith in an Age of Credulity* (New York: Free Press, 1992), 84.

5.   Ibid., 87.

6.   *Far Glory*, 40.

7.   Ibid., 88–89.

8. Ibid., 14.

9. Peter Berger, *The Heretical Imperative* (New York: Doubleday, 1979), 16.

10. Ibid., 28.

11. Brigitte Berger and Peter Berger, *The Homeless Mind* (New York: Random House, 1973), 52.

12. Peter Berger, *A Rumor of Angels* (New York: Doubleday, 1969), lx.

13. *Heretical Imperative*, 120.

14. *Rumor of Angels*, 47.

15. Ibid., 38.

16. *Heretical Imperative*, 57.

17. Ibid., 85–88.

18. *Far Glory*, 94.

19. Ibid., 95.

20. Ibid., 95–96.

21. *Heretical Imperative*, 154.

22. *Rumor of Angels*, 56.

23. Peter Berger, *Redeeming Laughter: The Comic Dimension of Human Experience* (New York: Walter de Gruyter, 1997), 153, n. 2.

24. Ibid., 214.

25. Ibid., 188.

26. *Far Glory*, 152.

27. Ibid., 82.

28. Ibid., 87.

29. Ibid., 200.

30. Ibid., 211.

31. *Far Glory*, 14. Berger makes exactly the same reading of St. Paul's offensiveness. The apostle scandalized his audiences, according to Berger, because of his inexplicable strangeness: "I doubt very much whether Paul impressed sophisticated people as an appealing character. To say the least, he must have embarrassed them. He was obsessed with his mission, unbending and endlessly aggressive in his religious views, absolutist and authoritarian in his dealings with others, and on top of that afflicted with a malady whose details we don't know, but which we may well imagine did not add to his social acceptability. We may reconstruct the phrases used to describe him at a cocktail party of the Corinthian elite (if the latter was aware of him at all) and in the pubs where his petit bourgeois clientele would gather—"fundamentalist," "simplistic," "compulsive," "asking too much of people," "never listening to the other side of any argument," "perhaps a little crazy"—in sum, something of a disagreeable fanatic" (ibid., 5).

Chapter 4

1. Mark A. Noll, *American Evangelical Christianity: An Introduction* (Malden, MA: Blackwell, 2001), 193.

2. Ibid., 194.

3. Ibid., 195.
4. David Morgan, *Protestants and Pictures: Religion, Visual Culture, and the Age of American Mass Production* (New York: Oxford University Press, 1999), 18.
5. Ibid., 24.
6. Quoted in ibid., 272–73.
7. Ibid., 340.
8. Allen C. Guelzo, *Abraham Lincoln: Redeemer President* (Grand Rapids, MI: Eerdmans, 1999), 20.
9. Quoted. in D. Bruce Lockerbie, *Dismissing God: Modern Writers' Struggle Against Religion* (Grand Rapids, MI: Baker, 1998), 11.
10. Ibid., 15.
11. Mark Twain, *Adventures of Huckleberry Finn* (New York: Ivy, 1997), 11.
12. William Placher, *The Domestication of God: How Modern Thinking about God Went Wrong* (Louisville, KY: Westminster John Knox, 1996), 135–36.
13. Twain, *Huckleberry Finn*, 11–12.
14. Lockerbie, *Dismissing God*, 119.
15. Both quotations are found in Placher, *Domestication of God*, 10.
16. Karl Barth, *The Epistle to the Romans*, 6th ed., tr. Edwyn C. Hoskyns (New York: Oxford University Press, 1968), 40.
17. Ibid., 44.
18. Lockerbie, *Dismissing God*, 11.
19. Barth, *Romans*, 40.
20. Quoted in Roger Lundin, *Emily Dickinson and the Art of Belief* (Grand Rapids, MI: Eerdmans, 1998), 37.
21. Ibid., 40–41.
22. Ibid., 52.
23. Quoted in Lockerbie, *Dismissing God*, 41.
24. Lundin, *Emily Dickinson*, 49.
25. Lockerbie, *Dismissing God*, 40, 47, 49.
26. Noll, *American Evangelical Christianity*, 21.
27. William B. McClain, "Introduction" to *Songs of Zion* (1981), quoted in Jon Michael Spencer, *Black Hymnody: A Hymnological History of the African-American Church* (Knoxville: University of Tennessee Press, 1992), 70. I am indebted to Robert Darden for this reference.
28. Dietrich Bonhoeffer, *No Rusty Swords* (London: Collins Fontana, 1970), 109. The work of the Alvin Ailey American Dance Theater is also noteworthy, especially its immensely popular Revelations, which more people have seen than Swan Lake. The ballet is deeply evangelical in its movements and rhythms, evoking the life of the small black Baptist churches that Ailey knew as a child in Texas. With remarkable effect, it links the gospel music of black spirituals with the moral passion of the civil rights movement. Audiences often weep rather than cheer, when they have not been stunned into silence after seeing it performed.
29. Noll, *American Evangelical Christianity*, 153.

30. Ibid., 150.

31. Ibid., 51.

32. Ibid., 253.

33. Mark A. Noll, *The Scandal of the Evangelical Mind* (Grand Rapids, MI: Eerdmans, 1994).

34. Bonhoeffer, *No Rusty Swords*, 92.

35. Robert E. Webber, *Ancient-Future Faith: Rethinking Evangelicalism for a Postmodern World* (Grand Rapids, MI: Baker, 1999) and D. H. Williams, *Retrieving the Tradition and Renewing Evangelicalism: A Primer for Suspicious Protestants* (Grand Rapids, MI: Eerdmans, 1999).

36. Even an Anglo-Catholic establishmentarian such as T. S. Eliot was worried about this danger. Writing in 1931, he warned that "One of the most deadening influences on the Church in the past, ever since the eighteenth century, was its acceptance, by the upper middle and aspiring classes, as a political necessity and as a requirement of respectability" ("Thoughts after Lambeth," in *Selected Essays*, 324).

37. Quoted by Mark A. Noll, *The Old Religion in a New World: The History of North American Christianity* (Grand Rapids, MI: Eerdmans, 2002), 24.

38. Ibid.

39. The review appeared in *First Things* 116 (October 2001): 43–46. James Nuechterlein's response was printed in the same issue, 8–9.

40. Ibid., 9.

41. I refer, of course, to the ground-breaking ecumenical declaration of 1994, "Evangelicals and Catholics Together: The Christian Mission and the Third Millennium," authored chiefly by Charles Colson and Richard John Neuhaus, but with the aid of thirteen other Protestants and Catholics, and endorsed by twenty-five other signatories. It initially appeared in *First Things* 43 (May 1994): 15–22.

42. Noll, *Old Religion*, 248.

43. Ibid., 128.

44. Ibid., 249.

45. Ibid., 250.

46. Another salutary sign is to be found in the *Ressourcement* series being issued by Eerdmans Publishing Company, a press with deep evangelical roots. It is bringing into English translation the oft-neglected works of important pre- and post-Vatican II theologians and literary figures. Rather than resorting to the traditional Thomist categories, these Catholic writers have sought to recover the patristic and medieval sources of Christianity, to offer fresh interpretations of St. Thomas, and thus to enter "dialogue with the major movements and thinkers of the twentieth century, with particular attention to the problems associated with the Enlightenment, modernity, liberalism." I believe that this "Retrieval and Renewal in Catholic Thought" will also bear immense fruit for Protestant faith and life.

Chapter 5

1. Burtchaell nowhere mentions Thomas, but there is little doubt that he alludes
    to the poem entitled "Do not go gentle into that good night." Thomas wrote
    it while observing the slow death of his father, as cancer turned the once ebul-
    lient English master at Swansea Grammar School into a semi-invalid who had
    lost his sight, his brilliance, and his pride. In addition to the title line itself, the
    poem's other refrain is an injunction that Burtchaell makes his own: "Rage, rage
    against the dying of the light."
2. James Tunstead Burtchaell, C.S.C, *The Dying of the Light: The Disengagement of
    Colleges and Universities from their Christian Churches* (Grand Rapids, MI:
    Eerdmans, 1998), 171.
3. Ibid., 607.
4. Ibid., 842.
5. Ibid., 794.
6. Quoted in ibid., 81.
7. I owe this observation to Mark Noll by way of e-mail correspondence.
8. Ibid., 712.
9. Ibid., 272.
10. Ibid., 613.
11. Ibid., 407.
12. Ibid., 611.
13. The work of the comparativist philosopher of religion Paul Griffiths is espe-
    cially helpful here. A specialist in both Buddhism and Christianity, he points
    out that all of the major religions make necessarily conflicting claims to being
    unsurpassable by any other way of life, comprehensive in their accounting for
    the whole of reality, and central rather than peripheral to the actual lives of their
    adherents (*Religious Reading: The Place of Reading in the Practice of Religion*
    [New York: Oxford University Press, 1999], 3–13).
14. Robert Benne, *Quality with Soul: How Six Premier Christian Colleges and
    Universities Keep Faith with Their Religious Traditions* (Grand Rapids, MI:
    Eerdmans, 2001), 15.
15. Ibid., 77.
16. Ibid., 190.
17. Ibid., 14
18. Ibid., 155.
19. Ibid., 10.
20. Ibid., 123.
21. The University of Chicago Divinity School, though intentionally pluralist in
    outlook, still makes a significant contribution to Christian scholarship, and I
    am its very grateful beneficiary. Sunday worship is also held in Rockefeller
    Chapel, while such school-sponsored services are virtually absent from the other
    formerly Baptist universities.
22. Ibid., 111.

23. Ibid., 184.
24. In the first half of the twentieth century, only two major works of theology were written by Baptists in the South: E. Y. Mullins's *The Christian Religion in Its Doctrinal Expression* and W. T. Conner's *The Gospel of Redemption.* Nor did the second half of the century prove much more promising. It produced only James Leo Garrett's *Systematic Theology: Biblical, Historical and Evangelical,* Dale Moody's *The Word of Truth,* and James Wm. McClendon's three-volume *Systematic Theology: Ethics, Doctrine, and Witness.* McClendon's work is by far the most compelling, though it is devoted to a lower-case "baptist" vision that seeks to make common cause with Mennonites and Pentecostals more than the Calvinist tradition whence the earliest British and American Baptists sprang.
25. Benne, *Quality with Soul,* 201.
26. Ibid., 112.
27. See, for example, Stanley Hauerwas, "How Universities Contribute to the Corruption of Youth," in *Christian Existence Today* (Durham, NC: Labyrinth, 1988): 237–52.
28. Knile, *As I Was Saying,* 37.
29. G. K. Chesterton, *Orthodoxy* (San Francisco: Ignatius, 1995; originally published 1908), 53.
30. Richard Strier, *Love Known: Theology and Experience in George Herbert's Poetry* (Chicago: University of Chicago Press, 1986).
31. Quoted in Knile, *As I Was Saying,* 271.

Chapter 6

1. Robert Wilken, "Roman Redux," an interview in *Christian History* XVII, 1 (Winter 1998): 44.
2. Burtchaell, *Dying of the Light,* 840.
3. Although this quote has the clear stamp of Chesterton on it, none of my Chestertonian friends has been able to help me locate it.
4. C. S. Lewis, "Introduction" to *St. Athanasius on the Incarnation* (Crestwood, NY: St. Vladimir's Orthodox Theological Seminary Press, 1993), 4–5.
5. Frank Lentricchia, "Last Will and Testament of an Ex-Literary Critic," *Lingua Franca* (September–October 1996): 60–63.
6. Hauerwas and Willimon, *Truth About God,* 89.
7. Thomas Fleming, "Cultural Revolutions," *Chronicles* 26, 1 (January 2002): 11.
8. Quoted in Knile, *As I Was Saying,* 70, 74.
9. G. K. Chesterton, *The Wisdom of Father Brown,* 6th ed. (New York: Dodd, Mead, 1906), 154.
10. G. K. Chesterton, *Charles Dickens* (New York: Dodd, Mead, 1906), 154.
11. Chesterton, *Orthodoxy,* 125. It must be confessed that Chesterton was often the exponent of a militarized Christendom, as in his 1915 poem celebrating the victory of the Holy League (Spain, Venice, and the Papal States) over the Ottoman Turks at Lepanto. It was led by the Emperor Don John of Austria.

The following lines from "Lepanto" are typical:

> Don John pounding from the slaughter-painted poop,
> Purpling all the ocean like a bloody pirate's sloop [. . . .]

The Collected Poems of G. K. Chesterton (New York: Dodd, Mead, 1980), 111.

12. Quoted in Raymond T. Bond, ed., *The Man Who was Chesterton* (Garden City, NY: Image, 1960), 82.

13. Percy, *Love in the Ruins*, 109.

14. Eric Donald Hirsch, *Cultural Literacy: What Every American Needs to Know* (New York: Vintage, 1988).

15. George Steiner demonstrates the distancing and objectifying effect of scientific research and literary high culture on those who practice them—so that well-educated people can come to sanction the most heinous of evils. Steiner makes this case in many of his essays and books, but nowhere more clearly than in his work on Martin Heidegger, the most important philosopher of the twentieth century: Is there anywhere in Heidegger's work a repudiation of Nazism, is there anywhere, from 1945 to his death, a single syllable on the realities and philosophical implications of the world of Auschwitz? These are the questions that count. And the answer would have to be, No" (*Martin Heidegger* [New York: Penguin Modern Masters, 1980], 121).

16. Twain, *Adventures of Huckleberry Finn*, 249.

17. It is sadly necessary to add, given the obloquy to which Huckleberry Finn has been subjected, that Twain employs the slur word not to demean Jim but to show Huck's initial conformity to Southern racial practice, the better to measure his eventual liberation from it.

18. William Faulkner, *Go Down, Moses* (New York: Modern Library, 1955), 267.

19. See John D. Sykes, Jr., *The Romance of Innocence and the Myth of History: Faulkner's Religious Critique of Southern Culture*, NABPR Dissertation Ser. 7 (Macon, GA: Mercer University Press, 1989).

20. Immanuel Kant is altogether typical: "For history tells how the mystical fanaticism in the lives of hermits and monks, and the glorification of the holiness of celibacy, rendered great masses of people useless to the world; how alleged miracles accompanying all this weighed down the people with heavy chains under a blind superstition; how, with a hierarchy forcing itself upon free men, the dreadful voice of orthodoxy was raised, out of the mouths of the presumptuous, exclusively 'called,' Scriptural expositors, and divided the Christian world into embittered parties over creedal opinions on matters of faith (upon which absolutely no general agreement can be reached without appeal to pure reason as the expositor)" (*Religion Within the Limits of Reason Alone* [New York: Harper Torchbooks, 1960], 121).

21. Rosemary Radford Ruether shows how we Christians, in the name of a falsely universalizing kind of Christendom, created an anti-Semitism which the Nazis could exploit (*Faith and Fratricide: The Theological Roots of Anti-Semitism* [Minneapolis, MN: Seabury, 1974], esp. 183–225).

22. "Introduction" to Athanasius on the *Incarnation*, 5.
23. Charles Scriven, "Schooling for the Tournament of Narratives: Postmodernism and the Idea of the Christian College," in *Theology Without Foundations*, ed. Stanley Hauerwas, Nancey Murphy, and Mark Nation (Nashville, TN: Abingdon, 1994), 283.

Chapter 7

1. O'Connor, *Collected Works*, 949.
2. Ibid., 1165.
3. Ibid., 930.
4. Flannery O'Connor, *Mystery and Manners: Occasional Prose*, ed. Sally and Robert Fitzgerald (New York: Farrar Straus & Giroux, 1970), 178.
5. Quoted by John Desmond in *Risen Sons: Flannery O'Connor's Vision of History* (Athens: University of Georgia Press, 1987), 9.
6. Quoted in Clifford Green, ed., *Karl Barth: Theologian of Freedom* (San Francisco: Harper Collins, 1989), 149.
7. His remarkable indictment of our entertainment-driven culture is to be found in *Amusing Ourselves to Death* (New York: Viking, 1986).
8. Wilken, "Roman Redux," 44.
9. Ibid.
10. Berger, *Far Glory*, 96
11. Kathleen Norris, *The Cloister Walk* (New York: Riverhead, 1996), 95.
12. Leander Keck, *The Church Confident* (Nashville, TN: Abingdon, 1993), 34–36.
13. Diogenes Allen, "Jesus as Lord, Jesus as Servant," *Christian Century* (March 18–25, 1998): 297.
14. Martin Luther, *Commentary on Galatians* (Grand Rapids, MI: Fleming H. Revell, 1988), 254.
15. Christopher Morse, *Not Every Spirit: A Dogmatics of Christian Disbelief* (Valley Forge, PA: Trinity, 1994), 9.
16. Ibid., 11.
17. Peter De Vries, *The Blood of the Lamb* (Boston: Little, Brown, 1961), 24–25.
18. Quoted by William Placher, *The Domestication of Transcendence: How Modern Thinking about God Went Wrong* (Louisville, KY: Westminster John Knox, 1996), 117.
19. Ibid., 237.

Chapter 8

1. Evelyn Underhill, *Worship* (New York: Harper & Brothers, 1936), 9.
2. James Kirwan, *Beauty* (New York: Manchester University Press, 1999), 32.
3. Jaroslav Pelikan, *The Illustrated Jesus Through the Centuries* (New Haven, CT: Yale, 1997), 101.

4. For the argument that classical conceptions of beauty can be translated into Christian categories, see Etienne Gilson, *The Arts of the Beautiful* (New York: Scribner's, 1965), esp. 23–34.

5. C. S. Lewis, ed., *George Macdonald: An Anthology* (London: Geoffrey Bles, 1955), 105–6.

6. "Dickens' Christmas Tales," in *The Spirit of Christmas*, selected and arranged by Marie Smith (New York: Dodd, Mead, 1985), 25.

7. Quoted in Bond, *The Man Who was Chesterton*, 17. Chesterton argues that the grotesque element in Gothic makes it "the only fighting architecture. All its spires are spears at rest; and all of its stones are stones asleep in a catapult. In that instant of illusion, I could hear the arches clash like swords as they crossed each other. The mighty and numberless columns seemed to go swinging by like the huge feet of imperial elephants. The graven foliage wreathed and blew like banners going into battle; the silence was deafening with all the mingled noises of a military march; the great bell shook down, as the organ shook up its thunder. The thirsty-throated gargoyles shouted like trumpets from all the roofs and pinnacles as they passed; and from the lectern in the core of the cathedral the eagle of the awful evangelist clashed his wings of brass" (ibid., 56–57).

8. Chesterton, *Orthodoxy*, 127–28.

9. Christopher Lasch, *The Culture of Narcissism* (New York: W. W. Norton, 1979).

10. Reynolds Price, *A Whole New Life* (New York: Atheneum, 1995), 98.

11. Geoffrey Galt Harpam, *On the Grotesque: Strategies of Contradiction in Art and Literature* (Princeton, NJ: Princeton University Press, 1982), 3. I owe this reference to John Sykes.

12. Flannery O'Connor, "A Temple of the Holy Ghost," in *A Good Man Is Hard to Find* (New York: Harcourt Brace Jovanovich, 1983), 94.

13. Ibid., 88.

14. I refer to the hermaphrodite as "he" even though the two cousins use the pronoun "it." Their neutered word reveals, all too clearly, that they have unthinkingly transformed a person created in the image of God into an impersonal thing. Medical dictionaries indicate that there is no pure hermaphroditism, no fully developed genitalia of both kinds, but always a predominance of one set of gender traits over the other. And since this particular hermaphrodite ends by playing a priestly role, it seems appropriate to envision the character in masculine terms.

15. O'Connor, *A Good Man*, 97.

16. Ibid., 98.

17. Ibid., 97.

18. The hermaphrodite has no way of knowing the important theological distinction between first and second causes. He does not understand, therefore, that not all natural events can be ascribed directly to the will of God. Nor does he know that the divinely ordered cosmos has room for chance—so that his deformed bodily condition could be the result of nature's impersonal probabil-

ities, even as his life itself remains the direct intention of the personal God. The hermaphrodite is surely right to insist, however, on the Prime Causality providentially ruling over all things, so that even chance events must cohere with the ultimate sovereignty and goodness of God. The man's faith thus enables him to see that he is not a mere physical body, as modern naturalists hold, but an inspirited body whose incorporeal soul provides him enormous moral freedom within the limits of his sorry sexual state.

19. O'Connor, "Temple to the Holy Ghost," p. 27. The Misfit is a cracker nihilist, and he thus employs perfect redneck pronunciation of his active verb.

20. I rely here largely on Francesca Murphy's clear and succinct account of von Balthasar's complex theological aesthetics (*Christ the Form of Beauty*).

21. Francis Bacon (1561–1626) also declared that there is "no excellent beauty that hath not some strangeness in the proportion" (quoted in Kirwan, *Beauty*, 132–33, n. 44).

22. The quotations in these last two paragraphs are drawn from "The King of the Birds," in *Mystery and Manners*, 3–21.

23. O'Connor, *A Good Man*, 239.

24. Kirwan, *Beauty*, 28.

25. I owe this summary of Shepherd's thesis to James Wm. McClendon, Jr., *Doctrine: Systematic Theology* II (Nashville, TN: Abingdon, 1994), 408.

Chapter 9

1. Jonathan Swift wickedly noted that, whatever else will occupy our lives in Paradise, we shall neither give nor be given in marriage.

2. Frederick Buechner, *Wishful Thinking: A Theological ABC* (New York: Harper & Row, 1973), 54.

3. C. S. Lewis, *The Screwtape Letters* (New York: Touchstone, 1996), 71.

4. G. K. Chesterton, *What's Wrong with the World* (San Francisco: Ignatius, 1993; orig. pub. 1910), 44.

5. It should be evident that marriage is no sure stronghold against sexual sin. As Calvin noted, it is possible to turn the marriage chamber into a brothel.

6. Quoted in Jim Forest, *Confession: Doorway to Forgiveness* (Maryknoll, NY: Orbis, 2002), 8–10.

7. Quoted in Helen Waddell, ed., *The Desert Fathers* (Ann Arbor: University of Michigan Press, 1957), 76.

8. Norris, *Cloister Walk*, 259.

9. William Rees-Mogg, *"An Humbler Heaven": The Beginnings of Hope* (London: Collins Fount, 1979), 65.

10. Kathleen Norris, *Amazing Grace* (New York: Riverhead, 1999), 75.

11. *Cloister Walk*, 200–1.

12. Edwin Muir, *Collected Poems* (London: Faber & Faber, 1960), 117. This poem is not to be confused with another by Muir that has the same title.

13. These Luther anecdotes are lifted from the chapter entitled "A School for Character" in Roland Bainton's biography of *Luther, Here I Stand* (Nashville, TN: Abingdon, 1950), 286–304.

14. *Screwtape Letters*, 72; emphasis added.

15. Dietrich Bonhoeffer, *Letters and Papers from Prison*, ed. Eberhard Bethge (New York: Macmillan, 1972), 42–43; emphasis added. Chesterton makes a similar claim about the fixed character of marriage and the ignominy that should accompany its dissolution: "In everything on this earth that is worth doing, there is a stage when no one would do it, except for necessity or honor. It is then that the Institution upholds a man and helps him on to firmer ground ahead. [. . .] Two people must be tied together to do themselves justice; for twenty minutes at a dance, for twenty years in a marriage. In both cases the point is, that if a man is bored in the first five minutes, he must go on and force himself to be happy. Coercion is a kind of encouragement; and anarchy (or what some call liberty) is essentially oppressive, because it is essentially discouraging" (*What's Wrong with the World*, 45).

16. Ibid., 46.

17. Chesterton, *What's Wrong with the World*, 46.

18. Graham Greene's novel *The End of the Affair* (New York: Viking, 1946) is, among other things, a searing study of the damnation inherent in romance for its own sake.

19. P. D. James, *Time to Be in Earnest* (New York: Knopf, 2000), 9.

20. *Catechism of the Catholic Church* (Mahwah, NJ: Paulist, 1994), ¶ 2362, p. 567.

Chapter 10

1. C. S. Lewis, *Perelandra* (New York: Macmillan, 1965), 91; emphasis added.

2. Art Ross and Martha Stevenson, *Romans, Interpretation Bible Studies* (Louisville, KY: Geneva, 1999), 30–31.

3. Declan Marmion, *A Spirituality of Everyday Faith* (Louvain: Peeters, 1998), 10–16.

4. Jacques Leclercq, *The Love of Learning and the Desire for God* (New York: Fordham University Press, 1982), 2–4.

5. Alven M. Neiman, "Self-Examination, Philosophical Education, and Spirituality," *Journal of Philosophy of Education*, 34, 4 (2000): 580.

6. For a fine philosophical account of this revolutionary development, see Taylor, *Sources of the Self*.

7. Karl Barth, *Protestant Thought: From Rousseau to Ritschl* (New York: Simon & Schuster, 1969), 52–54.

8. *The J. I. Packer Collection*, selected and introduced by Alister McGrath (Downers Grove, IL: InterVarsity, 1999), 198.

9. Diogenes Allen, "Academic Theology and Christian Spirituality," *inSpire* (Winter 2002): 11. Asked how contemporary spirituality might answer the Taliban's terrorist destruction of American lives on September 11, 2001, Allen

cites Sir Robert Shirley's response to the Puritans' terrorist destruction of English churches during the Civil War: he built a beautiful church in Staunton Harold, Leicester, above whose entrance are carved these words: "In the year 1653 when all things Sacred were throughout the nation Either demolisht or profaned Sir Robert Shirley, Barronet, Founded this church; Whose singular praise it is, to have done the best of things in the worst of times, and hoped them in the most callamitous. The righteous shall be in everlasting remembrance."

10. Quoted in David Lyle Jeffrey, ed., *English Spirituality in the Age of Wesley* (Grand Rapids, MI: Eerdmans, 1994), 383–84. George Herbert, a seventeenth-century Anglican poet, reveals how profoundly suggestive is the metaphor of "putting on Christ" in his poem entitled "Aaron."

11. New York: Oxford University Press, 2001. This same exaltation of the spiritual over the religious is thoroughly documented in the excellent study by Conrad Cherry, Betty A. DeBerg, and Amanda Porterfield, *Religion on Campus* (Chapel Hill: University of North Carolina Press, 2001).

12. See John David Dawson's excellent critique of Fuller in "Table for one," *Christian Century* (March 13–20, 2002): 30–34.

13. Quoted by Wuthnow in *After Heaven: Spirituality in America Since the 1950s* (Berkeley: University of California Press, 1998), 158.

14. Ibid., 162.

15. Quoted in Ramie Targoff, *Common Prayer: The Language of Public Devotion in Early Modern England* (Chicago: University of Chicago Press, 2001), 88.

16. Hauerwas and Willimon, *Truth About God*, 89.

17. C. S. Lewis, *Letters to Malcolm: Chiefly on Prayer* (London: Geoffrey Bles, 1964), 12.

18. Kallistos Ware, *The Orthodox Way* (Crestwood, NY: St. Vladimir's Seminary Press, 1995), 113.

19. Barth wittily observed that, whenever the musical angels play their harps before the throne of God, they resort to Bach. But when they're off to themselves, it's always Mozart.

20. Barth, *Church Dogmatics*, vol. IV, part 2, p. 552.

21. Richard Heyduck propounds this thesis in *The Recovery of Doctrine: An Essay in Philosophical Ecclesiology* (Waco, TX: Baylor University Press, 2002).

22. Leclercq, *Love of Learning*, 261.

23. Robert W. Burtner and Robert E. Chiles, eds., *John Wesley's Theology* (Nashville, TN: Abingdon, 1982), 26.

24. Ibid., 36.

25. Ibid., 248–49.

26. Frederick C. Gill, ed., *Selected Letters of John Wesley* (London: Epworth, 1956), 237.

27. John Bunyan stresses precisely this point when he has Christian and Hopeful confront one of the early Protestant spiritualizers, a Quaker-like figure named Ignorance. Ignorance is scandalized at the antinomian risk inherent in total

reliance on Christ's objective, all-efficacious atonement: "What! Would you have us trust to what Christ in his own person has done without us? This conceit would loosen the reines of our lust, and tollerate us to live as we list: For what matter how we live if we may be Justified by Christs personal righteousness from all, when we believe it?" (*The Pilgrim's Progress*, ed. N. H. Keeble [Oxford: Oxford University Press, 1984], 121; emphasis added).

28. Thomas Howard, "The Power of Wise Custom," *Touchstone* 13, 10 (December 2000): 11.

29. The late Moelwyn Merchant made this case in a lecture at the University of Chicago Divinity School in the mid-1960s.

Conclusion

1. Robert W. Jenson, "How the World Lost Its Story," *First Things* 36 (October 1993): 20.

2 . Ibid., 21, 23.

3. This is the central thesis of McIntyre's *After Virtue*.

4. Jenson makes the arresting point that Father-Son-Holy Spirit is the most compressed version of the divine story, and thus that well-meant substitutes replace it at the cost of heresy: "The triune name evokes God as three actors of His one story, and places the three in their actual narrative relation. Substitutes do not and cannot do this; 'Creator, Redeemer, and Sanctifier,' for example, neither narrates nor specifically names, for creating, redeeming, and sanctifying are timelessly actual aspects of the biblical God's [singular] activity, and are moreover things that all putative gods somehow do" ("How the World Lost Its Story," 23).

5. Ibid., 22.

6. Peter Taylor Forsyth, "Positive Preaching and the Modern Mind," The Lyman Beecher Lectures on Preaching delivered at Yale University in 1907 (Grand Rapids, MI: Baker, 1980), 212.

7. "Your Word Is Truth," *First Things* 125 (August/September 2002): 39.

8. Karl Barth, *The Göttingen Dogmatics: Instruction in the Christian Religion*, vol. I, ed. Hanelotte Reiffen, tr. Geoffrey W. Bromiley (Grand Rapids, MI: Eerdmans, 1991), 58.

9. As a Baptist, I have no trepidation about using the term "sacrament," since the word conveys exactly the right meaning: a sacred sign, a holy mystery. In both Baptism and the Supper, the grace of God is not merely humanly remembered or appropriated: it is divinely proffered through mortal instruments. As with salvation itself, so with its sacramental means: they are efficacious because God himself is the prime Actor.

10. Daniel T. Jenkins, *The Catholicity of the Church* (London: Faber & Faber, 1941), 7

Index